TRUMP:
MONSTER
OR HERO

SERIOUS QUESTION – SCARY ANSWER

MOHAMMAD O. ALANJARI

Published by Pin Mark Research Center

Mohammad O. AlAnjari
P.O. Box 33127
AlRawda, 73452
Kuwait

 info@MonsterOrHero.com

 Telephone/Whatsapp +965 98814555

 www.MonsterOrHero.com

ISBN 978-0-692-74457-4

Available On:

DEDICATION

To my mother and father, may God's mercy be upon them. They were in reality my school that helped enable me to accomplish what I have accomplished today. I would have loved to gift this book to them during their lives, but not everything a person hopes for comes about.

To my wife, my life-long companion, and to my son, daughters, daughter-in-law, and my lovely grandson Mohammad, may God preserve them all. They have stood by me patiently with both smiles and support.

To my friends, Nabil and Adam, who have helped me with this book, along with everyone else who contributed from their time and efforts to provide caring support along the way.

CONTENTS

WHO SUPPORTS TRUMP?

WHY IS TRUMP A PROBLEM?

DOES TRUMP EVEN UNDERSTAND THE ISSUES?

A DANGEROUS PRESIDENT

CONCLUSIONS

PREFACE:

THE IMPORTANCE OF KNOWING WHY A KUWAITI HAS WRITTEN ABOUT TRUMP

MY PURPOSE IN WRITING THIS BOOK IS TO INform the American people of an important issue facing the nation. Many would ask, "Why is a Kuwaiti person writing about Donald Trump?" America is currently at a very important and sensitive crossroads in the 2016 presidential campaign. There have been numerous candidates, but only one of them undoubtedly and incontestably stands out as being a true phenomenon. That candidate is, of course, Donald J. Trump.

Donald Trump, despite what a phenomenon he has become, is a man who harbors many despicable character traits which would be very dangerous for the American nation. He seems free from constraints of moral ethics, civility and basic courtesy. In the course of this book, those terrible traits are expounded upon and the risks of having someone so reckless and dangerous in power are clarified. The culmination of these traits can be called a disease, and that is why it is referred to numerous times in the book as the Disease of Trump.

YOU WILL FIND SIMILARITIES IN THE LIKES OF ADOLF HITLER, THE KU KLUX KLAN, AND EVEN IN THE SICK MENTALITIES OF ISIS AND AL-QAEDA.

Trump, however, is not alone in having this disease. He shares the same traits with other twisted individuals from the past and present. You will find similarities in the likes of Adolf Hitler, the Ku Klux Klan, and even in the sick mentalities of ISIS and Al-Qaeda. Trump may not have the same beliefs and faith as the aforementioned, but his mindset and way of thinking are similar.

The stakes are very high. The United States of America is the world's most powerful nation in almost all aspects. If the US decides to follow the ways of the Ku Klux Klan, Adolf Hitler, or Al-Qaeda, it will be a disaster for the whole world and would jeopardize the future of humanity.

No individual country alone can counter the turmoil that the world is facing. Because America remains the strongest of nations — economically, technologically, and militarily — if Trump and those like him were to cut pursue his hypernationalistic policies to cut America off from the rest of the

AMERICA REMAINS THE STRONGEST OF NATIONS - ECONOMICALLY, TECHNOLOGICALLY, MILITARILY

world, it would be a huge disaster. Without America, the rest of the world would not be able to overcome the threat of terrorism. To clarify this, it is my belief that if it had not been for America's involvement in World Wars I and II, they would not have come to an end.

In the current global situation, if the US and the militaries of the rest of the world came together, despite the tremendous costs, they would be able to overcome all the obstacles facing humanity. If, however, the US were to take a step back, as Trump's rhetoric suggests, the world's problems would likely fester and become much worse. And then, even if America were to rejoin the other countries in the future, none of the armies and the militaries would be able to make a difference at that delayed stage because it would be too late, and God knows best.

Here are just a couple examples of what Trump has said about some other nations:

"The Chinese leaders are not our friends. I've been criticized for calling them our enemy. But what else do you call the people who are destroying your children's future? What name would you prefer me to use for the people who are hell-bent on bankrupting our nation, stealing our jobs, who spy on us to steal our technology, who are undermining our currency, and who are ruining our way of life? To my mind that's an enemy." [1]

"Mexico is not our friend. Mexico is the new China." [2]

According to the US census, the population of America is approximately 323.25 million, while the global population is 7.313 billion. What is noteworthy in these facts is that Americans make up less than 4.5% of the world population. What about the other 95.5% of humanity whom Trump seeks to ostracize in regards to trade, cooperation, and many other arenas?*

If we look at recent history and the conflicts in which the US military has been involved, nearly all were without the full backing of the people that they were designed to help. The notable exception is the Kuwaiti people, who have been thankful to the Americans for the liberation of their country from the invading Iraqi army of Saddam Hussein. This sentiment is echoed around me from the men, women and children whom I

> ## WHAT ABOUT THE OTHER 95.5% OF HUMANITY WHO TRUMP SEEKS TO OSTRACIZE IN REGARDS TO TRADE, COOPERATION, AND MANY OTHER ARENAS?

---

* Trump has spoken out against: China, Japan, India, South Korea, Mexico, Saudi Arabia, Europe, Kuwait, Native Americans, and the Muslims, for example. Who's left?

know: they share the same opinion. To be precise, even if other people have been thankful for the American involvements in their lands, it was never to the extent of the Kuwaiti people who, even today, are completely thankful. Just as the Kuwaitis were helped by the US and our mutual allies, in whatever way they were able to, we too hope that the Americans accept this important advice from a Kuwaiti regarding the danger of Trump's disease. That's what we are able to offer.

IT IS THE RESPONSIBILITY OF THE NATION AND ITS ELECTORATE TO RECOGNIZE THE GRAVITY OF THIS AFFAIR.

My fear for America is a fear for the harm that would come about for its people. If Trump and those like him were to be in charge, it would lead to the collapse of the United States as we know it, and would plunge the world into a state of turmoil and confusion. It is the responsibility of the nation and its electorate to recognize the gravity of this affair. Therefore, it is both a fear for my people and a fear for this world from demise that has motivated me to compile this book for the American people.

A DANGEROUS
PRECEDENT

1

INTRODUCTION

I N 1935, FOUR YEARS BEFORE WORLD WAR II, BRITISH
Prime Minister Sir Winston Churchill* made an incredibly deep
observation and prediction. He was upset that the German people
had elected Adolf Hitler to power through their voting process. This
was especially surprising to him because he considered Germans to be
educated, scientific, philosophical, romantic, and open-minded. What
follows is some of what Churchill said about Hitler, in **bold letters**, followed by my comparison to what is occurring with Donald J. Trump
now.

"History will pronounce Hitler either a *monster* or a *hero*." 3

---

* Sir Winston Churchill (November 30, 1874 – January 24, 1965), British politician
and author, and best known as Prime Minister, was famous for his stubborn resistance to
Hitler during the darkest hours of World War II. He was a staunch American ally and
the first foreign national to receive honorary United States citizenship. He met various
presidents and President John F. Kennedy's presidential proclamation praised the man
whose "bravery, charity and valor, both in war and in peace, have been a flame of inspira-
tion."

Churchill presented this as a rhetorical statement, and his own stance and analysis of Hitler's traits made it absolutely clear that he considered him a monster. However, he raised the issue in this way to make his argument and remind people to consider the gravity of the situation. He called upon them to contemplate this question: "Is Hitler a monster, as I see him, or is he a hero, as the majority of those voters expected?"

> THE RESULT OF THE MAJORITY BELIEVING HITLER'S CHARADE OF BEING A HERO WAS THE HORROR OF WORLD WAR II, WHICH LED TO MORE THAN SEVENTY MILLION DEATHS.

The result of the majority believing Hitler's charade of being a hero was the horror of World War II, which led to more than seventy million deaths. That's seventy million, including soldiers, civilians, and those who died from diseases and starvation; so much pain and suffering, due to Germany's electing Hitler to power.

I therefore have decided to use the same comparison made by Churchill for the title of this book, as my opinion of Trump is the same as Churchill's opinion of Hitler. I believe Trump is a monster, and if I were to choose an alternate title for this book, it would be: *Trump, The New American Monster*.

"Hitler's triumphant career has been borne onwards, not only by a passionate love of Germany, but by currents of hatred so intense as to sear the souls of those who swim upon them." [4]

I believe that Trump's way of thinking will continue to spread across the world, and will have an effect in strengthening those in Europe who already share his sickness. The spread of his disease will no doubt have the far-reaching consequences of breeding enmity between people in a way both similar to and different from what resulted from Hitler's disease. As *The Economist* has pointed out: "Even if he loses Mr. Trump will have shown that there is a path to the nomination that runs via nativism and economic populism. Mountaineers know that the surest route to a summit is the one that has worked before."

"It is certainly not strange that everyone should want to know 'the truth about Hitler. What will he do with the tremendous powers already in his grasp and perfecting themselves week by week? If, as I have said, we look only at the past, which is all we have to judge by, we must indeed feel anxious." [5]

In this book, based on proof and evidence, I discuss from many angles the dangers of Trump and those Trumpians similar to him. If he succeeds in the November elections, it will be further proof how the voting process can be very dangerous and bring about monsters like Hitler, Mussolini, and Trump.

"He had long proclaimed that, if he came into power, he would do two things that no one else could do for Germany but himself. First, he would restore Germany to the height of her power in Europe, and secondly, he would cure the cruel unemployment that afflicted the people." [6]

Trump entices his followers with these very same huge empty promises, but time and again, whenever he speaks about his policies, we find no solutions. Anyone truly seeking to rectify the many problems that America and the world are currently facing would obviously be expected to have strategic plans. It is incomprehensible that after over a year of making speeches, he hasn't proposed a single actionable strategy that could be assumed to bring about positive results.

This book includes many studies and comparisons exposing the reality of Trump and his twisting of the real issues currently challenging the United States. These realities are clearly presented in the language of

THIS BOOK INCLUDES MANY STUDIES AND COMPARISONS EXPOSING THE REALITY OF TRUMP AND HIS TWISTING OF THE REAL ISSUES CURRENTLY CHALLENGING THE UNITED STATES.

numbers that cannot be misinterpreted. These calculations clearly expose Trump's blatant lack of focus on that which really counts: the numbers.

"Hitler had risen by violence and passion; he was surrounded by men as ruthless as he." [7]

If Trump takes the Oval Office, his presidency will usher in a period of great turmoil and difficulties for the world. Despite the pressure Trump would face from outside the United States, he can expect to be overwhelmed by the pressure from his supporters who have put all their hopes and trust in him. Those who follow him, such as the Ku Klux Klan and its sympathizers, are using him as a bridge to reach their own goals, and Trump will pay for that in the long run. He won't be able to fulfill his brazen, empty promises, and that is when there'll be a backlash against him.

These were Churchill's observations and predictions almost four years before Hitler started the war that caused the deaths of more than seventy million people. Nowadays, four years pass by very quickly, and we likewise would have four years to witness the disastrous effects of a Trump presidency, both in America and around the world. There wouldn't be any doubt about the aftermath.

If Trump is successful in the election, I will write a book at the end of his term, clearly showing the damage done during his years in power. And if he isn't successful, I will write a book after a certain period of time, highlighting what terrible effects and influence his campaign brings about.*

Trump's disease is here. Without vigorous opposition the disease will continue to spread, and if he achieves success at the ballot box its toxic effects will greatly intensify.

---

* *God willing.*

2

IF TRUMP WINS, IT WILL BE BECAUSE OF THE COUNT OF THE HEADS AND NOT THE **WEIGHT OF THE MINDS** OF THOSE WHO VOTE

I N KUWAIT, DURING PARLIAMENTARY ELECTIONS, I witnessed the victory of a Trumpian politician just like Donald J. Trump. When I was asked how people like him could have reached the Parliament, I contemplated and realized that such politicians have the same type of ignorant mentality as Trump, and resemble Trump's chemistry.

This is similar to how people are surprised that Trump is the nominee for the Republican Party.

Most people do not know, but this same kind of amazement was expressed by Sir Winston Churchill about Hitler in 1935, before the outbreak of World War II.

IF TRUMP SUCCEEDS, AMERICAN VOTERS WOULD SHARE THAT VERY SAME SHAME OF WHICH CHURCHILL SPOKE.

"The astounding thing is that the great German people," said Churchill, "educated, scientific, philosophical, romantic, the people of Christmas tree, the people of Goethe and Schiller, of Bach and Beethoven, Heine, Leibnitz, Kant and a hundred other great names, have not only not resented this horrible bloodbath, but have endorsed it and acclaimed its author with the honours not only of a sovereign but almost of a God. Here is the frightful fact before which what is left of European civilization must bow its head in shame, and what is to more practical purpose, in fear." [8]

I can see clearly the parallels between these individuals and how they have advanced in their respective careers, despite their complex problems. Just as Churchill pointed out how millions of highly educated and intelligent people had endorsed Hitler in his time, we see the same thing happening with versions of Trump in Kuwait and elsewhere. And just as it happens in Kuwait, we are now witnessing this in America amongst the supporters of Trump.

The Associated Press also understood these same meanings, which I have explained, as they summarized the following on October 30, 1935:

"Winston Churchill's article in *The Strand Magazine* said only time would tell whether Adolf Hitler would be a monster or a hero. Mr. Churchill professed to be astounded that

BETTMANN/GETTY IMAGES

the educated German people had endorsed Hitler's blood purges. The article said what was left of European civilization must hang its head in shame and fear before this fact." [9]

I believe the Kuwaiti voters who chose the minor Trump should also feel responsible, as Churchill said of those who voted for Hitler: "European civilization must bow its head in shame." If Trump succeeds, American voters would share that very same shame of which Churchill spoke.

These leaders are recognizable by their idiosyncrasies - their speech, writing, choice of words, way of speaking, body language, etc., right down to their fan base and entourage. They also have the common trait of being boastful of their lineage, even though that is something in which they had no choice in the matter. Donald Trump did not choose his parents, and it's well known that his father, Fred Trump, a successful developer in Brooklyn and Queens,   launched

CHURCHILL
MADE THESE INSIGHTFUL
OBSERVATIONS ABOUT HITLER IN 1935, BASED
ON HIS OWN TREMENDOUS POLITICAL AND LIFE EXPERIENCES. THESE
SIGNS WHICH CHURCHILL SAW IN HITLER ARE THOSE SAME SIGNS SEEN IN TRUMP TODAY.

his son in business.

Despite their terrible psychological traits, these leaders achieve success in the elections and gain many supporters. One cannot help but wonder why this is happening and in so many countries around the world.

The answer to that question of how people like Trump and Hitler get into power is that there is an inherent inadequacy in the voting process. It counts the *heads* of the voters without weighing their *minds*- in other words, quantity over quality. This is the problem with the philosophy of voting. I believe this disease will be recognized in the results of the polls. As Churchill said when he described Hitler after he gained power:

I CAN CLEARLY SEE AND RECOGNIZE THE DISEASE OF HITLER—ISIS—AL-QAEDA—KKK IN TRUMP

"It was not till 1935 that the full terror of this revelation broke upon the careless and imprudent world, and Hitler, casting aside concealment, sprang forward armed to the teeth, with his munitions factories roaring night and day, his aeroplane squadrons forming in ceaseless succession, his submarine crews exercising in the Baltic, and his armed hosts tramping the barrack squares from one end of the broad Reich to the other." [10]

That was how Churchill described Hitler's condition after 1935, when he cast aside his concealment and sprang out, armed to the teeth. It is a strength of Churchill that he recognized such detailed traits of Hitler, years before the war, even though he had never met him.

One of the first editors to see a draft of this book used the same argument with me – how could I speak about Trump when I have not met him personally. I expect that this editor may actually be a supporter of Trump – his statements gave signs that he had been affected. I can clearly see and recognize the disease of Hitler–ISIS–Al-Qaeda–KKK in Trump, and that is why I have written this book.

To see clearly the disease of Hitler and the depth of it, let us also examine the meetings Neville Chamberlain, prime minister of England before Churchill, had with Adolf Hitler. In 1938, "the two men met at the Munich Conference between Britain, Germany, Italy, and France ... [which] convened to decide the future of Czechoslovakia's Sudetenland.

BRITISH PRIME MINISTER NEVILLE CHAMBERLAIN READ OUT THE AGREEMENT TO JUBILANT CROWDS IN 1938, AFTER HE AND HIS TEAM OF NEGOTIATORS HAD BEEN DECEIVED BY HITLER'S LIE THAT HE WOULD REMAIN PEACEFUL.

BRITISH PRIME MINISTER NEVILLE CHAMBERLAIN

The Munich Agreement stated the German leader's desire never to go to war with Britain again."

"On September 30, 1938, British Prime Minister Neville Chamberlain declared the accord with the Germans signaled 'peace for our time,' after he had read it to a jubilant crowd gathered at Heston Aerodrome in West London."

"The German leader stated in the agreement: 'We are determined to continue our efforts to remove possible sources of difference and thus to contribute to assure the peace of Europe.'"

"Adolf Hitler did not keep the promises he made to Neville Chamberlain. A year later the German leader derided the agreement as just a 'scrap of paper,' and on September 1, 1939 the German Army invaded Poland. Britain and France declared war on Nazi Germany two days later, and the Second World War began." [11]

This is a clear example of how Hitler fraudulently presented himself as an ally who would remove national differences and contribute to finding peaceful resolutions. He did not only deceive everyday people, but also the prime minister and his whole team of negotiators who were attempting to avoid war.

HITLER REACHED HIS POSITION THROUGH VOTING, AND NONE OF THOSE VOTERS SAW HOW DANGEROUS AND DISEASED HE WAS.

So what about Trump, who openly strives to construct sources of discord amongst people?

TRUMP ON OBAMA

Trump himself has criticized President Obama for an alleged inability to effectively negotiate, despite the latter being a graduate of Columbia University and Harvard Law School, where he served as president of the Harvard Law Review.

Trump said in his book *Get Tough* that Obama *"may have been a good 'community organizer', but the man is a lousy international deal maker. This is hardly a surprise – he has never built or run a business in his life."* [12]

So that being the case, how was he able to reach the White House? Why did the voters not elect a president who possessed the negotiation skills befitting a president? It is because the voting public themselves are not experts in negotiation and are thus unable to evaluate one's skills in that regard. Likewise, Trump's supporters, who think he can solve the nation's problems through effective management, are not experts in management or administration themselves.

TRUMP'S SUPPORTERS, WHO THINK HE CAN SOLVE THE NATION'S PROBLEMS THROUGH EFFECTIVE MANAGEMENT, ARE NOT EXPERTS IN MANAGEMENT OR ADMINISTRATION THEMSELVES.

In either situation, whether electing Obama, Trump, or any other president, the average working class American is not and will not be truly qualified to make a decisive choice. It is a simple, undeniable fact that those who do not have detailed knowledge and understanding of all the intricacies involved in running a country – and global relations –also do not have the ability to adequately appraise a public servant's ability to do so. Just as it is impossible for the average citizen to evaluate someone's ability to perform brain surgery or pilot a space shuttle, the average citizen cannot evaluate a candidate's ability to manage a nation.

This explains why so many people are following Trump; they are

HE BRINGS NEITHER ACTUAL STRATEGIES NOR PROCEDURES TO CREATE THE MUCH-NEEDED JOBS

looking for solutions, but they themselves have no idea about any of the details required to run a country successfully. The voting public is not to be blamed for this, though, as indeed they are only hoping for what is best for them and their country. However, Trump is using their good intentions and hopes as bait to lure them

into his trap. He only provides empty promises to take advantage of their situation by claiming:

"We will have, if I get elected, you may get bored with winning!" [The crowd cheered with applause] "I agree we'll never get bored with winning!" [13]

So he makes this empty promise and blames other external entities for all the nation's problems. He blames foreign governments, nationalities, and Islam, claiming this is what will *"make America great again."* He brings neither actual strategies nor procedures to create the much-needed jobs for the people; this is a regrettable situation they are in.

These examples clearly illustrate that vast numbers of the voting public are not qualified to accurately evaluate and judge the suitability of a candidate to be president. They cannot evaluate accurately in areas where they are out of their depth. This is one of the weaknesses and problems with voting.

It's important to point out that many who come to power through the vote of the majority only bring hardship to their nations and the world. Hitler reached his position through voting, and none of those voters saw how dangerous and diseased he was. When they voted for Hitler, his mindset was just the same as Trump's. It was the same disease. Hitler was similar to the KKK, Al-Qaeda, and ISIS; they are all reflections of each other. He was successful in reaching the majority, as they bought into his anti-Communist rhetoric, but they could never have known how costly their votes would be to humanity. Take a good look at the end of the story – it was a disaster. Those who gave Hitler the power wanted to use his sickness against their enemy, which was Communism. In the same way, those empowering Trump do not know where it will take them. They're running from the fire into a volcano. The coming together of the majority could be the coming together of destruction. If the minority had overcome the majority, it would have been better and more merciful for Germany and its people.

IT WAS MANKIND, FROM AMONGST THE DIFFERENT RACES AND ETHNICITIES, WHO PAID THE PRICE FOR THE WRONGNESS CAUSED BY THE VOTES OF GERMANY'S MAJORITY.

The example of Hitler is sufficient to clarify that the majority who chose him were upon falsehood, even though they were the majority. The minority who were against Hitler's election were upon the truth, even though they were the minority. It was mankind, from amongst the different races and ethnicities, who paid the price for the wrongness caused by the votes of Germany's majority. This included the innocent lives of women, children, men, and the devastation of property.

We hear from many different politicians that voting isn't perfect, but rather it is from the best options they see available.

This analysis proves that indeed it is only the arbitrary count of the heads that is measured, as opposed to the weight of the minds. It invalidates the concept that the majority should rule. The majority are often not capable of choosing correctly, because they are not qualified and versed enough in the competencies of the presidential role.

"No one pretends democracy is perfect or all wise. Indeed, it has been said that democracy is the worst form of government, except for all the others that have been tried from time to time;"

– Sir Winston Churchill

WALTER STONEMAN/HULTON ARCHIVE/GETTY IMAGES

3

DANGERS OF THE TONGUE

IN A FASCINATING REPORT, CNN'S BRIAN STELTER revealed how an individual could guide ordinary people through his or her speech and actions to far reaching consequences. The March, 2016 report showcased the work of Ph.D. student Sam Barnett, who uses technology to see the emotional captivation each of the presidential candidates can have on their listeners – even if a listener does not like or agree with that candidate. [14]

The example of what happened in Jonestown, Guyana exposes the dangers of the tongue and how it can even lead to convincing people to commit mass suicide. This was accomplished by the evil use of a leader's tongue to control his followers, all in the name of religion. CNN reported that "the key to understanding the tragedy that was Jonestown lies in the oratory skills of the People's Temple founder, Jim Jones. With the cadence and fervor of a Baptist preacher, the charm and folksiness of a country storyteller and the zeal and fury of a maniacal dictator, Jones exhorted his followers to a fever pitch...."

"As he spoke, they applauded, shouted, cheered... "He was very charismatic, very charismatic," said Leslie Wilson, who survived that fateful

"HE WAS VERY CHAR-ISMATIC, VERY CHAR-ISMATIC," SAID LESLIE WILSON, WHO SURVIVED THAT FATEFUL DAY IN JONESTOWN BY WALK-ING AWAY FROM THE SETTLEMENT BEFORE THE CYANIDE THAT KILLED MORE THAN NINE HUNDRED MEMBERS OF THE PEOPLES TEMPLE WAS DISTRIBUTED.

day in Jonestown by walking away from the settlement before the cyanide that killed more than nine hundred members of the Peoples Temple was distributed. She was one of [only] 33 people who began the day in Jonestown and lived to tell the tale....»

"Jones further enraptured crowds with [so-called] faith healings – laying hands on disabled or sick people who would miraculously be cured of any ailments. Though insiders later revealed that these healings were staged, Jones' mastery of word and presentation left few in attendance with any doubts about his abilities.... And he justified his brand of socialism with the Bible for those recruited from more conservative religious factions." [15]

Is this what Jesus (peace be upon him) preached?

It is amazing that they could have believed that Jesus and Mary (peace be upon them) were upon the same way as them? Indeed, the message of Moses, Jesus, and Mohammad (all of them servants of God) was far away from the deviations taught by Jim Jones. All the prophets were placed on the earth to actualize their main message to single out God in worship and not to have any intermediaries in their connection and relation with God. No one on earth requires an intermediary between himself or herself and God, no matter how bad someone may be. Each individual needs to seek forgiveness from God alone and actualize his worship to his Lord.

"Jones' tone as a speaker changed. He constantly fed his followers in Guyana a steady diet of fatalism. 'I said, life is a f**king disease,' he said. 'It's worse than cancer. It's a disease. And there's only one cure for the son of a bitchin' disease. That's death. And socialists can only take one form of death. What is it? Fight a god-damn war, or revolutionary suicide. If you don't believe life's a disease, then you're dumb. Very dumb.' Spurred on by their leader's talk, Peoples Temple members were ready to follow Jones even into death. At his request, they even wrote personal notes to him expressing their willingness to die for their cause." [16]

Compare this with the compassionate call of the Prophets; they didn't come to order the people to work for them, kill children, or be oppressive to the people. Look to the call of Moses, Jesus, and Mohammad; they didn't call to worship themselves, rather to worship God alone. They didn't distinguish themselves from the rest of the people by wearing special clothes, nor did they go around collecting money from them as the holy and religious men and women of almost every religion do today. The Prophets worked for their living and spent on their belief. They came only with their message from God and did not introduce anything from themselves into it.

It is amazing how the followers of Rev. Jim Jones obeyed him. He made total submission and obedience to himself a part of his religion, and likened it to the worship of Jesus son of Mary (peace be upon them). He imprisoned their souls to the extent of eventually mak-

WE SEE A MASS OF PEOPLE GET MISGUIDED BY A PERSON WITH HIS TONGUE AND SPEECH, WHILE THE CALL OF THE PROPHET JESUS IS CLEAR AND, FAR FROM THAT

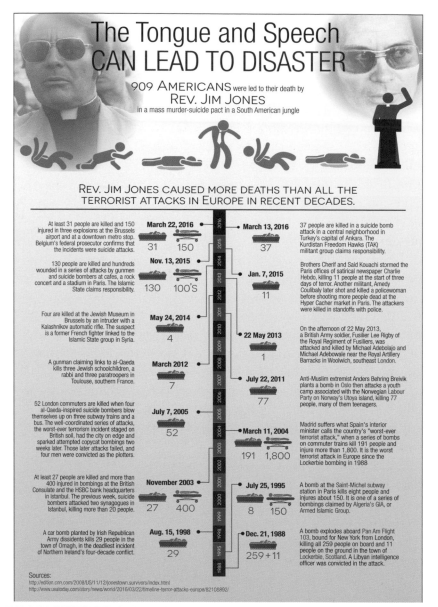

THIS IS AN EXAMPLE OF JUST HOW FAR THE SPEECH OF ONE MAN WAS ABLE TO CAPTIVATE THE HEARTS AND MINDS OF HUNDREDS OF SHORT-SIGHTED PEOPLE. THESE WERE NOT UNEDUCATED FOREIGNERS, THEY WERE BORN AND RAISED IN AMERICA. IF THIS WAS THE CASE WITH ONE MAN WHO LED SO MANY TO THEIR DEATH, THEN WHAT ABOUT THE VOTING PUBLIC? THE DANGERS UPON THOSE FROM THE ELECTORATE WHO MAY BE SHORT-SIGHTED WOULD BE TERRIBLE IF THEY BEGIN TO FOLLOW THE WRONG LEADER. THEY ARE NOT OF AN ADEQUATE LEVEL OF POLITICAL EXPERTISE IN ORDER TO EFFECTIVELY DECIPHER THE RHETORIC PRESENTED TO THEM. VOTING THUS PUTS THESE MASSES IN A POSITIONTHAT BRINGS ABOUT MORE HARM FOR THEM THAN GOOD. I BELIEVE TRUMP IS TRULY HARMFUL FOR THE FUTURE OF AMERICA.

ing them commit suicide. We see a mass of people get misguided by a person with his tongue and speech, while the call of the Prophet Jesus is clear and, far from that, for everyone to see. Sadly, we see from this story that these people of sick mindset are still able to find followers, just as Hitler found followers.

Trump and his disease will lead the US to virtual suicide. This will happen with the intent, will, and support of those who follow him, just as the followers of Rev. Jim Jones allowed him to lead them. This same thing is happening from some of the political leaders supporting Trump, like Ben Carson and Chris Christie.

I have confidence that the majority of the electorate will not vote for Trump and his way of thinking because they are

IT'S NOT JUST A MATTER OF THIS ONE PARTICULAR TRUMP; MORE TRUMPS WILL COME AND FOLLOW IN HIS WAY.

aware of the consequences that will result. It's not just a matter of this one particular Trump; more Trumps will come and follow in his way. This way of Trump/Hitler will keep spreading, and it will spread even more in the next thirty years if intelligent Americans do not stop it. It will be difficult to stop, not just in the US but in Europe also. The right-wing parties that are multiplying by leaps and bounds are another version of Trumpism.

Think about this: If you count all those who died in every terrorist attack in Europe in recent decades, it will not reach 909, the number of followers who committed suicide by their will and intent following Rev. Jim Jones.

Those terrorists are a filthy, evil, and misguided people. But was the Rev. Jim Jones really so different? For he, in the name of the Bible and using only his tongue and speech, was able to make 909 people kill themselves.

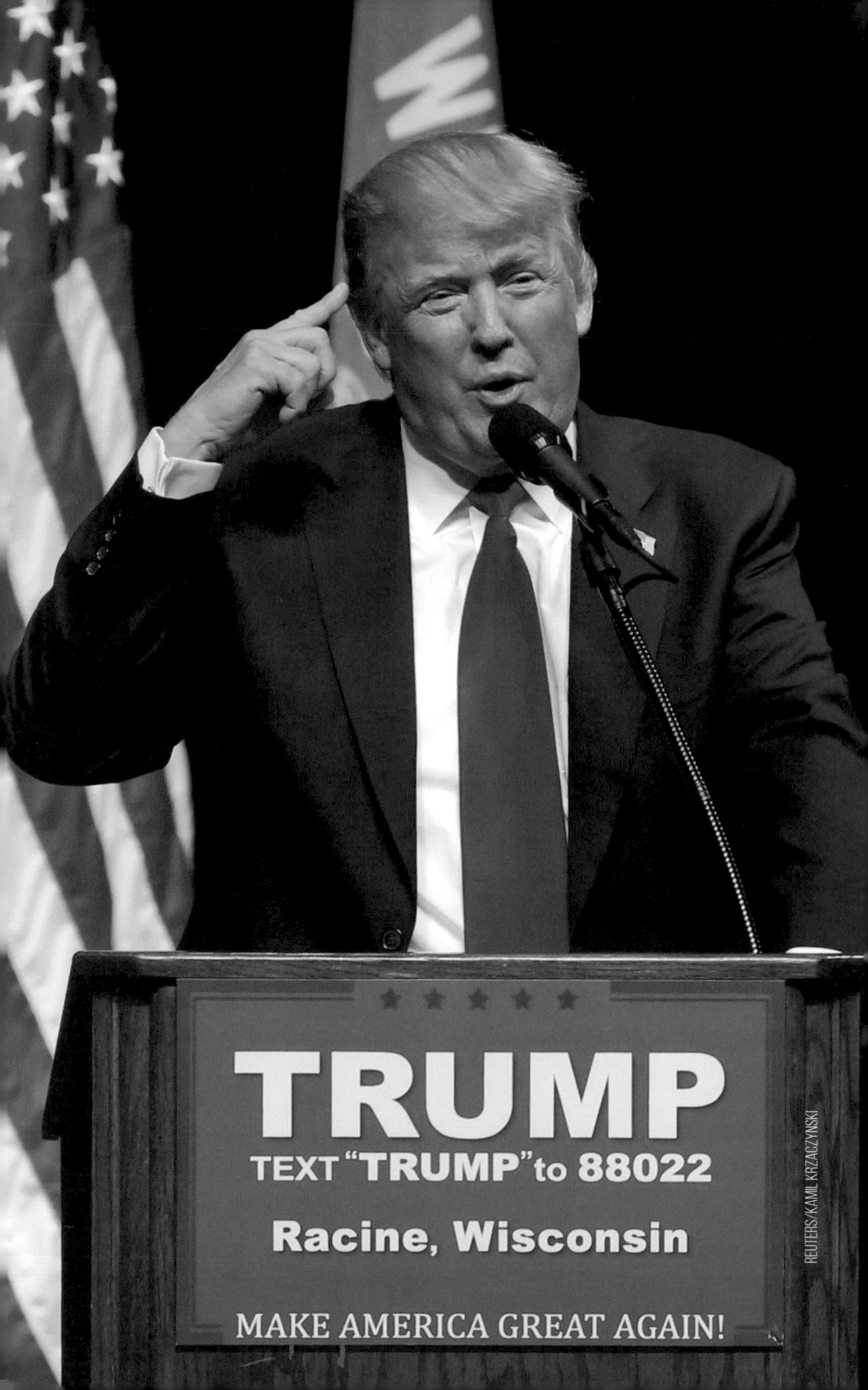

REUTERS/KAMIL KRZACZYNSKI

WHO IS THIS TRUMP? (IN HIS OWN WORDS)

4

IS THIS THE SPEECH OF
WHO YOU WANT TO BE
AMERICA'S PRESIDENT?

IVANKA, TRUMP'S DAUGHTER

"... she does have a very nice figure. I've said that if Ivanka weren't my daughter, perhaps, I would be dating her."[17] *What do you have in common with Ivanka? "Well I was going to say s-x, but I can't really."*[18]

HILLARY CLINTON, FORMER SECRETARY OF STATE

"If Hillary cannot even satisfy her husband, what makes you think she can satisfy America?"[19] *"got schlonged"*[20]

ROSIE O'DONNELL, TELEVISION ACTRESS

"Disgusting both inside and out. You take a look at her, she's a slob. She

talks like a truck driver." [21]* *"Rosie's a very unattractive person, both inside and out."* [22] Asked about his use of language like *"fat pigs," "dogs," "slobs"* and *"disgusting animals"* to describe some women, *"Only Rosie O'Donnell."* [23] *"If she ever fell in the wrong direction I wouldn't have a chance."* [24] *"She was at the wedding and I got extremely*

angry because she ate almost the entire wedding cake." [25] *"Rosie's a loser. A real loser. I look forward to taking lots of money from my nice fat little Rosie."* [26] *"Rosie is crude, rude, obnoxious and dumb — other than that I like her very much!"* [27] *"I mean she's a total trainwreck"* [28] *"I like to see bad people fail; Rosie failed, I'm happy about it."* [29] *"I'd look her right in that fat ugly face of hers and say Rosie, you're fired!"* [30] *"I'll probably sue her; I'd like to take some money out of her fat a** pockets."* [31]

TRUMP'S CHILDREN

"Cause I like kids, I mean, I won't do anything to take care of them. I'll supply funds and she'll take care of the kids. It's not like I'm gonna be walking the kids down Central Park." [32]

DIANA, PRINCESS OF WALES
(SHORTLY AFTER HER DEATH IN A CAR CRASH)

You could've gotten her, right? You could've nailed her. *"I think I could have."* [33]

HALF OF TRUMP'S FRIENDS

"What really fascinates me is email. I have friends — first of all — half of my friends are under indictment right now because they sent emails to each other about how they're screwing people, email is unbelievable. They'll talk on the phone, they can't even say hello, they don't want to say hello or goodbye, and yet they'll write you a message that they're having sex with 15 different married women." [34]

---

* Trump's showering of insults on Rosie O'Donnell included: **"She talks like a truck driver"** It's truly sad how he looks down upon hard-working blue-collar Americans, such as truck drivers.

BODY PARTS

"My fingers are long and beautiful, as, it has been well documented, are various other parts of my body." [35] *"You know, it really doesn't matter what the media write as long as you've got a young, and beautiful, piece of a*s."* [36]

CHINA

"Listen, you motherf--ers, we're going to tax you twenty-five percent" [37] *"We can't continue to allow China to rape our country, and that's what they're doing."* [38] *"China right now has $1.8 trillion of our debt! They're cheating us, and they're friends of mine!"* [39] *"The Chinese leaders are not our friends. I've been criticized for calling them our enemy. But what else do you call the people who are destroying your children's future? What name would you prefer me to use for the people who are hell bent on bankrupting our nation, stealing our jobs, who spy on us to steal our technology, who are undermining our currency, and who are ruining our way of life? To my mind that's an enemy."* [40]

MEXICO

"we get the killers, drugs & crime, they get the money!" [41] *"they're killing us"* [42] *"They are not our friend; believe me."* [43] *"Mexico is not our friend. Mexico is the new China."* [44] *"We're going to build a great wall and Mexico will pay for it."* [45] *"The wall just got ten feet taller, believe me. It just got ten feet taller."* [46]

INDIA

"India is taking our jobs. It is not going to happen anymore, folks!" [47]

SAUDI ARABIA

"You're not gonna raise that fuc*in' price!" [48]

AFRICAN AMERICANS

"Black guys counting my money; I hate it! The only kind of people I want counting my money are little short guys that wear yarmulkes every day." [49]

NATIVE AMERICANS AND ELIZABETH WARREN, SENATOR

"Pocahontas" [50] *"Goofy Elizabeth"* [51] *"weak and ineffective. Does nothing. All talk, no action – maybe her Native American name?"* [52]

BRANDE RODERICK, TELEVISION CONTESTANT

"must be a pretty picture, you dropping to your knees." [53]

JEB BUSH, FORMER FLORIDA GOVERNOR

"had to bring in mommy to take a slap at me" [54] *"a total embarrassment to himself and his family"* [55]

BEN CARSON, RETIRED NEUROSURGEON

"has never created a job in his life (well, maybe a nurse)" [56]

TED CRUZ, UNITED STATES SENATOR

"a nasty guy" [57] *"lies like a dog over and over again!"* [58] *"in bed with Wall St."* [59]

LINDSEY GRAHAM, UNITED STATES SENATOR

"should respect me" [60] *"nasty!"* [61]

JOHN KASICH, OHIO GOVERNOR

"I will sue him just for fun!" [62]

MARTIN O'MALLEY, DEMOCRATIC CANDIDATE, FORMER GOVERNOR OF MARYLAND

"a clown" [63]

GEORGE PATAKI, FORMER NEW YORK GOVERNOR

"couldn't be elected dog catcher if he ran again" [64]

RAND PAUL, UNITED STATES SENATOR

"reminds me of a spoiled brat without a properly functioning brain" [65]

RICK PERRY, FORMER TEXAS GOVERNOR

"should be forced to take an IQ test" [66]

MARCO RUBIO, UNITED STATES SENATOR

"a joke!" [67] *"perfect little puppet"* [68]

BERNIE SANDERS, UNITED STATES SENATOR

"wacko" [69]

SCOTT WALKER, WISCONSIN GOVERNOR

"puppet" [70]

MARIAH CAREY, SINGER

Would you bang her? "I would do it without hesitation." [71]

ANGELINA JOLIE, FILM ACTRESS

"I never thought she was good-looking. I don't think she's got good skin. I don't think she's got a great face. I think her lips are too big, to be honest with you, they look like too big." [72]

NICOLLETTE SHERIDAN, TELEVISION AC-TRESS

"A person who is very flat-chested is very hard to be a 10." [73]

CARMEN ELECTRA, TELEVISION ACTRESS

"The boob job is terrible — they look like two light posts coming out of a body." [74]

GLENN BECK, TELEVISION PERSONALITY

"wacko" [75] *"mental basketcase"* [76] *"a real nut job"* [77]

ELIZABETH BECK, LAWYER
"she wanted to breast pump in front of me at dep." [78]

BRENT BOZELL, PRESIDENT, MEDIA RESEARCH CENTER
"begging for money like a dog" [79]

DAVID BROOKS, COLUMNIST, THE NEW YORK TIMES
"a clown" [80] *"one of the dumbest of all pundits"* [81]

GRAYDON CARTER, EDITOR, VANITY FAIR
"sloppy" [82] *"grubby"* [83]

S.E. CUPP, COLUMNIST
"flunkie" [84]

ERICK ERICKSON, CONSERVATIVE COMMENTATOR
"got fired like a dog" [85] *"total low life"* [86] *"a major sleaze and buffoon"* [87]

DAVID GREGORY, POLITICAL ANALYST, CNN
"fired like a dog!" [88]

JEFF HORWITZ, REPORTER, THE ASSOCIATED PRESS
"wouldn't know the truth if it hit him in the face" [89]

SAMUEL L. JACKSON, ACTOR
"cheats" [90]

CHERI JACOBUS, G.O.P. CONSULTANT
"Begged my people for a job" [91] *"Major loser, zero credibility!"* [92]

PENN JILLETTE, PERFORMER
"hokey garbage" [93] *"goofball"* [94]

MEGYN KELLY, FOX NEWS ANCHOR

"Crazy" [95] *"I refuse to call Megyn Kelly a bimbo, because that would not be politically correct"* [96]

FRANK LUNTZ, POLITICAL CONSULTANT

"a total clown" [97] *"a low-class slob"* [98]

ANGELA MERKEL, GERMAN CHANCELLOR

"ruining Germany" [99]

ANA NAVARRO, CNN CONTRIBUTOR

"flunkie" [100]

COKIE ROBERTS, CONTRIBUTOR, "MORNING EDITION"

"kooky" [101]

MITT ROMNEY, FORMER MASSACHUSETTS GOVERNOR

"I could've said, 'Mitt, drop to your knees,' and he would've dropped to his knees." [102]

KARL ROVE, FORMER DEPUTY WHITE HOUSE CHIEF OF STAFF

"moron" [103] *"irrelevant clown, sweats and shakes nervously"* [104]

BEN SASSE, UNITED STATES SENATOR

"looks more like a gym rat than a U.S. Senator" [105]

STUART STEVENS, POLITICAL CONSULTANT

"a dumb guy who fails @ virtually everything he touches" [106] *"a clown!"* [107]

CHRIS STIREWALT, EDITOR, FOX NEWS CHANNEL

"really dumb puppet" [108]

JOHN SUNUNU, FORMER NEW HAMPSHIRE GOVERNOR

"couldn't get elected dog catcher" [109] *"forgot to mention my phenomenal biz success rate"* [110]

MARC THIESSEN, COLUMNIST AND FOX NEWS CONTRIBUTOR

"really dumb puppet" [111]

CHUCK TODD, MODERATOR, "MEET THE PRESS"

"will be fired like a dog" [112] *"pathetic"* [113] *"love watching him fail"* [114]

BOB VANDER PLAATS, PRESIDENT AND CHIEF EXECUTIVE, THE FAMILY LEADER

"a total phony and con man" [115]

RICK WILSON, REPUBLICAN POLITICAL CONSULTANT

"dumb as a rock" [116]

FOX NEWS, NEWS ORGANIZATION

"the only network that does not even mention my very successful event" [117]

THE NEW HAMPSHIRE UNION LEADER, NEWSPAPER

"kicked out of the ABC news debate like a dog" [118]

POLITICO, NEWS ORGANIZATION

"pure scum" [119] *"clowns"* [120]

AMERICAN COMPANIES THAT OUTSOURCED OVERSEAS

"come back to New Hampshire, and you can tell them to go f**k themselves!" [121]

MACY'S DEPARTMENT STORE

"very disloyal to me" [122] *"Macy's stores suck"* [123]

5

TRUMP AND HIS FILTHY SPEECH

THERE ARE MANY EXAMPLES IN WHICH TRUMP has chosen to use filthy, lewd, and disgusting speech publicly.

One example is his statement about his daughter on *The View* television show:

"Although she does have a very nice figure. I've said that if Ivanka weren't my daughter, perhaps, I would be dating her." [124]

And in another interview, when asked what he had in common with Ivanka, he replied:

"Well I was going to say s*x, but I can't really." [125]

Donald Trump attacked Mrs. Hillary Clinton stating she *"got schlonged"* [126] by Barack Obama in the 2008 presidential race at a rally in Grand Rapids, Michigan.

On *Celebrity Apprentice*, Trump commented to contestant Brande Roderick that it, *"must be a pretty picture, you dropping to your knees."* [127] This was after he was informed about how she had begged to her team members on his show.

In a 1991 *Esquire Magazine* interview, Trump stated, *"You know, it really doesn't matter what the media write as long as you've got a young, and beautiful, piece of ass."* [128]

At a New Hampshire rally, he said, *"We're gonna bring businesses back. We're gonna have businesses that used to be in New Hampshire, that are now in Mexico, come back to New Hampshire, and you can tell them to go f**k themselves!"* [129]

"My fingers are long and beautiful, as, it has been well documented, are various other parts of my body." [130]

These are the characteristics and manners of a presidential candidate that are exposed to everyone; to men and women, and even to children in their schools. Is this appropriate for a president? What does America want? His supporters must want a place where anything goes, no matter how inappropriate or unacceptable.

We see the way he speaks is parallel to the life his grandfather Friedrich Trump lived. The well-known German *DW News* reported Trump's grandfather built his restaurants on land that he did not own. In that time of the Gold Rush in the Klondike, it was the Wild West period. It was wide open, very raw, with lots of single men desperately trying to find gold; and prostitutes. Grandpa Trump's restaurants had liquor, food and access to women. His restaurants had little cubicles off to the sides with heavy curtains – so called private rooms for ladies – which was absolutely understood to mean prostitutes. [131]

TRUMP SAID ABOUT JOHN MCCAIN, UNITED STATES SENATOR: *"dummy"* [152] *"graduated last in his class"* [153]

TRUMP SAID ABOUT JOHN SUNUNU, FORMER NEW HAMPSHIRE GOVERNOR: *"dummy"* [134]

"Sorry losers and haters, but my I.Q. is one of the highest — and you all know it! Please don't feel so stupid or insecure, it's not your fault" [137]
- *@realDonaldTrump*

TRUMP SAID ABOUT ALWALEED BIN TALAL, PRINCE, SAUDI ARABIA: *"dopey"* [139]

TRUMP SAID ABOUT LINDSEY GRAHAM, UNITED STATES SENATOR: *"dumb mouthpiece"* [140]

TRUMP SAID ABOUT ARIANNA HUFFINGTON, FOUNDER, THE HUFFINGTON POST: *"dummy"* [23]

TRUMP SAID ABOUT MORT ZUCKERMAN, OWNER, THE NEW YORK DAILY NEWS: *"dopey clown"* [24]

"The final key to the way I promote is bravado. I play to people's fantasies... That's why a little hyperbole [exaggeration] never hurts. ... I call it truthful hyperbole." [25]

- Donald Trump in The Art of the Deal

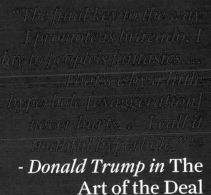

TRUMP SAID ABOUT MITT ROMNEY, FORMER MASS. GOVERNOR: *"one of the dumbest and worst"* [19] *"so awkward and goofy"* [20]

TRUMP SAID ABOUT KARL ROVE, FORMER DEPUTY WHITE HOUSE CHIEF OF STAFF: *"dummy"* [21] *"dopey"* [22] *"total fool"* [23] *"moron"* [24]

6

TRUMP'S AMAZEMENT WITH HIS OWN WEALTH

I N 1987, *FORBES MAGAZINE* IDENTIFIED 140 BILLION-aires, including 96 outside of the United States. Roughly 60% of that larger group were self-made, with only Europe having pre-dominantly old, inherited money.[147] Trump, of course, is from those who received their startup capital from their family, as he has said that he received from his wealthy father "a small loan of a million dollars."[148]

Since his early life, Trump's way is to be boastful and to show off about his money in a way not spoken by others who are much richer than he.

In 1987, David Letterman introduced Trump by joking, "Our next guest has

SINCE HIS EARLY LIFE, TRUMP'S WAY IS TO BE BOASTFUL AND TO SHOW OFF ABOUT HIS MONEY IN A WAY NOT SPOKEN BY OTHERS WHO ARE MUCH RICHER THAN HIM.

enough money to give everyone in the audience tonight a million dollars."[149]

Trump has also said, *"Part of the beauty of me is that I'm very rich."*[150]

He told CNN's Anderson Cooper, *"Hey Anderson, I'm a very rich guy... I'm a very, very, rich guy."*[151]

CNN Newsroom also broadcast him saying on April 17, 2016:

"Nobody has better toys than I do, I could put 'em in the best planes and bring 'em to the best resorts in the world... I could put 'em in the best places in the world – California, I have something that blows everything away."[152]

Trump has a long history of bragging about his money. Did any leaders in the United States' history talk like this about their own wealth? They did not, which shows us this is a disease that he carries inside himself. The people of intellect find this type of bragging repulsive.

It is as if Trump is saying: *"Everyone who does not have a billion dollars is dumb, and should follow me."*

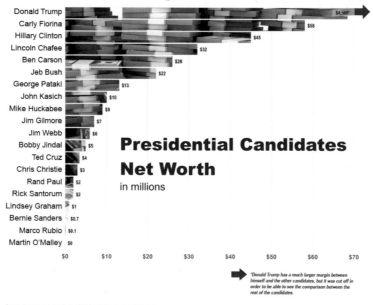

Presidential Candidates Net Worth

in millions

Donald Trump	$4,500*
Carly Fiorina	$58
Hillary Clinton	$45
Lincoln Chafee	$32
Ben Carson	$26
Jeb Bush	$22
George Pataki	$13
John Kasich	$10
Mike Huckabee	$9
Jim Gilmore	$7
Jim Webb	$6
Bobby Jindal	$5
Ted Cruz	$4
Chris Christie	$3
Rand Paul	$2
Rick Santorum	$2
Lindsey Graham	$1
Bernie Sanders	$0.7
Marco Rubio	$0.1
Martin O'Malley	$0

*Donald Trump has a much larger margin between himself and the other candidates, but it was cut off in order to be able to see the comparison between the rest of the candidates.

Source: Forbes.com; Article- Forbes' 2016 Presidential Candidate Wealth List
http://www.forbes.com/sites/afontevecchia/2015/09/29/forbes-2016-presidential-candidate-net-worth-list/#73f2edc7435d

TRUMP IS THE WEALTHIEST CANDIDATE, BUT HE'S ALSO THE MOST DANGEROUS FOR AMERICA.

7

CONTRADICTIONS

FUNDRAISING CONTRADICTION

WHEN I BEGAN WRITING THIS BOOK, TRUMP was often speaking out against candidates who sought donations. For months he portrayed his Republican opponents as "puppets" for relying on super PACs and taking contributions from wealthy donors that he said came with strings attached.

Trump said of current political leaders at an Iowa rally in February: *"You know a lot of times you see these really dumb deals, and you'll say that's dumb. It doesn't make sense. But then when you think, it does make sense because these politicians are representing interests, whether it's a country or a company, where doing the stupid deals actually makes sense only for that politician and for that company or country."* [153]

In contrast, he described himself, *"I'm self-funding my own campaign. It's my money."* [154]

WHY IS HE SOLICITING DONATIONS, WHILE HE HIMSELF HAS BILLIONS?

And the question at that time was: Why is he soliciting donations, while he himself has billions?

It is amazing that his followers didn't see that contradiction. There is a video exposing his disease in which he explains why he collected donations from the people:

"Small donations... we do accept that, because people want to invest in the campaign."[155]

The intelligent ones will see through these diseases of Trump clearly. How can Trump claim that he only accepted small donations, while it clearly stated on his official website otherwise? He would accept from any individual thousands of dollars for each stage of his campaign.

Despite Trump's repeated boasting that he didn't need anyone's money, he still invited people to donate. Even his own contributions to his campaign are in the form of loans which can be paid back to him from future donations,[156] as is in line with Federal Election Commission rules, which allow later contributions to be used to pay back loans.

IF CAMPAIGN DONATIONS ARE WRONG DUE TO THE CORRUPTION INVOLVED, THEN WHY HAS HE WILFULLY BECOME A PART OF THE PROBLEM?

Likewise, why did he himself contribute such large amounts to political campaigns in the past if he considers it corruption? Data from the Federal Election Commission and state elections offices show that Trump has given $584,850 to Democrats and $961,140 to the GOP over the last 26 years.[157]

As of May 2016 Trump's campaign has completely reversed gears in preparation for the general election, and is accepting massive donations from special interests. *"I'll be putting up money, but won't be completely self-funding,"* [158] Trump explained.

As just one example, on May 14, 2016, billionaire Republican donor Sheldon Adelson is reportedly willing to give Donald Trump as much as $100 million for his presidential campaign – a purported record-setting amount. [159] Trump even tweeted this news from his personal Twitter account. [160]

In April, candidate Ted Cruz was lamenting the American political process during a campaign stop in NH, saying, "Running for office is real simple: you just surgically disconnect your shame sensor, because you spend every day asking people for money." [161] By June, as the presumptive nominee, Trump has come to the same place: "Right now we're facing an emergency goal of $100,000 to help get our ads on the air." That is truly a relatively pathetic amount for a claimed multibillionaire to be begging from his supporters as an 'emergency'. [162] One wonders just how operational his shame sensor ever was!

What is Trump's philosophy in this regard – is it wrong or right? If campaign donations are wrong due to the corruption involved, then why has he wilfully become a part of the problem?

My personal message to Trump is:

You previously claimed that if you ordered Mitt Romney to get down on his knees, he would have obeyed you. [163] So now, will you be obeying Sheldon Adelson and be down on your knees before him in the very same way you expected of Romney? Your own situation is actually much more pathetic than the situation Romney was in before, as he was in need of support at the time. As for yourself, you're a billionaire scrounging for donations and that really doesn't befit someone who's wealthy by any standards. You likewise cannot claim that your opinions and stances cannot be bought, because you're proving that they can, otherwise you wouldn't be accepting these donations which you are not in need of. You have gone on record repeatedly that those who accept donations have strings attached.

TRUMP'S OVERSEAS DOUBLE STANDARD

Trump has said that he will force American companies that transferred their factories offshore to bring them back. This is while he himself knows well that he manufactures his clothing line in countries like Bangladesh, Mexico, and China. In other words, Trump's speech necessitates he'll need to launch a trade war against himself, as capably explained in *Forbes* by Stuart Anderson:

"Mr. Trump is either inexcusably hypocritical or inexcusably ignorant of economics," according to Donald J. Boudreaux, a professor of economics at George Mason University. "There is zero economic difference between, say, a U.S. car company's investments abroad in factories and Mr. Trump's own investments abroad in hotels: both are meant to improve the bottom line of companies headquartered in the U.S. by taking advantage of profitable economic opportunities outside of the U.S."

> 'THERE IS ZERO ECONOMIC DIFFERENCE BETWEEN, SAY, A U.S. CAR COMPANY'S INVESTMENTS ABROAD IN FACTORIES AND MR. TRUMP'S OWN INVESTMENTS ABROAD IN HOTELS'

"Trump has repeatedly said that if elected, he would not allow Ford to open a new plant in Mexico," reported the *Detroit News*. At his campaign announcement speech in New York in June, Trump said he would call [Ford CEO Mark] Fields to explain the "bad news."

"Let me give you the bad news: Every car, every truck and every part manufactured in this plant that comes across the border, we're going to charge you a 35% tax," Trump said. "They are going to take away thousands of jobs."

"When it comes to political hypocrisy, Donald Trump deserves a gold medal," said Mark J. Perry, a professor of economics and finance at the University of Michigan-Flint and creator of the economics

> **'WHEN IT COMES TO POLITICAL HYPOCRISY, DONALD TRUMP DESERVES A GOLD MEDAL,'**

blog Carpe Diem. "At the same time that the billionaire businessman criticizes Ford for producing some of its cars in Mexico, and threatens to stop any expansion there and impose a 35% tax on Ford imports from Mexico, he certainly has no trouble taking advantage of the global marketplace when it comes to his own businesses."

"For Trump to operate, outsource and invest globally while criticizing companies like Ford for doing the same is the ultimate hypocrisy. To be fair to Ford, Trump should either agree to impose a 35% tax on Trump Collection clothing and agree to stop investing overseas, or he should stop his threats against Ford for operating as a global carmaker."[164]

Forbes presented the following breakdown of Trump's foreign investments:

Under "Our Hotels" on the Trump Hotel Collection website, it lists six domestic hotels and six international hotels. Is the problem Ford is building something in Latin America? Well, there are Trump hotels in Panama and Rio de Janeiro. The other hotels abroad are in Toronto, Doonbeg, Ireland, Vancouver, and

Baku, Azerbaijan. (Toronto and Vancouver also have a Trump Tower.)

On the website for the Trump Real Estate Collection, nine international properties are listed, including two Trump Towers in India and one in Istanbul, another in Uruguay and another in the Philippines, as well as a Trump World in South Korea, among others.

If one argued the way Donald Trump argues on the campaign trail, then one could say that Donald Trump is costing America jobs by building hotels and commercial real estate in foreign countries instead of in the United States. In theory, the same money used to build and staff more than a dozen properties abroad could have supported thousands of jobs in America.[165]

TRUMP ON HIS COMPETITION

Trump has also been contradictory regarding key political personalities. I'll mention just the two examples of Hillary Clinton and Jeb Bush.

TRUMP ON HILLARY CLINTON BEFORE:

In 2012, as Obama was running for re-election, Trump called Clinton *"terrific"* again in an interview with Fox News, saying she performed well as Secretary of State.

'HILLARY CLINTON I THINK IS A TERRIFIC WOMAN,'

"Hillary Clinton I think is a terrific woman," he told Greta Van Susteren. *"I am biased because I have known her for years. I live in New York. She lives in New York. I really like her and her husband both a lot. I think she really works hard. And I think, again, she's given an agenda, it is not all of her, but I think she really works hard and I think she does a good job. I like her."*[166]

AFTER:

"Well, I think she's an embarrassment to our country," Trump said on CNN's *New Day. "She doesn't have the strength or the stamina to be president, frankly, as far as I'm concerned."*

"She talks about defeat our enemies. Well, where has she been for the last year? We can't even beat ISIS. She's not defeating our enemy. She wouldn't know how to defeat the enemy. It's ridiculous. ... I think she's an embarrassment, and we'll see what happens."[167]

DONALD TRUMP ON JEB BUSH BEFORE:

"Florida Governor Jeb Bush is a good man. I've held fundraisers for him. He's exactly the kind of political leader this country needs now and will very much need in the future. He, too, knows how to hang in there.

'FLORIDA GOVERNOR JEB BUSH IS A GOOD MAN.'

His first shot at Florida's governorship didn't work out, but he didn't give up. He was campaigning the day after his loss. He won the next race in a landslide. He's bright, tough, and princi- pled. I like the Bush family very much. I believe we could get another president from the Bushes. He may be the one."[168]

AFTER:

Trump tweeted: *"The last thing our country needs is another BUSH! Dumb as a rock!"*[169]

Trump said on *Meet the Press* with Chuck Todd: *"Jeb is a weak and ineffective person. He's also a low- energy person, which I've said before. But he's a weak and ineffective person. Jeb, if he were president, it would just be more of the same, it would be just—he's got money from all of the lobbyists and all of the special interests that run him like a puppet. He's got 2 percent in the polls; I have 41 percent in the latest poll. He has 2 percent. He's going to be off the stage soon. He's an embarrassment to the Bush family and, in fact, he doesn't even want to use the Bush name, which is interesting.*

Jeb is an embarrassment to himself and to his family and the Republican Party—they're not even listening to Jeb. Jeb is saying that—by the way, Chuck, Jeb is only saying that to try and get a little mojo going, but in the meantime, I went up 11 points in the new Fox poll. I went up 11 points after the debate, and he went down 2." [170]

REUTERS/BRENDAN MCDERMID

8

"THE ENDS JUSTIFY THE MEANS"

TRUMP CARRIES THE IDEOLOGY OF "THE ENDS justify the means." This ideology is a path for destruction of all values and manners. Due to that, the price of this to society would be destruction, especially if this principle becomes something commonplace and acceptable amongst the younger generation. If the president were to embody this idea and the methodology of the White House shifted in that direction, the results would be disastrous. If Trump uses this methodology and the people accept it with smiles, happiness, and support, what would come next? How will he deal with the economy, the military, and everything else? It is a long list, which will make the intelligent ones realize just how big the problem is.

The Telegraph reported Donald Trump has praised the leadership style of North Korea's dictator Kim Jong-un, for the "amazing" way he murders political rivals.

"You've got to give him credit. How many young guys – he was like 26 or 25 when his father died - take over these tough generals, and all of a sudden… he goes in, he takes over, he's the boss, it's incredible. He wiped out the uncle, he wiped out this one, that one. This guy doesn't play games" [171]

Not that it is surprising, Trump also described himself in the very same way as he described Kim Jong-un.

"They will know I'm not playing games." [172]

This was while discussing the issue of Iran on Fox News.

He does not want to show clearly his measuring stick. He said that Mexicans are drug dealers and rapists,[173] and then he said in February 2016, making an excuse for his own hiring of foreign workers:

"As far as the people that I've hired in various parts of Florida during the absolute prime season, like Palm Beach and other locations, you could not get help. It's the up season. People didn't want to have part-time jobs. There were part-time jobs, very seasonal, ninety-day jobs, one-hundred-and twenty-day jobs, and you couldn't get (them filled).

"Everybody agrees with me on that. They were part-time jobs. You needed them, or we just might as well close the doors, because you couldn't get help in those hot, hot sections of Florida." [174]

So how can we understand the first quote in relation to the second quote? He says this smiling, and people are accepting it and laughing about it, even if it is the principle of "the ends justify the means".

Likewise, when questioned about his hiring of illegal aliens from Poland, his only reply was, *"You haven't hired anybody,"*[175] without answering the actual question with anything relevant.

One of the topics Trump argues about the most is illegal immigration, so his evasive response without providing any clarification whatsoever makes no sense. Despite these tactics, his supporters still rally around him! Where will this take us and how can we understand it?

> NO SERIOUS PRESIDENTIAL CANDIDATE HAS EVER HAD TRUMP'S DEPTH OF DOCUMENTED BUSINESS RELATIONSHIPS WITH MOB-CONTROLLED ENTITIES."

We can see from this article from the *Washington Post* on February 29, 2016, that Trump's disease of corruption is widespread and that he is able to use unscrupulous means such as dealing with mobsters, even within the confines of the law:

> While Trump was never accused of doing anything illegal, he worked extensively with companies controlled by the mafia on properties in New York and Atlantic City, including Trump Tower and Trump Plaza.
>
> Some would say that was the only way to develop property in New York in the 1970s and 1980s – the mob controlled many parts of the city's construction industry, including concrete, labor unions and trash disposal. Still, the extent of Trump's involvement is certainly unique. No serious presidential candidate has ever had Trump's depth of documented business relationships with mob-controlled entities.[176]

> 'HE DID NOT SPECIFY WHICH ADDITIONAL METHODS OF TORTURE HE WOULD INTRODUCE

As another example, see his insistence on waterboarding prisoners and doing *"a whole lot more"* to them, as reported in *The Economist* on February 13, 2016:

"You bet your ass I would," Donald Trump said in November, addressing whether he might, if elected, bring back waterboarding, the interrogation technique used during the Bush administration in the early 2000s and abandoned, for its brutality and ineffectiveness, in 2009. Mr. Trump declared he'd embrace waterboarding *"in a heartbeat"* because *"it works."* The GOP presidential candidate then mused that the practice serves nicely as a punishment even if it fails to loosen suspects' lips: *"If it doesn't work, they deserve it anyway for what they do to us."*

HE IS THE EMBODIMENT OF A DEVIANT PHILOSOPHY THAT IS FAR REMOVED FROM SENSIBILITY AND FAIRNESS, PRINCIPLES WHICH ARE PARAMOUNT TO A HARMONIOUS WORLD.

On February 6th, at the most recent Republican presidential debate, Mr. Trump repeated his support for waterboarding and upped the ante on what George Bush's advisers euphemistically called 'enhanced interrogation' techniques fifteen years ago. *"They're chopping off heads of Christians and many other people in the Middle East. They're chopping heads off, they laugh at us when they hear we're not going to approve waterboarding."* he noted. To wage the war on terror, Mr. Trump said he would *"bring back a hell of a lot worse than waterboarding."* He did not specify which additional methods of torture he would introduce to bolster American intelligence-gathering. [177]

In this quote, we clearly see how Trump tries to justify being two-faced to Larry King in 2013, and he is not even ashamed:

"I got along with everybody. I got along with the Clintons, I got along with the Republicans, the Democrats, the liberals, the conservatives. That was my obligation. As a businessman, I had to get along with everybody, and I'll get along and do that as president," he continued, remarking, *"when I needed approvals, when I needed something from Washington, I always got what*

I wanted, and that's because I was able to get along with every-body." [178]

"I AM THE IMPORTANT ONE."

JABIN BOTSFORD/THE WASHINGTON POST VIA GETTY IMAGES

One aspect of Trump's campaign which stands out as unique and strange in comparison to other candidates is his 'loyalty pledges'. What is important is that we examine the specific wording he used and to what extent he wants his followers to go, even if that means risking their lives. Trump ordered his followers to repeat after him:

"I do solemnly swear that I, no matter how I feel, no matter what the conditions, if there are hurricanes or whatever, will vote on or before the 12th for Donald J. Trump for President." [179]

It is truly a pathetic situation that he would adamantly put his supporters' health and safety on the line. Even if they are feeling terrible, even in the case of a natural disaster, just so he can receive their votes. Where's his compassion?

Trump is a unique phenomenon of our times, one that we should not take lightly. He is the embodiment of a deviant philosophy that is far removed from sensibility and fairness, principles which are paramount to a harmonious world. Trump will have his day in the limelight, his fifteen minutes of fame, and we may even forget him in a few years, but his warped legacy will be reflected in the many Trumps, some of them among the nation's leaders, who will follow in his wake.

9

TIANANMEN SQUARE

TRUMP CLAIMS TO BE A PATRIOTIC CITIZEN WHO exemplifies American values. However, in 1990, when he was asked about the famous massacre of Tiananmen Square in a *Playboy* interview, he said:

"When the students poured into Tiananmen Square, the Chinese government almost blew it. Then they were vicious, they were horrible, but they put it down with strength. That shows you the power of strength." [180]

Likewise he said about the Soviet Union and Gorbachev:

"What you will see there soon is a revolution; the signs are all there with the demonstrations and picketing. Russia is out of control and the leadership knows it. That's my problem with Gorbachev. Not a firm enough hand." [181]

TRUMP SHOWS US THAT ONE OF HIS FACES RESEMBLES THE LIKES OF KIM JONG-IL FROM NORTH KOREA, SADDAM HUSSEIN FROM IRAQ, HAFITH ALASAD OF SYRIA, AND MUSSOLINI FROM ITALY.

Trump clearly shows his admiration for the strength of brute force and a "firm-handed" approach. Let us now examine what he said on April 14, 2016:

"Big protest march in Colorado on Friday afternoon! Don't let the bosses take your vote!" [182]

This brings about a very serious question regarding Trump's exemplification of American values, or lack thereof. Indeed, we repeatedly find him two-faced and having corrupt double standards. Thus, Trump shows us that one of his faces resembles the likes of Kim Jong-il from North Korea, Saddam Hussein from Iraq, Hafith AlAsad of Syria, and Mussolini from Italy

WHO SUPPORTS TRUMP?

10

"I LOVE THE POORLY EDUCATED!"

TRUMP DECLARES, *"I LOVE THE POORLY EDUCATED! They're the smartest people, the most loyal people."* [183]

It is easy for the people of intelligence to reflect upon why that is the case. Indeed, the reason is control. Trump sees himself as one of high intelligence and power, so he is excited by the opportunity to control those whom he sees to be below him. This is similar to how Khomeini and his successor Ali Khamenei control their subjects in Iran. The labor force there makes up 37% of the population. [184] It is especially these people which Khamenei finds easy to guide in whichever direction he wills. He is likewise able to hide his faults and keep the people oblivious to the country's many problems by using high-level speech and big words.

In the same way, Trump craves power, control, and the loyalty of his supporters. Just as Trump wants, he has led the polls in states with the lowest educational levels.

TRUMP SEES HIMSELF AS ONE OF HIGH INTELLIGENCE AND POWER, SO HE IS EXCITED BY THE OPPORTUNITY TO CONTROL THOSE WHOM HE SEES TO BE BELOW HIM.

Let us focus on what Trump intends behind his description of the poorly educated as being loyal. Indeed, what Trump craves is power and control over the people, and that becomes evident in the way he describes the degree of control that he has over those he believes are his loyal subjects.

Trump previously donated heavily to a foundation of Hillary Clinton, and due to that he considers her submissive and subordinate to himself:

"I'll tell you what, with Hillary Clinton I said, 'Be at my wedding' and she came to my wedding. You know why? She had no choice because I gave to a foundation that frankly, that foundation is supposed to do good. I didn't know her money would be used for private jets going all over the world -- it was." [185]

Trump also described the loyalty he felt he deserved from previous presidential candidate Mitt Romney, who had requested an endorsement from Trump, as reported in the *Washington Post:*

"I could've said, 'Mitt, drop to your knees,' and he would've dropped to his knees." [186]

So this is the foundation and basis of Trump's concept of loyalty. He believes that the poorly educated are the most loyal people. This is a facet of the disease of Trump/Hitler that they want to control the masses, and it is as if Trump is saying indirectly, "I am the person who has the right to control everyone and everything."

He is able to mesmerize his supporters with his bait of empty promises to the extent that he proudly boasts:

IT IS AS IF TRUMP IS SAYING INDIRECTLY, "I AM THE PERSON WHO HAS THE RIGHT TO CONTROL EVERYONE AND EVERYTHING."

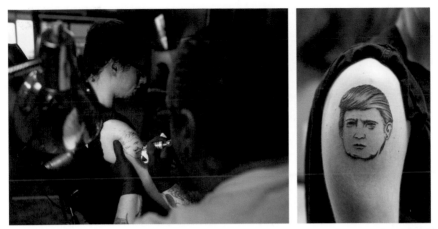

THERE IS SO MUCH AMAZING EVIDENCE SHOWING THE EXTENT TO WHICH PEOPLE BELIEVE IN TRUMP AND ARE INFATUATED BY HIM. PHOTOS BY SCOTT EISEN/GETTY IMAGES

"I could stand in the middle of Fifth Avenue and shoot somebody and I wouldn't lose any voters, okay?" [187]

He publicly announces this with confidence in front of his supporters! Trump has captivated them with his bait to the extent that he proudly tells them directly that if he shoots someone, they would still be committed to him. Even then, those people do not find anything wrong with that! It is truly a perplexing situation.

REUTERS/JOE SKIPPER

11

HOW DID TRUMP COME ABOUT?

T O ANSWER THIS QUESTION, I'LL QUOTE THE AR-
ticle of Nick Gass from Politico:

Republicans should not be surprised by the rise of Donald Trump, Senate Minority Leader Harry Reid (D-Nev.) said
Wednesday on the floor. The party has created a "Frankenstein
monster" in Donald Trump, he declared.

"Republicans have spent the last eight years stoking the fires
of resentment and hatred, building Trump piece by piece," said
Reid, referring to a Feb. 25 op-ed in The Washington Post by
Robert Kagan, a former official in the Reagan White House.

The piece, titled, "Trump is the GOP's Frankenstein monster. Now he's strong enough to destroy the party," framed Reid's
speech Wednesday, a day after Trump claimed victory in seven
states on Super Tuesday.

> **"REPUBLICANS HAVE SPENT THE LAST EIGHT YEARS STOKING THE FIRES OF RESENTMENT AND HATRED, BUILDING TRUMP PIECE BY PIECE,"**

"Today, the Republican establishment acts like it's surprised by Donald Trump and his victories around the country. They feign outrage that a demagogue spewing bile ... is somehow winning in a party that has spent years telling immigrants they are not welcome in America," Reid said, in reference to Trump's immigration plan to deport all undocumented immigrants and build a wall between the U.S. and Mexico, making the Mexican government pay for it.

"They act surprised that Republican voters are flocking to a birther candidate, even as Republican congressional leaders continue to support a man who refuses to distance himself from the Ku Klux Klan," Reid continued, alluding to Trump's reluctance to disavow David Duke and the Ku Klux Klan in a CNN interview earlier this week, despite having done so two days earlier. Trump later blamed the incident on a "lousy earpiece" provided by the network, and again disavowed Duke in subsequent remarks.

> **'REPUBLICANS CREATED HIM BY SPENDING SEVEN YEARS APPEALING TO SOME OF THE DARKEST FORCES IN AMERICA,'**

Reid tore into Republicans for being outraged at Trump's success among Republican voters while they refuse to hear a Supreme Court nominee for President Barack Obama.

"Republicans shouldn't be surprised. They spent eight years laying the groundwork for the rise of Donald Trump," Reid said. "The reality is that Republican leaders are reaping what they've sown."

The Nevada Democrat ran through a litany of Republican obstruction in Congress, slamming leaders and rank-and-file members for their failure to cooperate or come to the table on issues as varied as financial reform to health care.

Republicans "have set the Trump standard," Reid said, going on to say that the Republican Party "has long used Islam to fearmonger. Now, Donald Trump is doing the same thing."

"The Republican Party has spent years railing against Latinos and immigrants, trying to incite fear," Reid said, referring to comments from Rep. Steve King (R-Iowa) about undocumented immigrants with "calves the size of cantaloupes" in 2013.

It's not just Trump, Reid explained, arguing that Texas Sen. Ted Cruz, Florida Sen. Marco Rubio and Ben Carson "are saying basically the same thing," although more subtly. Reid also noted impishly that House Speaker Paul Ryan (R-Wis.) has said he would support Trump as the nominee and Senate Majority Leader Mitch McConnell (R-Ky.) has not said he would not vote for him, "publicly at least."

"Donald Trump is the standard bearer for

the Republican Party. Republicans created him by spending seven years appealing to some of the darkest forces in America," Reid said. "Now, it's up to the Republicans to undo what they've done by denouncing Donald Trump. It's time for Republicans to stop the Frankenstein they've created."

Reid concluded that if Republicans fail to do so, "he'll tear the party apart even more than it is now."[188]

WHO'S TO BLAME FOR THE RISE OF TRUMP?

A recent article published in *Spiegel International* proposed that the blame for Trump's popularity falls upon the shoulders of America's journalists.

> The longer this election continues, the more apparent it is becoming that this candidate is changing the fundamental relationship between the media and the American political world. The democratic public sphere, one of the pillars of every democracy, is facing two threats: Trump's brute attacks and the media's own failure. Many newsrooms didn't fulfill their democratic duty to monitor Trump, and to perform checks and balances, letting him get away with insults, lies and far-fetched promises. When it comes to Trump, the critical public sphere has shown itself to be dysfunctional far too often in the last few months.[189]

Due to its oversimplification, I profoundly disagree with the above assumption. Indeed, the disease of Trump is not something new. It has been long ingrained in some Americans for generations, as it has existed amongst other populations around the world. The followers of the KKK, Hitler, ISIS, and Al-Qaeda all share many aspects of the same mindset. It is not journalists who allowed these ideologies to spread and grow; it is the masses themselves.

REUTERS/JIM YOUNG

12

THE MAJORITY OF THOSE
REPUBLICANS WHO VOTED
ARE PLEASED BY TRUMP'S
STANCES AND SPEECH...
WHAT DOES THAT MEAN?

THERE IS A GROWING NUMBER OF INFLUENTIAL people who have openly endorsed or given support to Trump, and may be of the same mentality:

STATE GOVERNORS

- Chris Christie, New Jersey (former 2016 presidential candidate) [190]

- Sarah Palin, Alaska (former 2008 vice-presidential candidate) [191]
- Paul LePage, Maine [192]
- Rick Scott, Florida [193]

U.S. REPRESENTATIVES

- Lou Barletta of Pennsylvania [194]
- Chris Collins of New York [195]
- Scott DesJarlais of Tennessee [196]
- Renee Ellmers of North Carolina [197]
- Duncan D. Hunter of California [198]
- Tom Marino of Pennsylvania [199]
- Tom Reed of New York [200]

U.S. SENATORS

- Jeff Sessions, Senator of Alabama [201]
- Scott Brown, Former Senator of Massachusetts [202]
- Former GOP candidate and retired neurosurgeon Ben Carson [203]

FORMER EXECUTIVE BRANCH OFFICIALS:

- Pat Buchanan, White House Communications Director (1985-

JEFF SESSIONS   TAYLOR HILL/WIREIMAGE   SCOTT BROWN   JOE RAEDLE/GETTY IMAGES

JOE ARPAIO   REUTERS / BRIAN SNYDER

1987), senior advisor to Richard Nixon and Gerald Ford.[204]

- Michael T. Flynn, retired U.S. lieutenant general, director of the U.S. Defense Intelligence Agency (2012-2014), commander of the Joint Functional Component Command for Intelligence, Surveillance and Reconnaissance, and foreign policy adviser to the Trump campaign.[205]

- Jeffrey Lord, White House associate political director for the Reagan administration (1987–1988).[206]

- Robert C. Oaks, retired U.S. Air Force general, commander of Air Training Command and United States Air Forces in Europe (1986-1990).[207]

- Joseph E. Schmitz, inspector general of the Department of Defense (2002–2005), former executive with Blackwater Worldwide, and member of the foreign policy advising committee for the Trump campaign.[208]

There is also the likes of Joe Arpaio, the notorious Arizona Sheriff, who said of Trump: "I'm not trying to say he copies me, it just so happens we see eye to eye." He added: "He's somewhat like me. Or I'm like him. I don't know which way it goes."[209]

Trump could never have become the nominee for the Republican Party unless he offered something that pleased the majority of Republican primary voters. This proves that they accept and approve of his bom-

EVEN IF HIS SUPPORTERS TRY AND MAKE EXCUSES FOR THEMSELVES, THEY UNDENIABLY APPROVE OF HIS CRUDE AND DESPICABLE CHARACTER TRAITS AND MANNERS, OR ELSE THEY WOULD NOT HAVE VOTED FOR HIM.

bastic, crude, and foulmouthed ways. They agree with his bigotry, terrible manners, and his racial and national profiling. They approve of his mocking of women, the disabled, Native Americans, and of non-native English speakers. In general, even if his supporters try to make excuses for themselves, they undeniably approve of his crude and despicable character traits and manners, or else they would not have voted for him.

The fact that he has been chosen by this majority proves that in the realm of voting, there really is no clear frame for presidential candidates to fit into. Many people do have frames in their minds as to what the character and mannerisms of a candidate should be. We have as an example, the respectable George H. W. Bush and his wife Barbara, who are looked up to in how they carried themselves and how they presented themselves to the public. Trump, however, has completely broken this frame and has demonstrated that there's no limit to how low a candidate can go and how far he can stray from moral traditions and norms.

Trump of course, despite what many might assume, is not a phenomenon in and of himself. Rather, he is only a reflection of those who have voted for him. The nominee of any party, majority, or society is like a thermometer or litmus test that shows the condition of those who are supporting him. If the moral and ethical standards of a people sink down to the gutter, that's when they'll choose someone who fits those ideals to represent them.

Some may try to make excuses for the rise of Trump, and shift the blame away from that portion of society who has chosen him. They may claim, for example, that someone like him is needed due to the state of the American economy, and they are only turning to

THIS, IN REALITY, COMES FROM LAZINESS AND A LACK OF PATIENCE.

Trump due to this dire situation. They believe that for economic reasons, Trump is their answer, and whatever terrible policies and lack of values he exemplifies must be accepted for the greater good.

Regardless of who may make this lame excuse, it is without doubt baseless and invalid.

The U.S. economy remains the largest in the world in terms of nominal GDP. The $17.41 trillion U.S. economy is approximately 22.44% of the gross world product. The United States is an economic superpower that is highly advanced in terms of technology and infrastructure and has abundant natural resources. If someone from the low or middle class were to come and say that America has an excuse to "do whatever it takes" to strengthen its economy further, or must implement "any means necessary," then what about all the world's countries that are poorer than America? Would it be acceptable to the global community for poor countries to undertake rash, unacceptable, and nonsensical measures, all based on the excuse of having economic difficulties?

WOULD IT BE ACCEPTABLE TO THE GLOBAL COMMUNITY FOR POOR COUNTRIES TO UNDERTAKE RASH, UNACCEPTABLE, AND NONSENSICAL MEASURES, ALL BASED ON THE EXCUSE OF HAVING ECONOMIC DIFFICULTIES?

It would be both wrong and dangerous to allow the majority of the world's countries to implement "any means necessary" due to economic problems. Likewise, those claiming to be voting solely for Trump due to perceived economic difficulties do not really have a leg to stand on. If we can agree that it would be chaotic for all the poorer countries in the world to take rash, risky, and dangerous initiatives, then we should also agree that America shouldn't lead by example in taking actions out of desperation.

Trump has proposed many quick fixes that are appealing to many voters. He aims to quickly build a wall along the nation's southern border, raise international trading tariffs while cursing US allies, ban Muslims, and deport immigrants, among other hasty plans. What must be realized though is that quick fixes are what foolish people seek. It can even be called the language of dummies that people yearn for and expect results "now, now, now!" This mentality is from a very low-class, uneducated, and uninformed viewpoint that many people regretfully share. Even if someone is a successful university professor, their thought process may still be low-class if their reason is that Trump will vent their frustrations. This isn't an intellectual choice. This, in reality, comes from laziness and a lack of patience. That's what causes this hastiness and rushing into action without strategic planning that includes thoughtful contemplation about the ramifications or risks involved.

13

PREVIOUS CANDIDATES WERE RECOGNIZED FOR THEIR **GOOD CHARACTER**, AS OPPOSED TO THE NEW WAYS OF TRUMP

ANY AMERICAN LISTENING TO TRUMP NEEDS TO carefully consider the consequences of his crude character. He can clearly be seen as a man who wants to be considered a hero at any cost, without paying importance to manners, being respectful, or having good character.

In contrast, if we look back at the 2008 presidential election, a woman at a John McCain event insisted that Obama was "an Arab." "No ma'am," McCain replied. "He's a decent, family man, citizen that I just happen to have disagreements with on fundamental issues."[210]

Consider Senator John McCain's response when prompted with ill-mannered and derogatory questions regarding President Obama. This is also bearing in mind that Obama was McCain's fierce rival for the presidential election. There was none of the finger gesturing and sickening responses from Senator McCain like we see from Trump. Here is an example of how Trump reacted to a similar, even more demeaning statement:

At a Trump campaign rally in Rochester, New Hampshire a man in a "Trump" shirt took the microphone and said, "We have a problem in this country. It's called Muslims. We know our current president is one. You know he's not even an American."

"We need this question," Trump replied, smiling.[211]

And with these two opposite reactions the differences become distinct!

"We want to fight and I will fight," McCain told one of several questioners who demanded that he go after then Senator Obama harder. "But we will be respectful. I admire Senator Obama and his accomplishments. I will respect him."[212]

"WHEN SOMEONE SHOWS YOU WHO THEY ARE, BELIEVE THEM THE FIRST TIME."

These examples show us the high standards of character and manners typically expressed by America's leaders, even in situations of intense competition. This shows us the clear difference between their high level of manners and just how low Trump's are by comparison.

As Maya Angelou said, "When someone shows you who they are, believe them the first time."[213] Donald Trump has shown us clearly who he is, and if he becomes president, what we have seen is exactly what we'll get.

14

EVANGELICALS
FOR TRUMP

THERE ARE VARIOUS COLUMNISTS AND REPORT-
ers trying to make a connection between the evangelical Christians and Trump. For example, *The Atlantic* reported:

Donald Trump is immodest, arrogant, foul-mouthed, mon-
ey-obsessed, thrice-married, and until recently, pro-choice. By
conventional standards, evangelical Christians should despise
him. Yet somehow, the Manhattan billionaire has attracted their
support.

According to the most recent polls, Trump is one of the top
picks for president among evangelical Christians. One *Washington Post* poll even had him as the group's favorite by a margin of
six points. His first major rally in the Bible-Belt fortress town of
Mobile, Alabama, drew an estimated 18,000 attendees.

"Why do they love me?" Trump replied when asked about

the trend. *"You'll have to ask them. But they do. They do love me."*[214]

George Lakoff, professor of cognitive science and linguistics at the University of California at Berkeley, said of the white evangelicals:

Those whites who have a strict father personal worldview and who are religious tend toward Evangelical Christianity, since God, in Evangelical Christianity, is the Ultimate Strict Father: You follow His commandments and you go to heaven; you defy His commandments and you burn in hell for all eternity. If you are a sinner and want to go to heaven, you can be 'born again" by declaring your fealty by choosing His son, Jesus Christ, as your personal Savior.

Such a version of religion is natural for those with strict father morality. Evangelical Christians join the church because they are conservative; they are not conservative because they happen to

PASTOR DARRELL SCOTT

JOE RAEDLE/GETTY IMAGES

be in an evangelical church, though they may grow up with both together.

Evangelical Christianity is centered around family life. Hence, there are organizations like Focus on the Family and constant reference to "family values," which take to evangelical strict father values. In strict father morality, it is the father who controls sexuality and reproduction. Where the church has political control, there are laws that require parental and spousal notification in the case of proposed abortions.

HIS FOLLOWERS BECOME ATTRACTED TO HIS MENTALITY AND WAY OF THINKING, RATHER THAN A CONNECTION TO HIM RELIGIOUSLY.

Evangelicals are highly organized politically and exert control over a great many local political races. Thus Republican candidates mostly have to go along with the evangelicals if they want to be nominated and win local elections.[215]

Trump claims that he "won the Evangelicals".[216] However, I don't believe that religion really plays any major factor in people's decisions to support him. His followers become attracted to his mentality and way of thinking, rather than a connection to him religiously. It is a disease spreading across the world and becoming apparent across continents, irrespective of religions, cultures, or situations. As discussed previously in this book, Trumpians are appearing in the US, Kuwait, Europe, Africa, and everywhere in between.

The Atlantic also alluded to this point: "There is little about The Donald that would seem to align with evangelicals' values and beliefs. But when it comes to the famously coifed candidate, the faithful seem to be valuing style over substance or spirituality."[217]

The only ones we find actually attaching themselves to Trump on a religious basis are the followers of the KKK, and those of similarly prejudiced outlooks, as I have revealed earlier in this book. A *New York Times* reporter, Nate Cohn, proved that Trump's followers were bigots by coordinating a map of Trump support with a map of racist Google searches.[218] The teachings of the prophet Jesus (may God's peace be upon him) were far away and free from those ways.

15

THE **KU KLUX KLAN** AND RIGHT-WING NATIONALISTS' SUPPORT FOR DONALD TRUMP

DAVID DUKE, THE WHITE NATIONALIST AND FORmer Ku Klux Klan grand wizard, urged the listeners of his radio program to volunteer and vote for Donald Trump:

"Voting against Donald Trump at this point is really treason to your heritage," he said. "I'm not saying I endorse everything about Trump, and in fact I haven't formally endorsed him. But I do support his candidacy, and I support voting for him as a strategic action. I hope he does everything we hope he will do.

"And I am telling you that it is your job now to get active. Get off your duff. Get off your rear end that's getting fatter and fatter for many of you everyday on your chairs. When this show's over, go out, call the Republican Party, but call Donald Trump's headquarters, and volunteer. They're screaming for volunteers. Go in there, and *you're gonna meet people who are going to have the same kind of mindset that you have.*"[219]

TRUMP HAS ALSO EMERGED AS A HERO TO WHITE NATIONALISTS.

Please notice that I have been fair with David Duke and did not accuse him of "endorsing" Trump, as this is something he ridiculously denies. Duke clarified personally in February, 2016, that he is only encouraging his followers to "vote for him" and that he will vote for Trump:

"I have said specifically every time I've talked about his candidacy, that I am not endorsing Donald Trump. The point is, I have not endorsed him, but I do think that we should vote for him, and I will vote for him."[220]

An interview broadcast by NBC News on April 30, 2016, showcased current KKK members in Virginia showing their continued support for Trump. Their leader was asked: In your own personal opinion, who's best for the job (as president)? He replied: "I think Donald Trump would be best for the job. The reason a lotta' Klan members like Donald Trump is because a lotta' what he believes, we believe in. We want our country to be safe. If Donald Trump were to drop out tomorrow, I'd support Kasich before I'd support Ted Cruz, because he's not an American citizen."[221]

The New York Times reported on February 23, 2016 that nearly 20 percent of Trump's voters disagreed with Abraham Lincoln's Emancipation Proclamation,[222] which freed slaves in the Southern states during the Civil War. This example shows the gravity of this disease which has remained so widespread amongst the people. It is a danger not just for America, but for the rest of the world as well. Going forward, various proofs and evidences will be presented, consisting of many facts and figures. This will emphasize the importance of addressing it proactively from many dynamic angles.

Time Magazine reported April 14, 2016:

"Since the start of the 2016 campaign, Trump has built a broad coalition of supporters, attracting voters with his forceful personality and his willingness to challenge party doctrine. And while the vast majority are driven by reasons other than race, Trump has also emerged as a hero to white nationalists. "Trump has energized us," says Richard Spencer, president of National Policy Institute (NPI), a tiny think tank based in Arlington, Va., dedicated to the advancement of "people of European descent." For the first time since George Wallace in 1968, far-right activists in the U.S. are migrating toward mainstream electoral politics, stepping out of the shadows to attend rallies, offer endorsements and serve as volunteers. "It's bound to happen," Spencer says of white nationalists' running for office one day. "Not as conservatives but as Trump Republicans."

Extremists have latched on to Trump as a rallying cry and recruiting tool. Attendance at NPI events has jumped 75% over the past year, Spencer says. The white-supremacist website Stormfront reportedly had to upgrade its servers to handle a Trump-driven traffic spike. William Johnson, chairman of the racist American Freedom Party, paid for pro-Trump robocalls in six primary and caucus states. "Trump was the spark we needed," he says, citing a surge in membership.[223]

ABC News quoted from Mark Potok of the Southern Poverty Law Center, which tracks U.S. hate groups, says such support is no accident.

"He's appealing to the same constituency that the Ku Klux Klan appeals to," Potok said. "Not every supporter is sympathetic to them but that is the very same demographic." He notes that many of Trump's supporters are white, lower-middle class people who are "under a lot of economic pressure."

"He uses the same techniques, he hypes up the fear of the outsider, [the idea that] Muslims are out to destroy us, immigrants are rapists. Whether or not he is truly a white nationalist, I think is totally irrelevant," he said.[224]

This is a storyline that could shape more than the 2016 election. Trump's success with disaffected whites is a sign that the forces of xenophobia and nationalism, which fueled the rise of far-right populist parties across Europe, are gathering strength in the U.S. as well. At a moment of rising racial tensions, Trump's rhetoric of resentment has redrawn the boundaries of political speech in new and troubling ways.

16

TRUMP'S **VIOLENT INCITEMENT** AGAINST PROTESTERS

I T'S CLEAR WHERE TRUMP IS INEVITABLY GOING. IT will be difficult for him to win, but he will increase the spread of his disease.

For those who seek the truth, Trump has clearly shown that he is too dangerous and he wants to see blood. He has used harsh words regarding various protesters and encourages his supporters with violence, as is well documented:

"I'd like to punch him in the face."

"I love the old days, you know what they used to do to guys like that if they were in

> TRUMP HAS CLEARLY SHOWN THAT HE IS TOO DANGEROUS AND HE WANTS TO SEE BLOOD.

a place like this? They'd be carried out on a stretcher, folks!" [225]

"If you see somebody getting ready to throw a tomato, knock the crap out of them, would you? Seriously... just knock the hell... I promise you, I will pay for the legal fees, I promise." [226]

Trump will rile the crowd up even more, yelling at security to *"get them the hell out"* and saying once of a protester who was attacked at an Alabama rally, *"Maybe he should have been roughed up."* [227]

And to another protester at a rally he shouted: *"Go get a job!"* [228]

How did Trump know if that protester had a job or not? Was it because he is African American? This accusation shows that Trump has a resemblance to the KKK; here he has exposed his sickness.

TRUMP HAS A RESEMBLANCE TO THE KKK; HERE HE HAS EXPOSED HIS SICKNESS.

It is important for us to remember that before he became the presumptive nominee, when Trump was explaining what would happen if he did not get the nomination from the GOP, he said, *"I think you'd have problems like you've never seen before."* And, *"I think you'd have riots. I think you'd have riots,"* Trump said, on March 16, 2016, on CNN's *New Day*. *"I'm representing a tremendous many, many millions of people."* [229]

Ben Carson, the supporter and endorser of Trump, also said: "There's no question that there would be a lot of turmoil."[230]

In fact, another of Trump's supporters, Scottie N. Hughes, said there would be riots if Trump didn't win the nomination at the convention, though riots themselves "aren't necessarily a bad thing."[231]

Please realize that the definition of "riot" in the English language as stated by the *Merriam-Webster Dictionary* is this: "A situation

in which a large group of people behave in a violent and uncontrolled way."[232]

Look at the terrifying results of some recent riots in only the last decades:

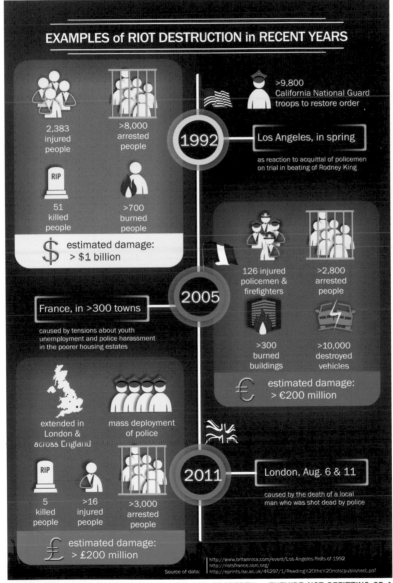

EXAMPLES of RIOT DESTRUCTION in RECENT YEARS

1992 — Los Angeles, in spring
as reaction to acquittal of policemen on trial in beating of Rodney King

2,383 injured people

>8,000 arrested people

51 killed people

>700 burned people

estimated damage: > $1 billion

>9,800 California National Guard troops to restore order

2005 — France, in >300 towns
caused by tensions about youth unemployment and police harassment in the poorer housing estates

126 injured policemen & firefighters

>2,800 arrested people

>300 burned buildings

>10,000 destroyed vehicles

estimated damage: > €200 million

2011 — London, Aug. 6 & 11
caused by the death of a local man who was shot dead by police

extended in London & across England

mass deployment of police

5 killed people

>16 injured people

>3,000 arrested people

estimated damage: > £200 million

Source of data: http://www.britannica.com/event/Los-Angeles-Riots-of-1992
http://riotsfrance.ssrc.org/
http://eprints.lse.ac.uk/46297/1/Reading%20the%20riots(published).pdf

THESE RIOTS CAUSE TRAGIC LOSS OF LIFE AND PROPERTY — THEY'RE NOT BEFITTING OF A CIVILIZED SOCIETY. TRUMP THREATENED THAT HIS SUPPORTERS WILL RIOT AND THIS IS THE RESULT OF HIS "ME" MENTALITY.

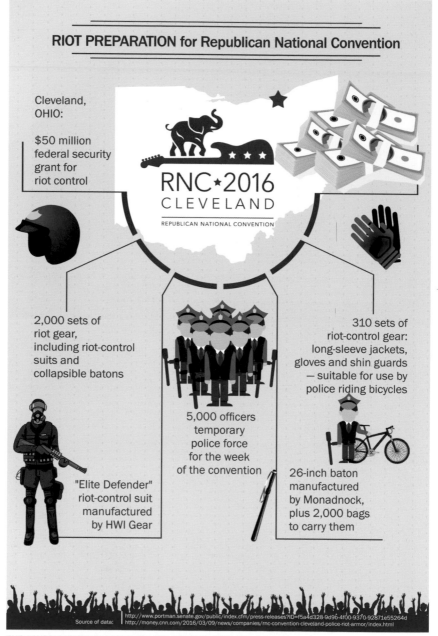

RIOT PREPARATION for Republican National Convention

Cleveland, OHIO:

$50 million federal security grant for riot control

RNC★2016
CLEVELAND
REPUBLICAN NATIONAL CONVENTION

2,000 sets of riot gear, including riot-control suits and collapsible batons

"Elite Defender" riot-control suit manufactured by HWI Gear

5,000 officers temporary police force for the week of the convention

310 sets of riot-control gear: long-sleeve jackets, gloves and shin guards — suitable for use by police riding bicycles

26-inch baton manufactured by Monadnock, plus 2,000 bags to carry them

Source of data: http://www.portman.senate.gov/public/index.cfm/press-releases?ID=f5a4d328-9d9b-4f00-9370-92871e55264d
http://money.cnn.com/2016/03/09/news/companies/rnc-convention-cleveland-police-riot-armor/index.html

THE GOVERNMENT'S PREPARATION FOR THE STUPIDITY AND THREATS OF TRUMP.

Whether or not Trump wins or loses the general election, his disease will remain and it will grow. If he is successful, his disease will become widespread, and if he fails his disease will spread to a lesser extent. This disease has already begun to manifest itself within America, so even if he fails, it will continue to grow because his campaign has provided a huge opportunity to spread it.

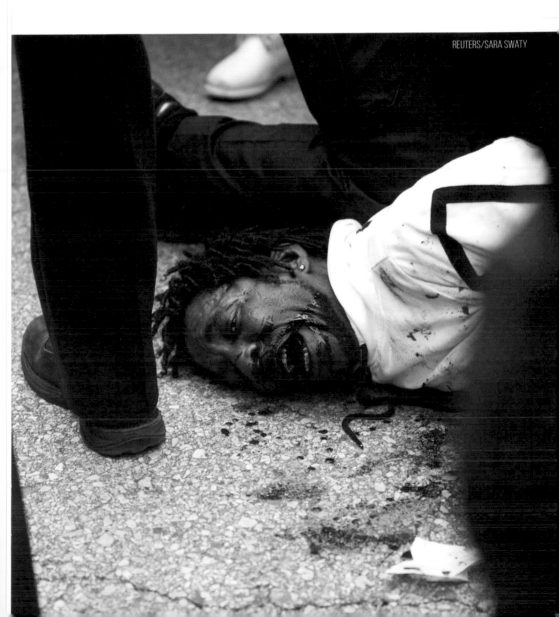

REUTERS/SARA SWATY

"And the other thing is with the terrorists, you have to take out their families. They, they care about their lives. Don't kid yourself. But they say they don't care about their lives. You have to take out their families" [240]

This is from his terrible speech that would only breed increased hostility amongst terrorists and potential terrorists. This gives the likes of ISIS, Al-Qaeda, and those like them, more fuel for their cause.

Boaz Ganor, who worked as part of an international anti-terror advisory group to the NYPD after 9/11 and has written extensively about terrorism, told CNN that killing the family members of terrorists would have little benefit in the effort to stop attacks.

"They might just spend more time and resources" on protecting family members, he told CNN on December 3, 2015. "Nevertheless, I don't think that the threat to kill their families will deter terrorist leaders from being engaged in terrorist activities."

"ONE OF THE MOST IMPORTANT PILLARS OF COUNTERTERRORISM: THE DIFFERENCES OF MORALITY."

Ganor argued that the real danger would be in squandering "one of the most important pillars of counterterrorism: the differences of morality."

"The American-led campaign in Syria and Iraq is too little and too late, and it will not lead as such to a military decisive victory on ISIS," he said. "This does not mean by any way that the U.S. should adopt savage policy, illegal or immoral military activity. There is a lot that still can be done and improve without adopting such policies." [241]

The terrorists will say, "What's the difference between us and Trump?" They will realize that Trump wants to kill the children, women, and other family members of the terrorists!

So they will say, "We believe in a certain way, and Trump believes in the same way and direction as we do!" So they will use this as an excuse for their own evil actions and to incite others against the United States.

God said in the Quran what means: "No bearer of a burden will bear the burden of another" (Surah Al-An'amAya 164).

FOREIGN FIGHTERS KEEP FLOCKING TO SYRIA

The number of foreign fighters in Syria and Iraq has more than doubled since last year to at least 27,000, according to a report by the Soufan Group security consultancy

Foreign fighters in syria and iraq *Estimates for selected countries*

2015 (2014)

Middle East

8,240 *(2,900)*

Africa

8,000 *(4,700)*

Western Europe

5,000 *(2.500)*

Former Soviet republics

4,700 *(800)*

Southeast Asia **900** *(50)*

Balkans **875** *(120)*

North America **280** *(100)*

WESTERN EUROPE	
France	**1,700**
Germany	**760**
United Kingdom	**760**
Belgium	**470**
Austria	**300**
Sweden	**300**
Netherlands	**220**
Spain	**133**
Denmark	**125**
Italy	**87**
Norway	**81**
Finland	**70**
Switzerland	**57**
Ireland	**30**
Portugal	**12**

NORTH AMERICA	
United States	**150**
Canada	**130**

MIDDLE EAST	
Saudi Arabia	**2,500**
Turkey	**2,000-2,200**
Jordan	**2,000+**
Lebanon	**900**
Kuwait	**70**
Israel	**40-50**

ASIA AND PACIFIC	
Indonesia	**700**
China	**300**
Maldives	**200**
Australia	**120**
Malaysia	**100**
Philippines	**100**
Pakistan	**70**
Afghanistan	**50**
India	**23**
New Zealand	**5-10**
Japan	**9**

FORMER EASTERN BLOC	
Russia	**2,400**
Kyrgyzstan	**500**
Uzbekistan	**500**
Tajikistan	**386**
Turkmenistan	**360**
Bosnia	**330**
Kazakhstan	**300**
Kosovo	**232**
Macedonia	**146**
Azerbaijan	**104+**
Albania	**90**
Serbia	**50-70**

AFRICA	
Tunisia	**6,000**
Morocco	**1,200**
Egypt	**600+**
Libya	**600**
Algeria	**170**

Sources: The Soufan Group, GN

I believe that no one should be killed or harmed due to the evil of someone else, even if that evil person may be a family member. That is nothing but oppression and far from justice.

Why isn't Trump held to account for this twisted ideology that he is encouraging and spreading?

19

WHY TRUMP?

TRUMP IS ESPECIALLY APPEALING TO THE PARticular class of Americans who are shortsighted, regardless of what their education level may be. Some of his supporters are professors, while others have not completed high school. They are burning inside with a fire of envy, and Trump's speeches, full of scaremongering and accusations, quench their thirst for what they consider justice. His followers are frustrated with their lives and confused about how they fit into this rapidly changing world.

I believe that deep inside, they surely recognize that Trump is not really offering any solutions, but they cannot resist the satisfaction he brings them. He is their release and their blowing off steam. They are frustrated with President Obama, an African American, who has been in the White House for nearly eight years. Many of Trump's supporters fear

HIS FOLLOWERS ARE FRUSTRATED WITH THEIR LIVES AND CONFUSED ABOUT HOW THEY FIT INTO THIS RAPIDLY CHANGING WORLD.

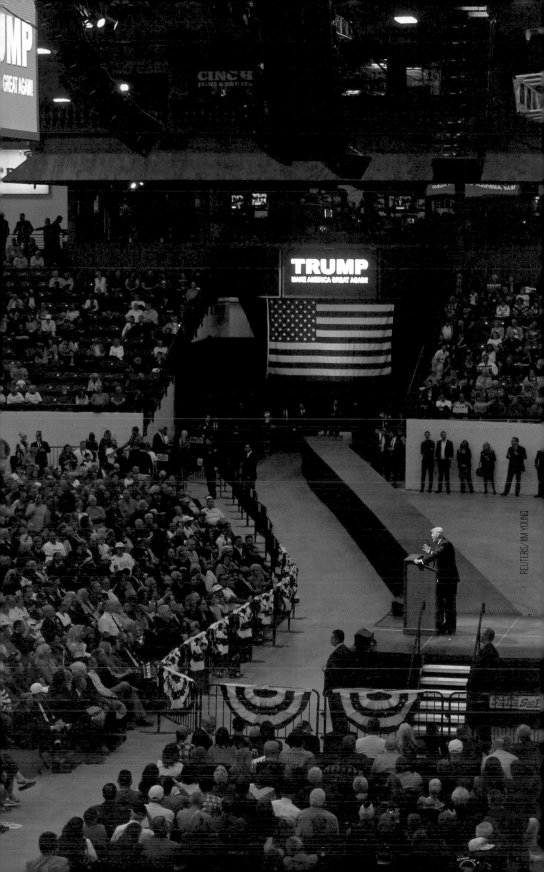

that whites are losing power and control, while also being scared that America is becoming even more diverse and multicultural. They are frustrated about the economy and recognize their future is uncertain, but they feel the need to hear someone vent for them, even though they are sure he won't do anything for them.

The emotion these people are feeling is similar to the satisfaction the envious feel if their enemy is spoken against or hurt in some way. Trump's attacks against foreign countries, nationalities, and religions do not tangibly benefit his supporters in any way at all, and they know that. It is simply the satisfaction of seeing someone other than themselves – an outsider, or an enemy – being degraded. It is often natural for people to wish harm for those they think are their enemies; but this is a weakness and disease of the heart which we must strive to control and repress. Envy does no good for the one feeling it. Rather, the envious should seek to rectify and improve their own situations, and not seek to block the opportunities of others just for the sake of self-gratification. This is why Trump has so many supporters from all levels of society.

REUTERS/MARIO ANZUONI

As an example of speech attractive to his followers, Trump tweeted:

"Sadly, the overwhelming amount of violent crime in our major cities is committed by blacks and hispanics – a tough subject – must be discussed." [242]

And: *"They (Mexico) send the bad ones over, because they don't want to pay for them, they don't want to take care of them."* [243]

WHY IS TRUMP A PROBLEM?

20

THE POLITICAL ATMOSPHERE SHOWS THAT **TRUMP IS THE BEGINNING** OF OTHER "TRUMPS" TO FOLLOW

THE TRUMP THOUGHT PROCESS EMBODIES A RE-curring disease of recent years. Over the course of the past four decades, I have traveled to the United States many times, most recently during the first quarter of 2016. During a nearly month-long period of business meetings with various companies, I had visited California, Washington, Pennsylvania, and New York. I had the pleasure of reacquainting myself with the American people, most of whom were helpful, friendly and courteous. I knew their open and smiling faces from previous visits, and for the most part, this has not changed.

However, at the same time, I found something very different than before. I saw the faces of some Trumpians– those who speak and act in the same way as Donald Trump, while also carrying his way of thinking.

I believe that some results of recent parliamentary elections in Europe have uncovered that this is a disease that has begun to spread. We are seeing similar support for right-wing parties or individuals all over the world: in Asia, Europe, the United States, and Africa.

NO RECENT DISEASE HAS REACHED WHAT HITLER'S DISEASE ACCOMPLISHED WITH HIS TONGUE

I'm a businessman and travel often. Yearly, I travel between twenty to thirty times throughout those regions I have mentioned, while meeting many people. I believe this disease of the Trump–Hitler–ISIS–Al-Qaeda–KKK mentality poses a very great danger for mankind. This is especially the case in light of the technological breakthroughs that can be seen in all business sectors. I am referring to technologies such as social media, digital communication, and what leads to increased disposable household income. Where will this mindset lead us to?

There are people who only look directly in front of them or into certain events of their choosing. They do not look at the big picture and where we would reach with the Trump–Hitler–ISIS–Al-Qaeda–KKK mindset. It is even more dangerous and caused more loss than the global flu outbreak of 1918,which killed 50 million people worldwide, ranking as one of the deadliest epidemics in history.[244] The deadly "Spanish flu" was one of the last great plagues to strike humanity. Now, compare that to what Hitler did, no recent disease has reached what Hitler's disease accomplished with his tongue, in the first half of the 20th century. Reflect on the fact that Hitler was not even German – he was an Austrian who convinced masses of people to follow him in his ideologies, leading to the deaths of many millions from various countries.

The normal, physical diseases are hated by everyone. Moreover, most people feel sorry for someone affected by a disease. But the ones affected by the Trump–Hitler–ISIS–Al-Qaeda–KKK disease bear hatred and

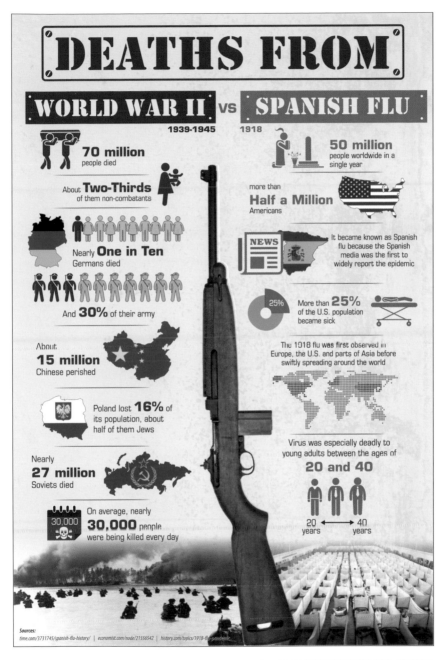

THESE ARE THE DETAILED LOSSES OF MORE THAN 70 MILLION LIVES LOST DUE TO THE WAR SPARKED BY HITLER'S DISEASE, IN COMPARISON TO THOSE WHO DIED OF THE DREADED SPANISH FLU, A NATURAL DISEASE.

hostility *to others.*

In the case of a normal disease, everyone fights it; all the people are on one side and the disease is on the other side. But the Trump–Hitler–ISIS–Al-Qaeda–KKK disease has split people up into groups, made them fight each other, and brought about much turmoil. The Hitler disease led to tens of millions of deaths, in addition to orphans and widows left behind to care for themselves. This disease of Hitler likewise leads to the destruction of animals, the environment, and buildings, along with the risk of nuclear war. It caused hatred to spread amongst the people and created enmity between them. Even normal infectious diseases spread amongst mankind due to the mass killings and torture; all this and more came about from the disease of Hitler.

HE WOULD BE OPPOSING EVERYONE; ENMITY TO OTHERS CREATES ENMITY IN RETURN.

Trump's political campaign has had fights, commotion, and disruption. If this is how he runs his political campaign, then how about the relations he would have with China, Russia, and the rest of the world? He would be opposing everyone; enmity to others creates enmity in return.

And if this methodology continues into the 21st century, where will it lead to? Indeed, to a more terrible disaster for the planet.

We, as human beings, need to stop this Trump–Hitler–ISIS–Al-Qaeda–KKK disease. We have a great example in another country which faced horrible terrorist attacks itself. Even though that country faced very big problems, I did not see a change in the stances of its leaders. That country is England. This shows us a good example of the right way to guide the people, which differs from how Trump deals with situations in his speech and actions.

On July 7, 2005, when terrorists attacked in London, setting off bombs in three subway stations and on one bus, the response of the government was laudable. I walked on Baker Street in downtown London at the time, and I experienced respect and courtesy from all levels of society. This is from the respect the police showed me, and including the merchants in the markets. I was an actual witness to how all the events unfolded from the attack and until two weeks thereafter in London. I was very happy to hear the response of Ken Livingstone, the then mayor of London. It is speech, as we say, that is worthy of being written in golden ink. Here I will share with the readers what he had to say as reported by the BBC:

IT IS SPEECH, AS WE SAY, THAT IS WORTHY OF BEING WRITTEN IN GOLDEN INK.

"I want to say one thing specifically to the world today. This was not a terrorist attack against the mighty and the powerful. It was not aimed at presidents or prime ministers. It was aimed at ordinary, working-class Londoners, black and white, Muslim and Christian, Hindu and Jew, young and old. It was an indiscriminate attempt to slaughter, irrespective of any considerations for age, for class, for religion, or whatever.

That isn't an ideology, it isn't even a perverted faith – it is just an indiscriminate attempt at mass murder, and we know what the objective is. They seek to divide Londoners. They seek to turn Londoners against each other. I said yesterday to the International Olympic Committee, that the city of London is

FORMER MAYOR OF LONDON, KEN LIVINGSTONE   ROB STOTHARD/GETTY IMAGES

the greatest in the world, because everybody lives side by side in harmony. Londoners will not be divided by this cowardly attack. They will stand together in solidarity alongside those who have been injured and those who have been bereaved, and that is why I'm proud to be the mayor of that city.

Finally, I wish to speak directly to those who came to London today to take life.

I know that you personally do not fear giving up your own life in order to take others – that is why you are so dangerous. But I know you fear that you may fail in your long-term objective to destroy our free society and I can show you why you will fail.

In the days that follow look at our airports, look at our seaports and look at our railway stations and, even after your cowardly attack, you will see that people from the rest of Britain, people

HERE WE FIND A BALANCED AND JUST REACTION BY THE GOVERNMENT IN THE UNITED KINGDOM

from around the world will arrive in London to become Londoners and to fulfil their dreams and achieve their potential.

They choose to come to London, as so many have come before because they come to be free, they come to live the life they choose, they come to be able to be themselves. They flee you because you tell them how they should live. They don't want that and nothing you do, however many of us you kill, will stop that flight to our city where freedom is strong and where people can live in harmony with one another. Whatever you do, however many you kill, you will fail."[245]

Here we find a balanced and just reaction by the government in the United Kingdom to the atrocities committed by those terrorists. This is far from the bullying and intimidating rhetoric of Trump.

Trump has a completely different approach in combating terrorism, as he cited what CNN described as "an apocryphal [highly debatable] story about a U.S. general who purportedly dipped bullets in pigs' blood to execute Muslim prisoners a century ago in an effort to deter Islamic terrorism":

TRUMP SHOULD HAVE DONE SOME BASIC FACT CHECKING. IT'S LIKELY MOST AMERICANS WOULD EXPECT THAT OF ANYONE RUNNING FOR POLITICAL OFFICE

Speaking at a rally in North Charleston, South Carolina, Trump reiterated his claim that the U.S. should *"go much further"* than waterboarding suspected terrorists, telling the story of Gen. John Pershing in the Philippines, who Trump said captured fifty Muslim prisoners a century ago. He then supposedly ordered fifty bullets dipped in blood.

"He lined up the fifty people and they shot forty-nine of those fifty people," said Trump to the attentive crowd, "and he said to the fiftieth, you go back to your people and you tell them what happened; and in twenty-five years there wasn't a problem." [246]

The historian Barney McCoy strongly debunks Trump's claim about General Pershing:

"I have found no evidence to support the pig's blood story told by Trump on the campaign trail, or others in print, social media, and on the web in the past several years. The story is of personal interest to me as a university professor who is producing a documentary on General John J. Pershing's life and has spent some time researching Pershing's career and personal life in the Library of Congress and National Archives.

"Pershing sent friendly Moros to urge the hostile Moros to surrender. 'He wanted only guns, not lives,' wrote Donald Smythe, a history professor at John Carroll University. 'If they would merely surrender their guns they could go home in peace.'

"It's fair to ask if Donald Trump knew the pig's blood story was false when he told it to his campaign audience. To be accurate, Trump should have done some basic fact checking. It's likely most Americans would expect that of anyone running for political office, much less the presidency of the United States.

"Had Trump done better fact checking, he might have learned that General Pershing preferred negotiation and diplomacy with his foes in the Philippines. Only if negotiations failed did Pershing use military force to end further lawlessness, loss of life, and property.

"Trump could issue a formal correction, and an apology for his erroneous comments.

"The correction should accurately state the facts.

"The Trump apology should account for his misrepresentation of General Pershing's legacy, and for the resulting ethnic and religious divisiveness his political rhetoric has caused."[247]

To further clarify Trump's oppressive stance and statements which are far from the justice shown by UK's leaders, he was recently asked the following question regarding the terror suspect in Belgium, after the terrible and saddening attack that occurred in France 2015:

"So would you start torturing him right away, or would you see if he would cooperate and share information, because Belgian Police say he has been talking?"

Trump replied: *"Well, he may be talking, but he'll talk a lot faster with the torture."*[248]

In that same interview he also referenced the fabricated story about General Pershing again.

Trump's confrontational way in dealing with different countries and people is well-documented in the media. He throws slurs and expresses a hostile stance towards China, Japan, Mex-

IF THIS MAN IS ABLE TO REACH THE WHITE HOUSE, THEN IT WILL REFLECT POORLY UPON THE NATION.

ico, and the Muslims (who together constitute almost half of the world's population). He does this with a pessimistic outlook that creates a big problem for the future. Does Trump want to live in the world alone?

It is necessary for the United States and the world to protect the people from this Trump–Hitler–ISIS–Al-Qaeda–KKK disease, especially the younger generations. People see this disease, yet they are heedless and smiling about it. People laugh at Trump's speeches, his interviews, his cursing, his body language, finger gestures, and his crazy ideas. It is a serious and dangerous matter. If this man is able to reach the White House, then it will reflect poorly upon the nation.

Do you believe if the Trump–Hitler–ISIS–Al-Qaeda–KKK mindset grows, it will not have a reaction from Asia, Africa, and Europe? Maybe not today, but it will certainly happen tomorrow.

I present to you this example of someone who endorses Trump:

I read from the Florida governor, Rick Scott, the reason why he endorsed Trump, thus helping to propagate this disease. I found that there is something clear in what he mentioned that exposes and unravels a common attitude. Essentially, he wants guns in the streets of America, in accordance with

DO THE AMERICANS REALLY NEED TO OWN MORE GUNS TODAY?

his interpretation of the Second Amendment of the US Constitution.[249] It reads: "A well-regulated Militia, being necessary to the security of a free State, the right of the people to keep and bear arms, shall not be infringed."[250] Trump himself has also tweeted: *"We already have tremendous regulations. Now, if you look at my opponents, they're very weak on the Second Amendment. I'm very, very strong."*[251]

Do the Americans really need to own more guns today? Why would he think that is a primary concern in the midst of America's many problems? Despite all it's been through, America has experienced yet another terrible example of gun violence in Orlando, Florida at the hands of a crazed lunatic in the early morning hours of June 12, 2016. Even a mother who was desperately searching for her son among the victims was sobbing and pleading on ABC News: "Please, can we do something with the assault weapons so that we can stop this."[252] Trump, however, strives to keep this kind of deadly firepower as easily accessible as possible. I include this article from Fox Business News to demonstrate that certain leaders have been affected by the disease of Trump in America.

USA Guns, Violence, & Accidents

Since 1968, "more Americans have died from gunfire than died in… all the wars of this country's history."

— *Mark Shields, PBS commentator*[1]

1.4 MILLION   FIREARM DEATHS IN US BETWEEN THE PERIOD 1968-2011[2]

1.2 MILLION   DEATHS IN EVERY CONFLICT FROM THE WAR OF INDEPENDENCE[2]

GUNS HELD BY CIVILIANS[3]

310,000,000

Handguns 114,000,000

Rifles 110,000,000

Shotguns 86,000,000

31%
OF HOUSEHOLDS WITH GUNS

HIGHEST GUN OWNERSHIP IN THE WORLD'S 178 COUNTRIES

101.052
GUNS PER 100 PEOPLE

DEATHS RELATED TO GUNS[4] in 2013   33,169

SUICIDES 21,175

HOMICIDES 11,208

ACCIDENTAL DISCHARGE 505

17.4% OF ALL INJURY DEATHS

+ 84,258 NONFATAL INJURIES   26.65 PER 100,000

"A well regulated militia being necessary to the security of a free state, the right of the people to keep and bear arms shall not be infringed."

Second Amendment of US Constitution

COMPARE TO TERRORISM 2001-2011[5]

11,385 PEOPLE DIED ON AVERAGE ANNUALLY IN GUN INCIDENTS VS.

517 ANNUALLY IN TERROR-RELATED INCIDENTS, BUT…

…REMOVING 2001 (9/11)   **31** ANNUAL AVERAGE

1) On Friday, December 21st, 2012 in the PBS NewsHour; 2) Politifact (www.politifact.com/truth-o-meter/statements/2013/jan/18/mark-shields/pbs-commentator-mark-shields-says-more-killed-guns); 3) Gun Policy (www.gunpolicy.org/firearms/region/united-states); 4) Centers for Disease Control and Prevention (www.cdc.gov/nchs/data/nvsr/nvsr64/nvsr64_02.pdf); 5) Figures from the US Department of Justice and the Council on Foreign Affairs;

SINCE 1968, "MORE AMERICANS HAVE DIED FROM GUNFIRE THAN DIED IN… ALL THE WARS OF THIS COUNTRY'S HISTORY."

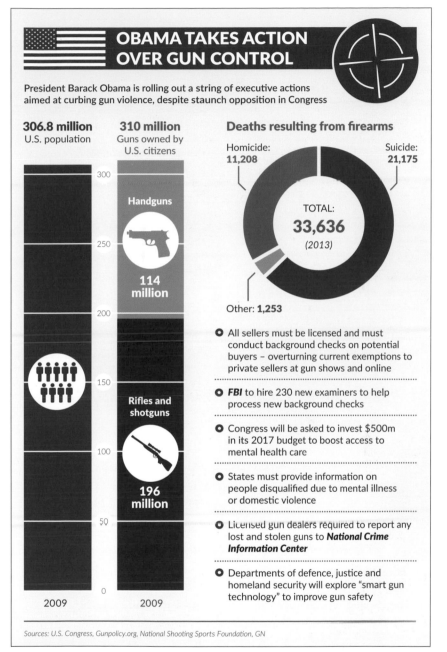

OBAMA TAKES ACTION OVER GUN CONTROL

President Barack Obama is rolling out a string of executive actions aimed at curbing gun violence, despite staunch opposition in Congress

306.8 million
U.S. population

310 million
Guns owned by
U.S. citizens

Handguns

114 million

Rifles and shotguns

196 million

2009   2009

Deaths resulting from firearms

Homicide:
11,208

Suicide:
21,175

TOTAL:
33,636
(2013)

Other: **1,253**

- All sellers must be licensed and must conduct background checks on potential buyers – overturning current exemptions to private sellers at gun shows and online
- *FBI* to hire 230 new examiners to help process new background checks
- Congress will be asked to invest $500m in its 2017 budget to boost access to mental health care
- States must provide information on people disqualified due to mental illness or domestic violence
- Licensed gun dealers required to report any lost and stolen guns to *National Crime Information Center*
- Departments of defence, justice and homeland security will explore "smart gun technology" to improve gun safety

Sources: U.S. Congress, Gunpolicy.org, National Shooting Sports Foundation, GN

HOW CAN THIS TOPIC BE OF SUCH FERVENT DEBATE WITH SO MANY TERRIBLE REALITIES SEEN IN OUR TIMES?

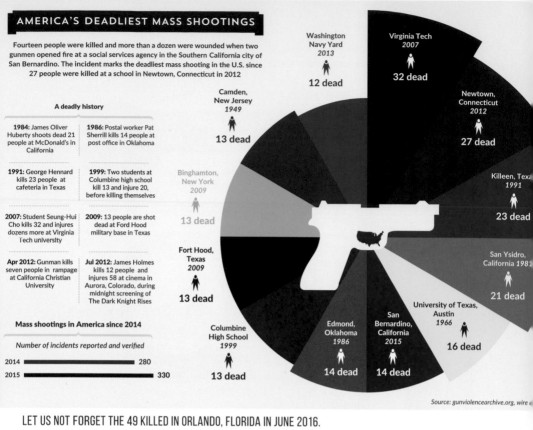

AMERICA'S DEADLIEST MASS SHOOTINGS

Fourteen people were killed and more than a dozen were wounded when two gunmen opened fire at a social services agency in the Southern California city of San Bernardino. The incident marks the deadliest mass shooting in the U.S. since 27 people were killed at a school in Newtown, Connecticut in 2012

A deadly history

1984: James Oliver Huberty shoots dead 21 people at McDonald's in California	**1986:** Postal worker Pat Sherrill kills 14 people at post office in Oklahoma
1991: George Hennard kills 23 people at cafeteria in Texas	**1999:** Two students at Columbine high school kill 13 and injure 20, before killing themselves
2007: Student Seung-Hui Cho kills 32 and injures dozens more at Virginia Tech university	**2009:** 13 people are shot dead at Ford Hood military base in Texas
Apr 2012: Gunman kills seven people in rampage at California Christian University	**Jul 2012:** James Holmes kills 12 people and injures 58 at cinema in Aurora, Colorado, during midnight screening of The Dark Knight Rises

Mass shootings in America since 2014

Number of incidents reported and verified

2014	280
2015	330

Washington Navy Yard 2013 — 12 dead

Virginia Tech 2007 — 32 dead

Camden, New Jersey 1949 — 13 dead

Newtown, Connecticut 2012 — 27 dead

Binghamton, New York 2009 — 13 dead

Killeen, Texas 1991 — 23 dead

Fort Hood, Texas 2009 — 13 dead

San Ysidro, California 1984 — 21 dead

Columbine High School 1999 — 13 dead

Edmond, Oklahoma 1986 — 14 dead

San Bernardino, California 2015 — 14 dead

University of Texas, Austin 1966 — 16 dead

Source: gunviolencearchive.org, wire

LET US NOT FORGET THE 49 KILLED IN ORLANDO, FLORIDA IN JUNE 2016.
IT'S SCARY THAT ONE MAN AND ONE GUN CAN KILL SO MANY PEOPLE; EVERYONE WHO OWNS A GUN ENABLES THIS TO HAPP

FLORIDA GOV. RICK SCOTT ON WHY HE'S ENDORSING TRUMP

By Matthew Kazin
Published March 17, 2016

One day after Donald Trump's victory in Florida, the state's governor, Rick Scott, has decided to endorse the GOP front-runner. He explained why he is backing the candidate on the FOX Business Network's *Cavuto: Coast to Coast*.

"We have to win in November," Scott said. "If we want a president that's going to focus on jobs, defending the Second Amendment, having somebody on the Supreme Court that believes in the Constitution, and rebuild the military, then we've got to start focusing on winning in November. The only way to do that is get behind Donald Trump today."

Scott, like Trump, is a businessman-turned-politician and is currently serving his second term in office.

The "Sunshine State's" governor is looking forward to seeing Trump win the White House, as he doesn't believe the current Administration has been of much help since he assumed the governorship in 2011.

"I need a partner in D.C. that cares about jobs," Scott said. "Barack Obama has not helped me build jobs in this country since I've been the governor for five years. He's never been a help to me. I need somebody that's going to defend the Second Amendment. I need somebody that's going to focus on the right things."[253]

Indeed there is a severe warning in the examples above. If we do not comprehend them correctly and take the necessary measures, then more people with the Trump–Hitler–ISIS–Al-Qaeda–KKK disease will appear to lead the people.

I have already spoken about this in detail, and more examples of this disease keep surfacing. I will quote here an article from the *Wall Street Journal* published April 18, 2016 which further proves that Trump's influential disease is spreading to world leaders:

IS BELGIUM'S INTERIOR MINISTER COPYING TRUMP?

"A significant part of the Muslim community danced in response to the attacks."

That statement, made by Belgian Interior Minister Jan Jambon in an interview with Flemish daily *De Standaard* published Saturday, may sound familiar to American readers. It closely echoes a claim made repeatedly by Republican frontrunner Donald Trump that "thousands of people were cheering" in Jersey City, N.J., when the World Trade Center towers fell on Sept. 11, 2001.

And just like Mr. Trump's claim — which has been denied vehemently by U.S. authorities — Mr. Jambon's comments, which refer to the deadly bombings at Brussels Airport and a subway station on March 22, have prompted political pushback, as well as an examination of whether they are true.

So what did Mr. Jambon, a member of the right-wing Flemish nationalist N-VA party, actually say?

In the interview, Mr. Jambon was asked whether Belgium, as a society, had to take responsibility for the attacks. After explaining that there were some oversights in the years leading up to the attacks, the minister launched into the following:

"A significant part of the Muslim community danced in response to the attacks. They threw stones and bottles at police and the press during the arrest of Salah Abdeslam (a suspected participant in the Nov. 13 attacks in Paris). That's the real problem. We can apprehend terrorists, extract them from society. But they are merely a pimple. Underneath, there is a cancer that is much harder to treat. We can do it. But not overnight. And those involved in politics will have to transcend themselves."

A few bottles and some other objects were indeed thrown at police in the hours after Mr. Abdeslam's arrest on March 18 in the Brussels district of Molenbeek, as witnessed by this reporter. But those incidents appeared to be mostly spontaneous and random — following an hours long siege of several residential blocks by riot police a neighborhood that has long had difficult relations with law enforcement — rather than part of a unified reaction to the arrest.

IT ISN'T APPROPRIATE TO MAKE GENERALIZATIONS

Was the reaction to the March 22 bombings, which killed at least 32 people, including a Muslim mother of three from Molenbeek, any broader?

Charles Michel, Belgium's prime minister, said Sunday that "there were expressions of support for the authors of the attacks." Mr. Michel told state-run news agency Belga that those incidents had been reported to the national security council, which includes key ministers including Mr. Jambon as well as OCAM, Belgium's coordination agency for threat analysis.

However, the prime minister also played down their significance. "These were acts coming from people who were in the minority and it isn't appropriate to make generalizations," he said.

The Brussels' prosecutor's office, under whose jurisdiction any post-attack dance parties would fall, said it is aware of just one incident, in which no one was charged. Six people were arrested on Avenue de Versailles, a street that has been linked to one of the alleged Paris attackers, following reports of a support demonstration.

However, the six people were later released, since "we don't have enough elements to prove that they were involved in such an incident," said spokeswoman Ine Van Wymersch.

In comments to Belgian media Monday, Mr. Jambon stood by his statement.[254]

We have also the example of Maine Governor Paul LePage as reported in *New York Daily News*:

Donald Trump doesn't like listening to Indian people talk — and neither does one of his most prominent supporters, Maine Gov. Paul LePage.

LePage — one of three sitting governors who has endorsed Trump for president — described Indian workers as "the worst

REUTERS/JOEL PAGE

ones" to understand during a xenophobic rant at the state's Republican convention Saturday.

His callous comments came just one day after Trump targeted Indians as well — using a fake accent to mock them during a Delaware campaign stop.

He complained about how workers with accents — whom he apparently assumes are all making minimum wage — are too difficult to understand.

LEPAGE — AS ONE WOULD EXPECT FOR A TRUMP-LOVING GOVERNOR — HAS A LONG HISTORY OF MAKING RACIST OR IDIOTIC REMARKS.

"It's hard to hear what they're saying. Have you ever tried to say, 'What's the special today?' to somebody from Bulgaria?" LePage said, drawing laughing from the audience.

"And the worst ones — if they're from India. I mean, they're all lovely people, but you gotta have an interpreter. Or how many of you try to return something on Amazon on a telephone?"

Earlier in the speech, LePage joked that "Obama" stands for "One Big Ass Mistake, America." LePage's shameful speech is a clear copy of Trump's campaign trail comments a day earlier.

Trump briefly used a cartoonish Indian accent while imitating a worker with an outsourced customer service job.

LePage — as one would expect for a Trump-loving governor — has a long history of making racist or idiotic remarks. He said asylum seekers bring AIDS and an imaginary disease called "ziki fly" to Maine, and blamed Maine's heroin problem on "guys with the name D-Money, Smoothy, Shifty" who come from other states and "impregnate a young white girl before they leave."[255]

Even in a place as far away from the US as Australia, Trumpians are expressing their infatuation with Trump and his ways:

DONALD TRUMP'S POPULARITY IS SPREADING TO AUSTRA-LIA, AND HIS SUPPORTERS ARE ALL AROUND US

March 2, 2016

YOUNG, educated, professional, and dissatisfied with Malcolm Turnbull.

These are the Aussies who are getting behind Donald Trump, and want a slice of the US Republican presidential nominee's flamboyant leadership style all for ourselves.

While discussions of the eccentric billionaire's lofty ambitions for presidential candidacy were only months ago reserved for the punch lines of bad jokes, Trump looks set to romp it in when 12 states vote for their presidential candidates in tomorrow's Super Tuesday.

More than 800 points ahead of his nearest competitor, and the most likely Republican to take on democrat Hillary Clinton, Trump is confident he'll take the White House.

But while the prospect of President Trump is terrifying to many, coming with warnings of economic turmoil and global conflict, to Trump supporters — and there are clearly a few of them — it just makes sense.

The supporters aren't just wacky Americans, jaded with the performance of the Obama administration that fell short of many voters' expectations, and excited by a celebrity candidate that's basically Barack's polar opposite.

As news.com.au discovered, the The Trump Effect has gone international, and supporters are all around us.

Not quite confident enough to campaign on the streets, closet Trump fans are converging on social media to throw their support across the equator and behind the man they believe can "make America great again".

A Facebook group for Australians supporting the surprise candidate keeps its members identities secret, but in an interview conducted over the site's messenger service, one of its ad-

THE
SUPPORTERS AREN'T
JUST WACKY AMERICANS,
JADED WITH THE PERFORMANCE
OF THE OBAMA ADMINISTRATION
THAT FELL SHORT OF MANY VOTERS'
EXPECTATIONS, AND EXCITED BY
A CELEBRITY CANDIDATE THAT'S
BASICALLY BARACK'S POLAR OPPOSITE.
AS NEWS.COM.AU DISCOVERED,
THE THE TRUMP EFFECT HAS GONE
INTERNATIONAL, AND SUPPORTERS
ARE ALL AROUND US.

ministrators outlined its fan base.

"I've been in contact with Trump supporters both in my city and around the country (believe me when I say we're everywhere), and as a general rule, we're under 40, male, and well-educated," he said.

The administrator himself is a right-wing bloke in his 20s. He has a graduate degree, lives and works in an Australian state's capital city and doesn't want to reveal much else about himself.

He says young Australian Trump supporters, including himself, consider themselves conservative but haven't found a politician or party that reflects their views in Canberra.

"We tend not to be members of the Liberals, either because we've always found them to be against our interests, or because of Malcolm Turnbull," he said.

"He represents everything that's wrong with the centre-right, and just like (John) Kasich, the Republican who Democrats could see themselves voting for, he'll never get left-leaning votes when there's an actual left-wing candidate in the race."

The fan club leader says he knew Trump was "something special" from the moment he announced his candidacy.

"We're about 10-15 years behind the States in our politics (think LBJ-Whitlam, Reagan-Howard), but I really think Trump becoming president will turn the tide more quickly," he said.

"Trump loves the military and the vets, but he's the least bellicose candidate left in this race. A military that's so big and so powerful that you don't have to use it is exactly what we want.

"I think most importantly, he is bringing back a culture of free speech. Legal protections like the First Amendment mean nothing if you could lose your job, your security, and so on, for having an unpopular opinion."

Trump supporters are not ignorant of the fact that in many mainstream circles, supporting Trump is itself an unpopular opinion.

Most fans approached by news.com.au were unwilling to identify themselves, or agreed only to speak "after Trump's inauguration".

Western Sydney man David McBride was one of the few open to discussing Trump's appeal, and said he's used to defending his opinion.

"I went back to my relatives for Christmas in Brisbane and one of the first things that was said to me was 'I looked at your Facebook and I see you've supported this Trump post', so I had to defend myself," the 46-year-old bank worker told news.com.au.

"I did so very easily, because I think the situation in the US is not very good and I think Trump offers an opportunity for possibilities. It hasn't been hostile, but I've of course come across people who are definitely not supporters."

Mr. McBride said he's been disappointed in the media fascination with Trump's celebrity character when he has so much more to offer.

UNIVERSITY OF SYDNEY'S UNITED STATES STUDIES CENTRE, DAVID SMITH, TOLD NEWS.COM.AU A TRUMP PRESIDENCY COULD BE A "GLOBAL DISASTER".

"When I hear accounts about Trump in the media or social media, what I hear is he's a reality TV star, but I know Trump from the '80s, and I remember he was world wide famous and not for reality TV, for owning a lot of money, being very flamboyant etc., and being very successful.

"So I was aware of him and I take him more seriously than others because I never watched *The Apprentice*," he said.

Mr. Trump has courted conservative US voters with his hard line views on immigration, even proposing to build a wall along the border the US shares with Mexico to prevent unauthorized migration.

With immigration and refugee issues also timely to Australian voters, his dramatic views have caused conservative ears to prick up closer to home as well.

"I remember back then people were talking about immigration and the war, and it was a problem that concerned me. They said we're going to fix it, we're going to fix it. I like that someone is calling the political establishment on both sides. That someone's calling them out on that and that something might actually be done," Mr. McBride said.

"When (Trump) came down the escalators that's one thing that he said on that day that differentiated him and put a red flag up for me, in terms of 'this is a guy to follow and maybe to support'."

Trump supporters believe a Trump presidency would have a huge impact on Australia, and experts agree.

Members of his support base hope his success inspires our politicians or new politicians to adopt some of his views, while others fear the effect his generally aggressive attitude, coupled with the power that comes with the US presidency, will have on trade and the global economy.

THE GOOD NEWS FOR HIM IS, THERE'S LITTLE PRESSURE FROM SOME OF HIS SUPPORTERS FOR HIM TO ACTUALLY PERFORM

Senior lecturer at the University of Sydney's United States Studies Centre, David Smith, told news.com.au a Trump presidency could be a "global disaster".

"It's very likely that Trump is going to get the Republican nomination at this stage," Dr Smith said. "His likely opposition would be Hillary Clinton, and instinctively most feel that Hillary Clinton would beat him fairly easily. But then again everyone felt he wasn't going to get far in the nomination race either.

"We really just don't know how he would behave as president. It's quite possible that Trump could spook markets in a way that could have negative effects for the economy overall. If he's going to get involved in the trade war with China, really, nobody is going to win that war."

But Trump is unpredictable. He's changed his positions on issues in the past, and he may do so on immigration and the other issues he's campaigning on. The good news for him is, there's little pressure from some of his supporters for him to actually perform, Mr. McBride explains.

IT IS THIS AUDACITY THAT ENCOURAGES THE MANIFESTATION OF THIS DISEASE IN SOCIETY.

"If all he does is just be a George W Bush or an Obama in office, if he doesn't fulfill anything of what he says, the fact that he's been able to do what he's done to get into the nomination and into the presidency, if only that occurs, that in itself will be good."[256]

This mindset is indeed something of old, and it is widespread amongst many of the people. However, it is Trump who has the audacity to announce and broadcast his corrupt views openly. It is this audacity that encourages the manifestation of this disease in society. This seems sure to happen, whether he wins or loses the election, because he has opened its door. It is now upon us to consider and plan on how to deal with it, for surely it is a disease that must be treated; and I believe that every disease has a cure. It is to the extent that a council should be established to study this important matter, just as various countries establish research committees for the rehabilitation of terrorists.

21

AMERICA SHOULD BE MORE **AFRAID** OF SOME OF THE **PEOPLE** SUPPORTING TRUMP THAN TRUMP HIMSELF

TRUMP'S CAMPAIGN CONTINUALLY ATTRACTS those with the same disease as him. Those who are infected by it love how he has set up numerous targets to go after. They want him to take on China, Mexico, the Gulf States, Japan, India, South Korea, the Muslims, and whomever else they feel like assaulting on any given day.

THESE SUPPORTERS MAY SEEM LIKE DIEHARD FANS RIGHT NOW, BUT WE FEEL THAT TRUMP WILL BE CLASHING WITH THEM IN THE NEAR FUTURE.

These supporters may seem like diehard fans right now, but we feel that Trump will be clashing with them in the near future. Many of his right-wing followers are supporting him because of the agenda he's put forward, such as building the wall, banning Muslims, and raising tariffs on foreign allies. But what will happen when he's unable to deliver these results to appease those who showed him support?

If Trump fails in the election, it really won't affect his life. He'll be able to go away and relax, back to his penthouses and golf courses, leaving his supporters behind. He will have used them to try to reach the White House and he won't need them afterwards, just as he didn't need them before his campaign.

The danger is that even if he loses, he's already had the opportunity to spread his disease. It's a very dangerous door he has opened with his campaign. He has brought to the surface much of the prejudice and sectarianism that still exists amongst some of the population. And that pent-up frustration and anger can boil over and erupt at any time, just as it did in Algeria only a few decades ago.

In 1987, the oil prices plummeted in Algeria from forty dollars per barrel all the way down to nine dollars per barrel. This caused a ripple effect through the economy, and the country was plunged into a very difficult situation. This brought about great frustration amongst the population and in 1988, protests began.

SOME OF TRUMP'S SUPPORTERS ARE LIKELY MUCH MORE DANGEROUS THAN HIM, AND THEY ARE ONLY USING HIM AS A LADDER TO REACH THEIR OWN GOALS.

Abbas Madani, who held a PhD, and Ali Belhaj, an eloquent speaker, saw these protests and demonstrations that were completely random, and they tried to take control of them. While the protesters had purely economic reasons for their actions at that time, these two leaders made the situation even worse by converting it to an organized movement.

In 1989, Abbas Madani and Ali Belhaj founded a political party, the FIS. Then, in 1991, they were on the verge of being elected. But, just before the final results in January 1992, the military called off the election and detained many FIS leaders. Thereafter, many groups and factions formed and proceeded to fight and kill each other for power, even turning against those two men who organized and formed their movement.[257]

Likewise, America should beware of some of those hiding behind Trump's ideas and helping him to spread their disease and be their voice. Some of Trump's supporters are likely much more dangerous than him, and they are only using him as a ladder to reach their own goals.

Playing off Trump's earlier words, Mayor Rick Kriseman of St. Petersburg, Florida, tweeted that he was banning Trump "until we fully understand the dangerous threat posed by all Trumps."[258]

22

TRUMP HAS EVEN
INFECTED OBAMA

IN AUGUST 2016, AS REPORTED BY BLOOMBERG, Trump said of the oil-rich nation Saudi Arabia,

"They should pay us. Like it or don't like it, people have backed Saudi Arabia. What I really mind, though, is we back it at tremendous expense. We get nothing for it.

"The primary reason we're with Saudi Arabia is because we need the oil. Now we don't need the oil so much, and if we let our people really go, we wouldn't need the oil at all and we could let everybody else fight it out." [259]

According to the U.S. State Department, [260] the U.S. currently imports more than one million barrels of Saudi Arabian oil each day.

"Saudi Arabia is going to be in big trouble pretty soon and they're going to need help, because if you look at Yemen and you look at that border," said Trump, *"you don't have to be an expert to know that is*

one long border, and they're not going in for Yemen, they're going in for the oil, they're going in for Saudi Arabia, so Saudi Arabia is going to need help. Saudi Arabia, if it weren't for us, they wouldn't be here. They wouldn't exist." [261]

> # NO ONE, NO MATTER HOW HIGH THEIR STATUS, IS SAFE FROM BEING AFFECTED BY THIS DISEASE.

No one, no matter how high their status, is safe from being affected by this disease. Even President Obama exposed his true feelings and spoke in a way provoking disunity amongst the nations, even though he previously did not speak in the way of Trump/Hitler.

In May 2015, in an exclusive interview with *AlArabiya*, he said:

"I think it is U.S. policy that in the Gulf, because of the wide range of interests and the deep friendship and security relations that we have with those countries, that if there was an external threat, our military would be working with the GCC, and hopefully a broad range of other international actors, to prevent that kind of violation of the basic norms of international behavior." [262]

Then, after becoming infected by the disease of Trump/Hitler, the president changed his tone to one of distrust, suspicion, and scare mongering, as was reported in an article by Jeffrey Goldberg in *The Atlantic*, April 2016, in which the President said that "The Saudis and other Gulf Arabs have funneled money, and large numbers of imams and teachers, into the country [Indonesia]. In the 1990s, the Saudis heavily funded Wahhabist madrassas, seminaries that teach the fundamentalist version of Islam favored by the Saudi ruling family."

The president said, "A country cannot function in the modern world when it is repressing half of its population." In meetings with foreign leaders, he said, "You can gauge the success of a society by how it treats its women." [263]

Throughout Obama's more than seven years as president, he never spoke in this tone against his allies. It has only been after Trump has begun his propagation of hate and fear that Obama has had to stoop down to this level in order to keep up with the competition. This has become the thought process of the US leaders due to this infectious mindset. In my opinion, this is running away from reality.

THROUGHOUT OBAMA'S MORE THAN SEVEN YEARS AS PRESIDENT, HE NEVER SPOKE IN THIS TONE AGAINST HIS ALLIES.

Saudi Arabia has continually supported the United States and other nations in their war against terrorism. The US has praised the Saudi Kingdom for blacklisting twelve Hezbollah-affiliated individuals including military officials and financiers. Joseph W. Westphal, US ambassador to Saudi Arabia, said in a statement that the United States "looks forward to further strengthening our partnership with Saudi Arabia as we work toward the common goal of exposing Hezbollah's nefarious activity and disrupting the group's ability to raise and move funds."

"Many of these figures were previously sanctioned by the United States and this action demonstrates our shared focus on targeting this violent terrorist organization and its support apparatus. These designations by Saudi Arabia are yet another example of close United States-Saudi coordination on countering terrorist financing in the Middle East and around the world," he said.[264]

UK Prime Minister David Cameron said in February 2015: "I can tell you one time since I've been prime minister, a piece of information that we have been given by that country (Saudi Arabia) has saved potentially hundreds of lives here in Britain."[265]

Trump does not think in a comprehensive way: he only thinks from one angle – and this is from his disease.

Prince Turki Al-Faisal, of Saudi Arabia, wrote the following reply rebutting the President Obama's allegations:

TRUMP DOES NOT THINK IN A COMPREHENSIVE WAY: HE ONLY THINKS FROM ONE ANGLE – AND THIS IS FROM HIS DISEASE.

> No, Mr. Obama. We are not 'free riders.' We shared with you our intelligence that prevented deadly terrorist attacks on America. We initiated the meetings that led to the coalition that is fighting Fahish (ISIL), and we train and fund the Syrian freedom fighters, who fight the biggest terrorist, Bashar Assad and

the other terrorists, Al-Nusrah and Fahish (ISIL). We offered boots on the ground to make that coalition more effective in eliminating the terrorists.

We initiated the support — military, political and humanitarian — that is helping the Yemeni people reclaim their country from the murderous militia, the Houthis, who, with the support of the Iranian leadership, tried to occupy Yemen; without calling for American forces. We established a coalition of more than thirty Muslim countries to fight all shades of terrorism in the world.

YOUR TREASURY DEPARTMENT OFFICIALS HAVE PUBLICLY PRAISED SAUDI ARABIA'S MEASURES TO CURTAIL ANY FINANCING THAT MIGHT REACH TERRORISTS.

We are the biggest contributors to the humanitarian relief efforts to help refugees from Syria, Yemen and Iraq. We combat extremist ideology that attempts to hijack our religion, on all levels. We are the sole funders of the United Nations Counter-terrorism Center, which pools intelligence, political, economic, and human resources, worldwide. We buy US treasury bonds, with small interest returns, that help your country's economy.

We send thousands of our students to your universities, at enormous expense, to acquire knowledge and knowhow. We host over 30,000 American citizens and pay them top dollar in our businesses and industry for their skills. Your secretaries of state and defense have often publicly praised the level of cooperation between our two countries.

Your Treasury Department officials have publicly praised Saudi Arabia's measures to curtail any financing that might reach terrorists. Our King Salman met with you, last September, and accepted your assurances that the nuclear deal you struck with the Iranian leadership will prevent their acquiring nuclear weapons for the duration of the deal. You noted "the Kingdom's leadership role in the Arab and Islamic world."

PRINCE TURKI AL-FAISAL

NO, MR. OBAMA. WE ARE NOT THE 'FREE RIDERS' THAT TO WHOM YOU REFER. WE LEAD FROM THE FRONT AND WE ACCEPT OUR MISTAKES AND RECTIFY THEM. WE WILL CONTINUE TO HOLD THE AMERICAN PEOPLE AS OUR ALLY

DOES TRUMP EVEN UNDERSTAND THE ISSUES?

23

THE WORLD IS
HIERARCHICAL

WHEN WE LOOK AT THE STARS, PLANETS, AND galaxies, we always find that the largest are few and the smallest are numerous. God created this earth as a hierarchy. You can always count the largest ones of anything, but the smallest cannot be counted, as they are too many in number. This is true of the trees, fish, and birds. Amongst the trees, fish, and birds, the largest are few and can be counted, while the smallest ones are too many. Likewise, the mountains are numerous, but the largest ones, such as the Himalayas, are few. In the wild, the lions are a limited number, and can be counted, but the other animals, which are their prey, are numerous. The small diamonds are many, but the large diamonds are few in number.

Also, consider the minds; the exceptional minds are few in number, while the average minds are plenty. How many Einsteins are there in the world? How many Bill Gates, Steve Jobs, or Isaac Newtons have we seen? How many Thomas Edisons or Bin Nafis? (For those unfamiliar with the last name, he is the Arab physician who discovered the human circulatory system.)

HOW WILL SMART PEOPLE IN THIS CENTURY USE THE ADVANCEMENTS IN TECHNOLOGY AND THE FACILITIES THAT HAVE NEVER EXISTED BEFORE?

How will smart people in this century use the advancements in technology and the facilities that have never existed before?

The connected nature of our world – the iPhones, present modern day logistics, IT and software, the advancements in economics and modern day trading – represents a situation that didn't exist before. How will leaders manage these for the benefit of humanity? It's something to think about deeply. To clarify this more, let's look at the example of Ford Motors reported by the BBC:

> Ford makes cars but that is now only part of its operations.
>
> The company's chief executive has revealed that it's working on the assumption that its major rivals in the future may not be General Motors or Chrysler, but Google and Apple. And that the latter is probably building a car.
>
> "Our working assumption is that they are," Mark Fields said.
>
> Ford, which made record profits of $10.8bn last year, says that "Level 4" driverless cars will be available by the end of the decade.
>
> "Level 4" cars can drive autonomously in a pre-defined area fully mapped by computers.
>
> "Level 5" cars, much further away, can take over completely from the driver and "take you home", wherever that may be.
>
> "A Level 4 vehicle is where the passenger does not have to take control of the vehicle, but it's a vehicle that's in a pre-defined area, that's been 3D mapped, and what we call geo-fenced," Mr. Fields said.
>
> "And we believe when we look at the advancements in the sensors and advancements in the software algorithms which are

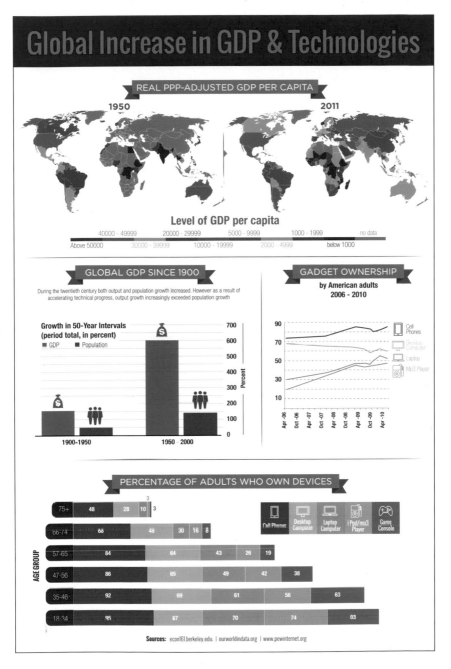

Global Increase in GDP & Technologies

REAL PPP-ADJUSTED GDP PER CAPITA

1950

2011

Level of GDP per capita

| Above 50000 | 40000 - 49999 | 30000 - 39999 | 20000 - 29999 | 10000 - 19999 | 5000 - 9999 | 2000 - 4999 | 1000 - 1999 | below 1000 | no data |

GLOBAL GDP SINCE 1900

During the twentieth century both output and population growth increased. However as a result of accelerating technical progress, output growth increasingly exceeded population growth

Growth in 50-Year Intervals (period total, in percent)

■ GDP ■ Population

1900-1950   1950 - 2000

GADGET OWNERSHIP

by American adults 2006 - 2010

Cell Phones
Desktop Computer
Laptop
Mp3 Player

PERCENTAGE OF ADULTS WHO OWN DEVICES

Cell Phones | Desktop Computer | Laptop Computer | iPod/mp3 Player | Game Console

AGE GROUP

75+	48	28	10	3	3
66-74	68	48	30	16	8
57-65	84	64	43	26	19
47-56	86	65	49	42	38
35-46	92	69	61	56	63
18-34	95	67	70	74	63

Sources: econ161.berkeley.edu. | ourworldindata.org | www.pewinternet.org

THESE RESULTS COME ABOUT WHEN INTELLIGENT PEOPLE OPTIMIZE THEIR USE OF EMERGING TECHNOLOGIES AND COMMUNICATIONS PLATFORMS IN THE OPEN MARKET.

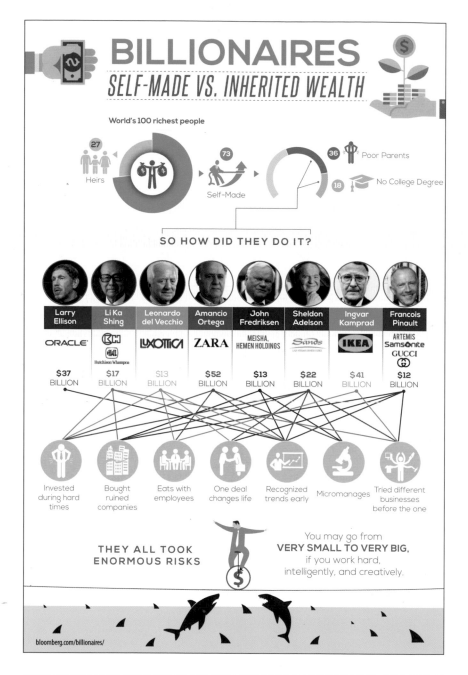

THESE RESULTS COME ABOUT DUE TO THE INTELLIGENT PEOPLE OPTIMIZING THEIR UTILIZATION OF EMERGING TECHNOLOGIES AND COMMUNICATIONS PLATFORMS IN THE OPEN MARKET.

necessary for the vehicle to navigate, that probably by the end of the decade, in the next four years or so, someone in the industry may have a Level 4 vehicle.[269]

I believe that if these same intelligent people were to become affected by the disease of Trump–Hitler–KKK–ISIS–Al-Qaeda, it will increase its spread in the years to come. This is a subject that I would like to expand upon, and perhaps it might be the subject of a future book.

Most of the rich people in the last twenty years did not make money by inheriting their wealth from their forefathers. They made it themselves. This is totally different to what it was before that period.

I will give you a great example to clarify this affair of smart minds further.

Consider the operation of taxicabs. For years people have been driving taxis, earning a median of $11.16 an hour, or a median salary of $23,210 (in 2014).

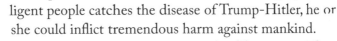

TRUMP CONSIDERS HIMSELF TO BE SMARTER THAN EVERYONE ELSE.

A man, such as the founder of Uber, then comes with an idea and an app and controls the business operations of thousands of drivers operating like taxis — all while sitting in his chair and sipping on his drink. The driver drives around all day in the sun and rain while the man who had the idea for the app can sit in his chair and make billions, due to his smart mind. This example is to show the risk if one of these highly intel-

ligent people catches the disease of Trump-Hitler, he or she could inflict tremendous harm against mankind.

It is important to point out that Trump considers himself to be smarter than everyone else. That is why he repeats the word "smart" about himself so many times.

He tweeted from his official *Twitter* account: *"Sorry losers and haters, but my I.Q. is one of the highest and you all know it! Please don't feel so stupid or insecure, it's not your fault".* [270]

On *Good Morning Britain*, Trump told Piers Morgan, *"I happen to be intelligent, very intelligent, based on the results I get while doing things"* [271]

Let me prove, though, that you do not need to be as smart as Trump believes he is in order to become very rich. As reported in 2007 by *CBS News*:

"Leona Helmsley left her beloved white Maltese, named Trouble, a $12 million trust fund, according to her will. But two of Helmsley's grandchildren got zilch from the late luxury hotelier and real estate billionaire's estate."[272]

Even though these kinds of people may be worth millions, they clearly are not all of sound minds.

24

UNDERSTANDING
JUSTICE AND EQUALITY

HOW CAN IT BE THAT THE COUNTRY THAT IS the fountain of technology, the global economy, and spring of education, where more than three hundred million people reside, you find that the Republican Party's nominee for the presidential race is such a bombastic individual? The reason, in my opinion, is that the leaders of the countries that won the Second World War guided our planet towards certain ideologies. They did this through those understandings they created while establishing the United Nations and World Trade Organization.

The world today is getting harder and harder for the hard-working middle class and the poor. At the same time, it's also getting harder for the shortsighted and the lazy people who expect the world to be handed to them. These freeloaders blindly cling onto the disease of Trump and those similar to him, in hopes that they will find a cure for their unhappiness.

THESE FREELOADERS BLINDLY CLING ONTO THE DISEASE OF TRUMP AND THOSE SIMILAR TO HIM, IN HOPES THAT THEY WILL FIND A CURE FOR THEIR UNHAPPINESS.

To explain this complicated situation clearly, I believe we need to remember that in the beginning, all of us in this world were born without choosing anything. We did not choose our father or our mother, or our roots, or our skin color, or the country we are born in, or if we are to be male or female. We could not choose when we were born, nor could we choose our body, nor our mind, nor choose our strength. Yes, we can increase and improve some of these things, but we cannot choose them from birth. So the people have become lost between these realities and the ideologies put upon them by the United Nations. These include the interpretations of freedom, equality, and human rights. This is something that clashes with the natural hierarchy of life, the form of the human body, and how our communities and countries are made up.

How can it be expected for ordinary people to understand equality? When a person is born to a father who is a multimillionaire like Trump, and he did not have a choice to choose his own father; this is from God. There are people who were born in Somalia who have very different opportunities compared to the people born in Japan; this is not by their choice. Look at the countries like Norway, which has great oil reserves available for it, without any effort from its own part.

So how can we actually reach equality? How do we actualize equality between the male and female while a man does not get pregnant with children, and a woman gets pregnant with each child and carries it in her womb for nine months? How do we actualize equality between the naturally intelligent and those born with lesser intelligence?

We can have *justice*, but *equality* is an unrealistic expectation. I will clarify it more with this example:

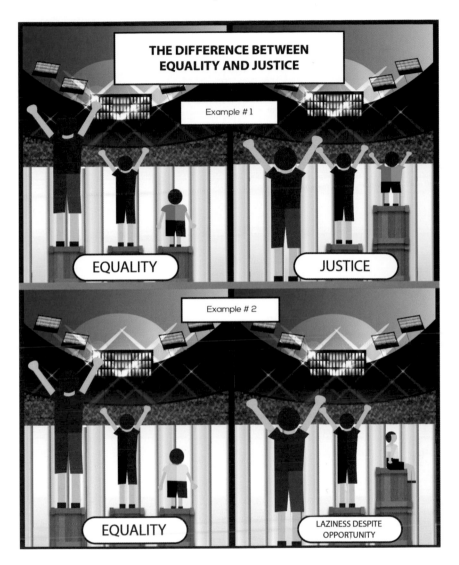

TRUMP – KUWAIT – CALIFORNIA

During his 1988 interview on the Oprah Winfrey Show, Trump asserted, *"In Kuwait, they live like kings. The poorest person in Kuwait- they live like kings!"* [273]

I can tell you first-hand that not every Kuwaiti lives like a king; however, it has been the decision of the government that each and every Kuwaiti is generously taken care of in many aspects of their lives. All Kuwaitis receive free or subsidized food staples, free education through the university level, money for getting married, money for each child, and money to build a house. A government employee can never be fired from his or her job. There is a clear reason why the economic situation is so different: it is because the policies of the governments differ.

TRUMP NEEDS TO STOP TRYING TO DISTRACT THE AMERICAN PEOPLE AWAY FROM THE DOMESTIC PROBLEMS WITHIN AMERICA. HE REPEATEDLY DOES THIS BY TURNING THEIR ATTENTION TO HOW PEOPLE LIVE IN FOREIGN COUNTRIES.

Trump needs to stop trying to distract the American people away from the domestic problems within America. He repeatedly does this by turning their attention to how people live in foreign countries. Let us look at the example of California, which among the fifty states has the highest gross domestic product (GDP).

The state can boast of tremendous wealth. Over 13,000 Californians are ultra-high net worth individuals, each owning over $30 million, and *Bloomberg* reported California had 777,624 households with at least $1 million in assets in 2013.[274] *Forbes* also reported:

> It not only has more billionaires than any other U.S. state, but also tops the nations of Germany, India, Russia, and the UK. In fact, if California were a country, it would be home to the third-highest number of billionaires in the world, surpassed only by the United States (which has 541) and China (which has 223). California's billionaires own a combined $560.1 billion in wealth, which is more than the GDP of 49 countries, including Argentina, Poland and Taiwan.[275]

While tremendous wealth exists in California, the poverty level is also very high. The Public Policy Institute of California reported that "according to official poverty statistics, 16.4% of Californians lacked enough resources – about $24,000 per year for a family of four – to meet basic needs in 2014. ... [That] is well above the recent low of 12.4%

CALIFORNIA'S BILLIONAIRES OWN A COMBINED $560.1 BILLION IN WEALTH, WHICH IS MORE THAN THE GDP OF 49 COUNTRIES, INCLUDING ARGENTINA, POLAND AND TAIWAN.

reached in 2007. Moreover, the official poverty line does not account for California's housing costs or other key family needs and resources. ... About one in five (19.8%) Californians were not in poverty but lived fairly close to the poverty line. All told, 40.8% of state residents were poor or near poor in 2013. But the share of Californians in families with less than half the resources needed to meet basic needs was 5.9%, a deep poverty rate that is smaller than official poverty statistics indicate."276

These are the types of real problems currently faced by millions of Americans in only one state. What about the many millions more in other states that are not as rich as California? Trump has not offered any systematic approaches for improvement, and we only see him pointing the finger outside, to foreign lands.

Here is a real plan which, in as little as one year, would completely change the lives of all 46.7 million Americans currently living in poverty. To eliminate poverty in America within such a quick period, this plan would take 2.5 % from the money of the rich and distribute it directly without intermediary amongst the poor.

HERE IS A REAL PLAN WHICH, IN AS LITTLE AS ONE YEAR, WOULD COMPLETELY CHANGE THE LIVES OF ALL 46.7 MILLION AMERICANS CURRENTLY LIVING IN POVERTY.

America will be left with *zero* poor people.

Millions of poor Americans can be given the opportunity to open new factories, new businesses, and to cover the costs of their households. This would create a huge turnover for the economy, and it would recur each year. In this solution, you find that there is a direct relation be-

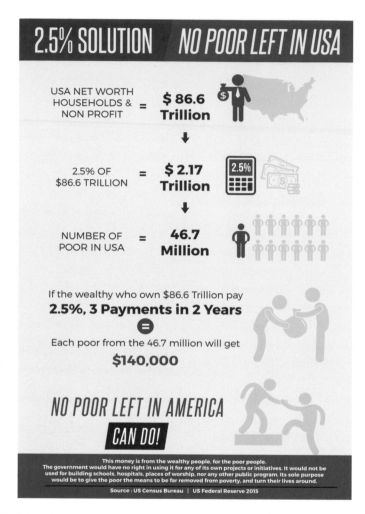

WHO WOULD HAVE EXPECTED THAT THIS SIMPLE 2.5% SOLUTION WOULD COMPLETELY ELIMINATE POVERTY IN AMERICA WITHIN A TIMESPAN OF AS LITTLE AS TWO YEARS? TO CLARIFY HOW IT WORKS: THE WEALTHY WHO POSSESS $86.6 TRILLION WOULD EACH CONTRIBUTE THEIR 2.5% OF WHAT THEY OWN TO HELP LIFT AMERICA'S POOR OUT OF POVERTY. THIS PAYMENT WOULD OCCUR THREE TIMES: AT THE START OF IMPLEMENTING THIS SOLUTION, AFTER ONE YEAR, AND FINALLY AT THE END OF THE SECOND YEAR. EACH AND EVERY POOR PERSON OF THE 46.7 MILLION WOULD RECEIVE OVER $140,000, SO A FAMILY OF FIVE WOULD RECEIVE $700,000. THE GOVERNMENT WOULD HAVE NO RIGHT TO ANY OF THOSE FUNDS, BUT IT WOULD ESTABLISH AN ADVISORY BOARD TO HELP THE PEOPLE TO OPEN BUSINESSES OR INVEST IN THEIR EDUCATION, TO CHANGE THEIR LIVES.

SOME MAY WONDER WHY THIS AMOUNT OF $140,000 WAS CHOSEN FOR THIS EXAMPLE; IT IS JUST TO SHOW HOW YOU CAN COMPLETELY CHANGE THE LIVES OF SO MANY AMERICANS. HOWEVER, IF YOU WANTED TO GIVE EACH POOR PERSON $46,000, THEN THAT CAN BE DONE AT ONLY ONE TIME. THIS WILL HELP ESTABLISH LOVE, SYNERGY, AND COHESIVENESS ACROSS ALL LEVELS OF SOCIETY. THIS CALCULATION HAS BEEN DONE INCLUSIVE OF REAL ESTATE VALUES, BUT EVEN IF WE REMOVED THAT FROM THE EQUATION, IT WOULD STILL BE ENOUGH MONEY TO END POVERTY. NO POOR LEFT IN AMERICA!

tween the rich and poor, which creates love between the people. Those who have been helped would be thankful to those who helped them, and those who helped would be happy to see the positive change in the country and those people's lives. The money is from the people, for the people – completely separate from the government's money.

There is an interesting example in one of the richest men in the world, Ikea founder Ingvar Kamprad. Known to be very generous and socially conscious, he said, "I learned one thing: if I were to succeed with my little ideas and become a businessman, I had to never abandon the poor." That being said, *The Local* in Sweden reported that Kamprad was an admirer of the humble classes who bends over backwards to avoid paying taxes; despite being one of the world's richest people, he has been described as an obsessive penny-pincher.[277] We benefit from this that the rich would often much prefer to aid the poor with their excess wealth, rather than pay it to their governments.

> THE RICH WOULD OFTEN MUCH PREFER TO AID THE POOR WITH THEIR EXCESS WEALTH, RATHER THAN PAY IT TO THEIR GOVERNMENTS.

I believe that each able person should give, but should give in such a way that you can remove someone from poverty – not to give them just one dollar or even a thousand dollars, but to give them enough so that they can get out of poverty. Enough to help them to build businesses, factories, or homes, or invest in their education.

The result would be that in as little as one year there would be no poor people in America. You will see all those who were poor from the street corners turn to running businesses, running supermarkets, and they will be investing in their children's education. You will find that crime will be reduced and people won't be in need of guns and focusing so much on the Second Amendment. The businesspeople will work harder in order to cover that 2.5%, which would push them to amplify research and development, production, and delivery of innovative approaches to solve the world's problems.

Don't reject this concept just because it may be foreign to you. America has achieved success in various fields through implementing a mixture of strategies from around the globe. Be like the Japanese, when they heard about an Arab man named Ghosn, and they embraced his methods with open arms. *Forbes* reported the story:

AMERICA HAS ACHIEVED SUCCESS IN VARIOUS FIELDS THROUGH IMPLE- MENTING A MIXTURE OF STRATEGIES FROM AROUND THE GLOBE.

"In 1999, Nissan was practically bankrupt. Renault, itself practically bankrupt and state-owned just a few years before, invested $5 billion into Nissan for a one-third stake. Carlos Ghosn, deputy of Renault's legendary President Louis Sch- weitzer, rounded up 22 superstars at Renault and air-dropped with them into Tokyo. As the French foreign legion arrived in Japan, experts pre- dicted a disaster, and that the proud Japanese would rather cut their bowels than work under the yoke of 23 Frenchmen who couldn't even hold a chopstick.

"But the hard-charging results-man Ghosn, himself a walk- ing culture-clash, made a miracle happen. Firmly believing that mergers are the work of the devil, Nissan was kept as a separate company that later was integrated more tightly through the Re- nault-Nissan Alliance. Ghosn promised to make Nissan profit- able within a year, or he would leave. He didn't leave, taking over as CEO in 2001... Instead of being maligned in Japan, he was revered."[278]

Ghosn's culture and educational background were completely dif- ferent from that of his Japanese hosts. No one would have expected him to have so positive an impact on such a huge powerhouse of a company in Japan.

We also have a great example in the numerous multinational cor- porations benefiting from the exceptional leadership qualities of Indian executives.

PepsiCo likewise benefitted greatly by hiring Mr. Zein Abdalla from Sudan, in Africa, who served as the President of Pepsico Inc. from September 2012 to December 31, 2014. Mr. Abdalla is responsible for PepsiCo's food and beverage businesses in Continental Europe as well as the UK and sub-Saharan Africa, which together generated approximately $10 billion in revenues in 2010. Mr. Abdalla oversees PepsiCo's global category groups (Global Beverages, Global Snacks and Global Nutrition), Global Operations (IT, Global Procurement, Supply Chain and Productivity), Global Marketing Services and Corporate Strategy.

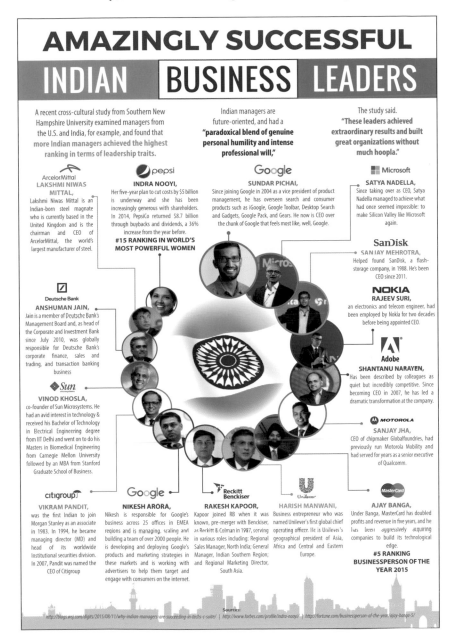

He previously served as the Chief Executive Officer at PepsiCo Europe until 2012.[276]

This is the world we are currently living in, and people need to maintain an open mindset to benefit from the innovations developed in other lands. It is only these people and countries that will be able to lead us successfully through the 21st century.

Let's examine the following example how the United Kingdom benefited from Canadian weapons technology to protect their nuclear arms. This is how the countries and governments coordinate between themselves in positive ways.

Now, in a negative light, we see the great harm that can come about due to the lack of effective coordination between the world's leaders. The crisis faced by Syria's children affected by the war in their country is truly dreadful, and it is so important for America's leaders to proactively push and influence other world leaders to help. To leave so many millions of children in a state of such instability risks future disaster; each may become a ticking time bomb of antisocial behavior. The US must engage proactively to prevent further damage.

> **THIS IS THE WORLD WE ARE CURRENTLY LIVING IN, AND PEOPLE NEED TO MAINTAIN AN OPEN MINDSET TO BENEFIT FROM THE INNOVATIONS DEVELOPED IN OTHER LANDS.**

I believe that the Trump disease has been in existence for many years. It has been festering in those who killed six million Jews, those who caused the deaths of seventy million in the Second World War, and those millions killed in various colonial conquests. Also, in the many millions who were killed in the medieval Crusades. Indeed this has all resulted from the same disease carried by Trump, Hitler, KKK, and ISIS.

Trump said, *"And ISIS is taking over a lot of the oil. You go and knock the hell out of the oil. Take back the oil. We take over the oil, which we should have done in the first place."*[280]

Trump is like one face of a coin, and ISIS the other face. Just as ISIS stole the oil from Syria, Trump too wants to steal it, and he is proud of it.

Likewise, Trump is one face of a coin to which the KKK is the other face. To prove this point:

ROYAL MARINE UNIT DITCHES ARMY RIFLE

A high-profile British Royal Marine unit tasked with protecting the UK's nuclear weapons is the first non-special forces unit to completely drop the standard SA-80 rifle for the Colt Canada C8 Diemaco carbine

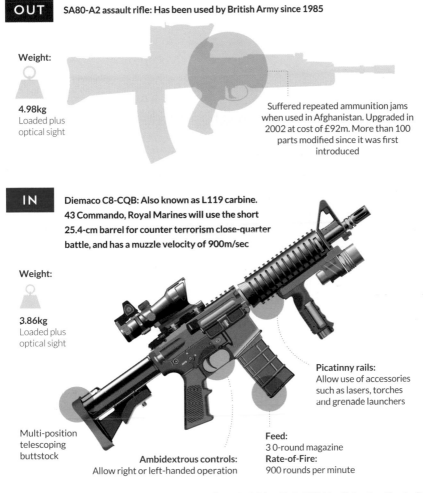

OUT SA80-A2 assault rifle: Has been used by British Army since 1985

Weight:

4.98kg
Loaded plus
optical sight

Suffered repeated ammunition jams when used in Afghanistan. Upgraded in 2002 at cost of £92m. More than 100 parts modified since it was first introduced

IN Diemaco C8-CQB: Also known as L119 carbine. 43 Commando, Royal Marines will use the short 25.4-cm barrel for counter terrorism close-quarter battle, and has a muzzle velocity of 900m/sec

Weight:

3.86kg
Loaded plus
optical sight

Picatinny rails:
Allow use of accessories such as lasers, torches and grenade launchers

Multi-position
telescoping
buttstock

Ambidextrous controls:
Allow right or left-handed operation

Feed:
3 0-round magazine
Rate-of-Fire:
900 rounds per minute

Sources: Jane's Defence Weekly, UK Ministry of Defence Focus Magazine, GN

THE UNITED KINGDOM ALREADY HAS EXPERTISE IN WEAPONS MANUFACTURING; HOWEVER, IT TURNED TO CANADA AFTER REALIZING THAT THESE PARTICULAR CANADIAN GUNS WERE BETTER. THIS IS THE WORLD WE LIVE IN, WHERE THE NATIONS COOPERATE AND AID EACH OTHER. AS FOR TRUMP, HIS WAYS AND METHODS WOULD ONLY LEAD TO CONFLICTS AND DISPUTES BETWEEN THE COUNTRIES OF THE WORLD.

Syrian children harmed by war

The 3.7 million Syrian children born since the conflict began five years ago have known nothing but a lifetime of war. In total, Unicef estimates that 8.4m children, or 80% of Syrians aged under 18, urgently need humanitarian aid.

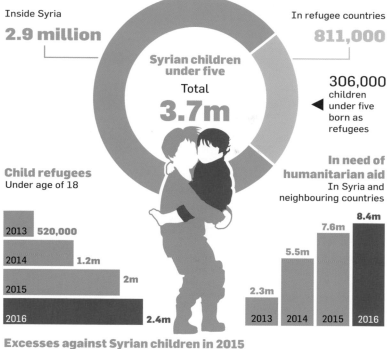

Inside Syria

2.9 million

In refugee countries

811,000

Syrian children
under five

Total

3.7m

306,000
children
under five
born as
refugees

◀

**In need of
humanitarian aid**
In Syria and
neighbouring countries

Child refugees
Under age of 18

2013	520,000
2014	1.2m
2015	2m
2016	2.4m

2.3m	5.5m	7.6m	8.4m
2013	2014	2015	2016

Excesses against Syrian children in 2015

1,500 — Grave violations verified by UNICEF – including 400 deaths and 500 instances of maiming due to explosive weapons in populated areas

7m — Children living in poverty in Syria. Children as young as three are working

50% — More than half of children recruited by warring sides in UNICEF-verified cases aged under 15, compared to 20% in 2014

2.8m — Out of school in Syria or neighbouring countries

Source: UNICEF Report "No Place for Children", GN

AS AMERICA IS THE STRONGEST WORLD POWER, IT IS REGRETFUL THAT IT HAS NOT BEEN PROACTIVE IN RECTIFYING THE PROBLEMS IN SYRIA. THESE STATISTICS SHOW SOME OF THOSE TERRIBLE EFFECTS OF ITS LACK OF RESPONSIVENESS TO THE SITUATION THERE. IT IS TRULY DANGEROUS BECAUSE EACH CHILD IS POTENTIALLY A TIME BOMB STORED AWAY; ESPECIALLY SINCE 50% ARE ALREADY BEING RECRUITED BY THE LOCAL WARRING SIDES. ABRAHAM LINCOLN IS KNOWN TO HAVE SAID: "YOU CANNOT ESCAPE THE RESPONSIBILITY OF TOMORROW BY EVADING IT TODAY."

Over one in 10 Syrians killed or injured

More than 11.5 percent of Syria's population have been killed or injured since the bloody crisis in the country erupted in March 2011, according to a new report by the Syrian Centre for Policy Research (SCPR)

Structure of Syrian population*

55% Non-displaced residents
26% IDPs
12% Refugees
Migrants 5%
Conflict-related deaths 2%

470,000
Number of conflict-related deaths – far higher than figure of 250,000 used by UN until it stopped collecting statistics in 2014

1.88 million
Expected number of wounded people by end of 2015

85.2%
Percentage of people expected to be living in poverty by end of 2015. More than 69 percent living in extreme poverty, unable to secure basic food and other items necessary for survival

21%
Real decrease in population since 2010*

6.36m
Number of individuals continuing to live in Syria as internally displaced persons (IDPs) – up from 5.65 million at end of 2014

1.17m
Projected number of migrants leaving Syria by end of 2015

3.11m
Estimated total refugee population by end of 2015. Majority of refugees hosted by Turkey, Lebanon and Jordan

55.4 years
Estimated life expectancy in 2015 (down from 70.5 years in 2010)

$254.7bn
Estimate of accumulated total economic loss at end of 2015

45.2%
Percentage of school-age children no longer attending school. Loss of schooling at all educational levels by end of 2015 represents 24.5m lost years

*Figures based on counterfactual population in 2015 (if Syrian conflict had not emerged)

Source: SCPR, Picture: Volodymyr Borodin / Shutterstock.com, GN

THE SITUATION HAS A SNOWBALL EFFECT AND WILL CONTINUE TO GROW. THE ENGLISH HAVE A WELL-KNOWN PROVERB: "A STITCH IN TIME SAVES NINE"– MEANING TO MAKE ONE STITCH WHEN IT'S NEEDED PREVENTS THE NEED TO MAKE NINE STITCHES AFTER IT'S TOO LATE. THE US AND ITS ALLIES MUST STEP IN NOW, AS THEY ARE THE MOST POWERFUL AND CAPABLE TO DO SO, BEFORE MORE LIVES ARE LOST.

Millions of African slaves were stolen from their families and taken to the New World, the Americas. This is from the Trump disease. Look at what Trump said to John R O'Donnell, who worked closely with Trump at the Trump Plaza Hotel:

"Black guys counting my money; I hate it! The only kind of people I want counting my money are little short guys that wear yarmulkes every day." [281]

When Trump was asked about the contents of O'Donnell's book, entitled *Trumped!*, he affirmed that the statements were *"probably true."* [282]

THERE'S NO VIRTUE OF WHITE OVER BLACK OR ANY RACE OVER ANY OTHER RACE. TRUMP MUST ACCEPT THAT AND RECTIFY HIMSELF TO LIVE IN TODAY'S WORLD.

How, then, will Trump feel when the portraits of respected African American leaders appear on his money? Will he accept it? An example of his thought process that degrades others is how he stated that the plan to put Harriet Tubman on the twenty-dollar bill was an idea based in "political correctness," and suggested that it may be more fitting to use her image on the two-dollar bill. [283] Of course, the two-dollar bill is rarely used and is known strictly for its souvenir value.

When America first designed the dollar, it chose collectively to inscribe upon it for generations to come the phrase, "In God we trust." So Trump should realize and accept that it was God himself who created all races, and individuals have no choice in which skin color they were born with. So there's no virtue of white over black or any race over any other race. Trump must accept that and rectify himself to live in today's world.

25

PRISONS IN AMERICA

RUMP HAS ADMITTED TO THE DISASTROUS state of the US prison system in an MSNBC interview: *"Our prison system is a disaster, it's a complete disaster all over the country."*[284]

Upon examining Trump's above answer, we see that he passes by this tremendous issue without giving it due attention. If we look at the population of the US which is 323.4 million and deduct the 74.3 million who are under eighteen years old, we find that approximately 249 million are 'of age' to be imprisoned. There are over 2.2 million Americans currently imprisoned in the US, which is almost 1% of those who are over eighteen.[285]

> **THERE ARE OVER 2.2 MILLION AMERICANS CURRENTLY IMPRISONED IN THE US, WHICH IS ALMOST 1% OF THOSE WHO ARE OVER EIGHTEEN.**

The revenue of the prison system in America is seventy four billion dollars annually which is more than the gross domestic product (GDP) of one hundred thirty three nations. It's also more than the combined annual military spending of both Germany and Italy.[286]

These numbers show the seriousness of the matter and it is imperative that proactive strategies for change are proposed and implemented.

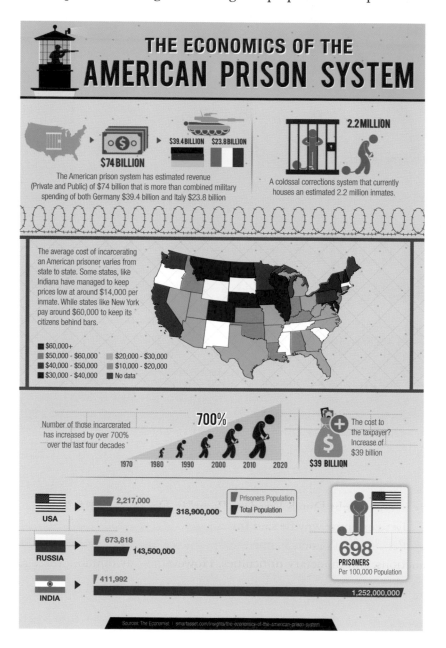

26

UNCOVERING THE ACTUAL REASON TRUMP FINDS SUPPORTERS

MANY SOURCES INCLUDING THE *TIMES OF INDIA* have reported that "the only leaders welcoming the prospect of Trump's election are right-wing demagogues. 'I hope @realDonaldTrump will be the next US President. Good for America, good for Europe. We need brave leaders,' tweeted Geert Wilders, the head of the extreme right Dutch Freedom Party," in December 2015.[287]

Let's examine why he said this.

People like Wilders blame their problems on immigration, refugees, sanctions, and monetary difficulties. However, in my opinion, these are not truly the roots of their problems. The truth is that the world has indeed changed and will continue to do so; people need to adapt to these changes, rather than use them as a camouflage for their real problems.

> # THE TRUTH IS THAT THE WORLD HAS INDEED CHANGED AND WILL CONTINUE TO DO SO; PEOPLE NEED TO ADAPT TO THESE CHANGES, RATHER THAN USING THEM AS A CAMOUFLAGE FOR THEIR REAL PROBLEMS.

On a recent trip to Iceland, I visited a water bottling plant that cost its owner millions of dollars to set up, but something about this plant was very different from others I have seen. There was not a single employee who was tasked to carry out any sort of manual labor; the plant was vacant of blue-collar workers. The entire facility was designed to be managed by only three or four people, in contrast to similar ones in Europe and Asia, which typically require forty or fifty skilled workers stationed at each plant.

The very near future will show us more and more innovations that will become commonplace: driverless cars, trucks, and busses, pilotless planes, along with factories and hotels without workers.

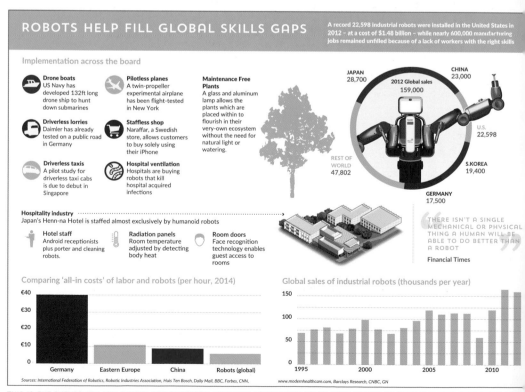

ROBOTS HELP FILL GLOBAL SKILLS GAPS

A record 22,598 industrial robots were installed in the United States in 2012 – at a cost of $1.48 billion – while nearly 600,000 manufacturing jobs remained unfilled because of a lack of workers with the right skills

Implementation across the board

Drone boats
US Navy has developed 132ft long drone ship to hunt down submarines

Driverless lorries
Daimler has already tested on a public road in Germany

Driverless taxis
A pilot study for driverless taxi cabs is due to debut in Singapore

Pilotless planes
A twin-propeller experimental airplane has been flight-tested in New York

Staffless shop
Naraffar, a Swedish store, allows customers to buy solely using their iPhone

Hospital ventilation
Hospitals are buying robots that kill hospital acquired infections

Maintenance Free Plants
A glass and aluminum lamp allows the plants which are placed within to flourish in their very-own ecosystem without the need for natural light or watering.

JAPAN 28,700
CHINA 23,000
2012 Global sales 159,000
U.S. 22,598
REST OF WORLD 47,802
S.KOREA 19,400
GERMANY 17,500

Hospitality industry
Japan's Henn-na Hotel is staffed almost exclusively by humanoid robots

Hotel staff
Android receptionists plus porter and cleaning robots.

Radiation panels
Room temperature adjusted by detecting body heat

Room doors
Face recognition technology enables guest access to rooms

> THERE ISN'T A SINGLE MECHANICAL OR PHYSICAL THING A HUMAN WILL BE ABLE TO DO BETTER THAN A ROBOT
>
> **Financial Times**

Comparing 'all-in costs' of labor and robots (per hour, 2014)

€40, €30, €20, €10, 0 — Germany, Eastern Europe, China, Robots (global)

Global sales of industrial robots (thousands per year)

150, 100, 50, 0 — 1995, 2000, 2005, 2010

Sources: International Federation of Robotics, Robotic Industries Association, Huis Ten Bosch, Daily Mail, BBC, Forbes, CNN, www.modernhealthcare.com, Barclays Research, CNBC, GN

THIS IS THE FUTURE WE ARE FACING AND EVERYONE NEEDS TO UNDERSTAND WHAT THAT MEANS SO THEY CAN PREPARE THEMSELVES SUCCEED IN THE JOB MARKET OF THE NEW ECONOMY.

Highly advanced robots are being developed which can take over many jobs. CNN has reported from the Bank of England that smarter robots can put a staggering fifty percent of all jobs at risk. It has warned that over the next ten to twenty years, machines could take over eighty million American and fifteen million British jobs.[288] Likewise, according to a Citigroup report, thirty percent of all bank jobs could be lost by 2025.[289]

What group of people is spearheading and taking advantage of these new technologies and opportunities? They are the smart and highly educated people in the world, and those who want results. They seek to minimize the potential for human error, labor-related costs, and the challenges involved with the rollercoaster of employee emotions. They want to help guide people to that which would be better for them. These intelligent and highly educated ones are not anyone's enemy; they are merely smart and trying to apply their gifted abilities towards developing beneficial solutions in completely acceptable and sustainable ways.

THESE INTELLIGENT AND HIGHLY EDUCATED ONES ARE NOT ANYONE'S ENEMY; THEY ARE MERELY SMART AND TRYING TO UTILIZE THEIR GIFTED ABILITIES TOWARDS DEVELOPING BENEFICIAL SOLUTIONS IN COMPLETELY ACCEPTABLE AND SUSTAINABLE WAYS.

Allow me to give the clear example of Steve Jobs. How many Steve Jobs are in America? How many Steve Jobs are in Europe? How many Steve Jobs are in Asia? The answer is: not many.

Jobs ordained that Apple would make their laptops and iPhones with built-in batteries that no one could change except for them. This highly intelligent person abandoned the world's common norms to follow what he wanted to do, rather than what the world thought it needed. No one was able to tell him that he couldn't do it. He carried out what he was determined to do, and that came from his intelligence and his training.

It is not a matter of money today; it is a matter of intelligence. The world has changed and the smart people are few in number. To understand this more clearly, how many billionaires are in the world today? Most people do not know that the first billionaires only came about in this world as recently as the twentieth century, with the Rockefellers.

When we look today at the world's billionaires and millionaires, we find that most of them built their fortunes through their own hard work. Most did not inherit their wealth and were from middle-class backgrounds, or even lower.

We can understand from this that intelligent people tend to have much bigger opportunities in this century than those of lesser intelligence.

> WE CAN UNDERSTAND FROM THIS THAT INTELLIGENT PEOPLE TEND TO HAVE MUCH BIGGER OPPORTUNITIES IN THIS CENTURY THAN THOSE OF LESSER INTELLIGENCE.

Let us now go back to where I first began. I believe today, the right-wing parties attract three main types of supporters.

First, the "lazy smart" people who aren't willing to work hard. They prefer to stay away from competition and do not want to invest the required efforts into building their lives.

Second, blue-collar workers who lack the feeling of security in their careers. This is because they have either already lost their jobs, or realize that they are at a high risk of losing them.

Third, all the shortsighted people who face the problem of having to deal with a new way of life, due to all of these changes. They feel that they're stuck and they're hoping for someone to rescue them. They need to put in more effort to establish themselves in this life with something they can be successful in.

These are the three main types of people who are supporting Trump and right-wing organizations, along with their motivations. In order to convince you of the seriousness of what these groups are facing, one statistic really stands out as important and should be reflected upon. Unemployment levels are rising globally for all three of these categories, especially amongst the youth. *The Economist* has reported the global rate of youth who are *NEET*s (not in employment, education, or training) is a staggering 24.9%.[290] Even with that being the case, nearly 600,000 manufacturing jobs remained unfilled in the US because of a lack of workers with the right skills, as reported by the Robotic Industries Association in

2012.[291] This is just one example to demonstrate that there are, and will be, opportunities for those who continually upgrade themselves to exceed existing standards.

Then there are those who are seekers of power. They themselves do not fit into the former three categories, because they are not short-sighted, they are not blue-collar workers, nor are they lazy. Rather, they cynically use the people in those three categories to rally support for themselves to reach positions of power over them. How do they do that? They play the blame game and set up causes that they convince the people they need to rally around. These causes include immigration, migration, fear of religions, and others I mentioned previously. They convince the people to focus on these issues rather than on their own real problems. Having fostered this support, they are often able to reach the level of power they crave.

> **THERE ARE, AND WILL BE, OPPORTUNITIES FOR THOSE WHO CONTINUALLY UPGRADE THEMSELVES TO EXCEED EXISTING STANDARDS.**

> **THEY CONVINCE THE PEOPLE TO FOCUS ON THESE ISSUES RATHER THAN ON THEIR OWN REAL PROBLEMS.**

In 2009 I was in Switzerland with my family, staying at the Four Seasons Hotel. The day was going nicely and everything in the hotel was normal. But then I found a message from the hotel's management under the door to our room, advising us not to go out of the hotel during a specific span of a few hours that afternoon. This worried me, and we were confused as to why the hotel would give such a warning to its guests. I called the front desk to investigate, and was informed that there would be a labor strike. This was something new for me, and thought it would be something very interesting to watch. After all, we were in Geneva, a place where the people enjoy one of the highest household incomes compared to the rest of the world. Surely everyone would be acting responsibly, respectably, and highly civilized, right?

The hotel is located on a busy street with high-end shops on it, with a small river on the other side of the street. In order to have a good, clear view, I took my family across a small bridge to the other side of the river, so we could watch the protesters as they proceeded down the street. We took our seats on a bench, eager to see how upper class Europeans carry themselves in this situation.

After a short time, we began to hear loud noises, but much louder than we would have expected; it sounded like explosions. My daughters hugged me tightly and began crying in fear. Vehicles began to appear with people shouting with megaphones and violently swinging sickles in the air. I could not understand what they were shouting about, because they were not speaking English.

Before long, the street was full of rioting people striking havoc and causing mass destruction. Windows of the luxury shops were smashed and high-end cars were blown up and burned. Surprisingly, the rioters were only smashing the glass of high-end shops, while leaving more affordable shops unharmed; they burned the expensive cars like Mercedes, while leaving the Toyotas alone. We witnessed cars blasted up four to six feet into the air. It was truly a frightening experience because my family and I were stranded on the other side of the river, and all we could do was hold each other and wait it out. Finally, once the commotion had passed, we made our way back to our hotel, where all the ground floor windows had been shattered.

MANY LET THEIR LAZINESS TAKE ADVANTAGE OF THEM AND BELIEVE THAT IF THEY ARE UNSUCCESSFUL, IT IS SOMEHOW THE FAULT OF THOSE WHO ARE SUCCESSFUL.

After viewing the destruction of the shops, cars, and hotel, I began to think about the psychology behind the riots. What must they have been shouting about, and what must have motivated them to vandalize and destroy only those things that could be considered signs of wealth? It did not make any sense at all. How could anyone of intellect consider it to be fair? The person who works hard enough to be able to afford a nice car, why should it be destroyed while the car of someone else is left untouched?

It could only have come from their hatred and jealousy towards those who have more than them. Likewise, many let their laziness take advantage of them and believe that if they are unsuccessful, it is somehow the fault of those who are successful.

There are various motivations for these right-wing groups and they often choose a different outlet to vent their frustrations and place their blame. *The Wall Street Journal* reported on May 1, 2016 about one such group heightening their attacks against Islam:

> Germany's upstart Alternative for Germany (AfD) party on Sunday adopted a clear anti-Islam stance in a platform that lays the foundation for the populist party's bid to win parliamentary seats in federal elections next year.

> The manifesto adopted by members gathered in Stuttgart for a party conference states that "Islam is not a part of Germany" and rejects minarets and the Muslim call to prayer—the clearest move yet by the party to harness widespread concern in Europe's largest country about steeply rising refugee numbers in recent years.

> Islam is foreign to Germany and for that reason it can't invoke the principle of religious freedom in the same way as Christianity," Hans-Thomas Tillschneider, an AfD lawmaker from Saxony-Anhalt responded, earning loud applause.[292]

The group AfD claims to be targeting Islam because it is foreign to Germany and the group is not intending to target Muslims. However, it was pointed out on the *BBC World Service* May 2, 2016[293] that Islam is the only religion being targeted by AfD, despite many other world religions existing in Germany which are not native to it.

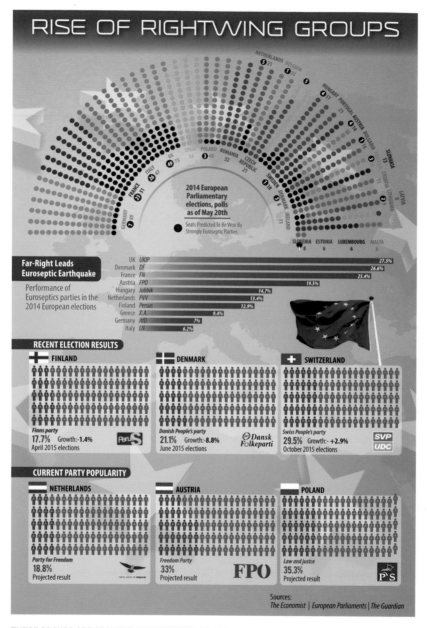

RISE OF RIGHTWING GROUPS

2014 European
Parliamentary
elections, polls
as of May 20th

Seats Predicted To Be Won By
Strongly Euroseptic Parties

**Far-Right Leads
Euroseptic Earthquake**

Performance of
Euroseptics parties in the
2014 European elections

UK	UKIP	27.5%
Denmark	DF	26.6%
France	FN	25.4%
Austria	FPO	19.5%
Hungary	Jobbik	14.7%
Netherlands	PVV	13.4%
Finland	Persus	12.9%
Greece	X.A.	9.4%
Germany	AfD	7%
Italy	LN	6.2%

RECENT ELECTION RESULTS

FINLAND

Finns party
17.7% Growth:-**1.4%**
April 2015 elections

DENMARK

Danish People's party
21.1% Growth:-**8.8%**
June 2015 elections

SWITZERLAND

Swiss People's party
29.5% Growth:- +**2.9%**
October 2015 elections

CURRENT PARTY POPULARITY

NETHERLANDS

Party for Freedom
18.8%
Projected result

AUSTRIA

Freedom Party
33%
Projected result

POLAND

Law and Justice
35.3%
Projected result

Sources:
The Economist | European Parliaments | The Guardian

THESE GROUPS ARE GROWING AND THEY FEED OFF SICK-MINDED INDIVIDUALS WHO SHARE TRUMP'S
MINDSET. THEY FEED INTO THE FEARS OF THE PEOPLE BY BLAMING SECONDARY PROBLEMS IN
THEIR COUNTRIES, MAKING THOSE SECONDARY PROBLEMS THE PILLAR OF THEIR PLATFORM. THEY
DO THAT WHILE COMPLETELY IGNORING THE ACTUAL ROOT CAUSES OF THEIR PROBLEMS AND NOT
SEEKING ANY SOLUTIONS FOR THEM.

Social media driving right-wing Europe

The rise of the far right across Europe is linked to the impact of social media, as a new generation of young supporters embrace hardline nationalist extremism and anti-immigrant groups

Austria

1. Freedom Party
Right-wing, anti-immigration. Support up **50%** since April

↓ Facebook likes Nov 2015

f 260,360

Denmark

2. Danish People's Party
Far-right. Has 37 seats in 179-seat parliament and 4 Members of European Parliament. Social media support up **76%** since April

f 58,290

France

3. Front National
Far-right. Has 24 Members of European Parliament. Facebook support has surged **66%** since April. Leader **Marine Le Pen** is high in polls for presidential election

f 281,320

Germany

Four years ago German BfV security agency estimated there were 25,000 right-wing extremists, of which 5,600 were neo-Nazis

4. Pegida
Anti-Islamic movement founded in Dresden, October 2014. Since February, number of supporters on its official Facebook profile has grown by **13%**

f 179,580

5. National Democratic Party of Germany
Neo-Nazi party has one Member of European Parliament

f 140,560

Hungary

6. Jobbik
Extremist party is third largest in National Assembly

f 301,460

Norway

7. Progress Party
Right-wing party has 29 seats in 169-seat parliment. Facebook support up **22%**

f 83,170

Sweden

8. Sweden Democrats
Anti-immigration. 49 seats in 349-seat parliament, 2 Members of European Parliament. Facebook support up **17%** since April

f 103,090

United Kingdom

9. Britain First
Far-right, anti-Islamist, nationalist party. Facebook support has grown **37%** since April

f 1,000,380

10. English Defence League
Far-right, anti-Islamist. Support has grown **22%** since April

f 232,000

Every time someone "likes" a Facebook page or comment, it is exposed to an average 136 other people, who then can "like" it to others

Facebook likes Nov 2015

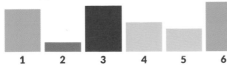

| 1 | 2 | 3 | 4 | 5 | 6 | 7 | 8 | 9 | 10 |

Source: Facebook, Spiegel, vocativ.com, GN

Right-Wing Europes's Support for Trump

Name *Country*	Known For	Quote
Jean-Marie Le Pen *France*	The former leader of France's far-right, anti-immigration party, the National Front.	"If I were American, I would vote Donald Trump."
Geert Wilders *Netherlands*	The anti-immigrant and anti-Muslim leader of the Dutch Freedom Party.	"good for America, good for Europe. We need brave leaders."
Jayda Fransen *United Kingdom*	The Deputy Leader of Britain First.	• "I think he's fantastic," "Vote Trump." • "Trump has a fortune that he can be sitting on very comfortably in a remote island somewhere, without worrying about the fact that you currently have, you know, a corrupt president who in my opinion is a Muslim, but at the very least is a Muslim appeaser," • "I'm not American, but we're all brothers and sisters, and we're in a common battle, okay?"
Kronc Blanc *France*	A white nationalist rapper from Paris.	"Ah, I love Trump," "Because he says he won't take any more Muslims in America. It's so, so nice."
Tommy Robinson *United Kingdom*	The founder of the right-wing English Defense League and current leader of the U.K. chapter of PEGIDA.	• "I think he's honest," • "NAZISM = ISLAMISM" and "TRUMP IS RIGHT." • "has moved the debate forward. So I'm grateful for him doing it."
Mischaël Modrikamen *Belgium*	A Belgian lawyer and leader of the small, right-wing People's Party. Also serves as vice president of the Alliance for Direct Democracy in Europe.	"A Message from BRUSSELS – Mischaël Modrikamen supports TRUMP"
Jimmie Åkesson *Sweden*	A Swedish politician and leader of the anti-mass migration Eurosceptic Sweden Democrats party.	"I agree with Trump that we should reduce immigration, reinforce border controls and keep better track of who is coming into our country,"

Jean-Marie and Geert Wilders found at: http://www.usatoday.com/story/news/world/2016/03/08/donald-trump-world-leaders-republican-gop/81312520/
Jayda Fransen and Kroc Blanc found at: http://fusion.net/story/285163/europe-right-wing-donald-trump-islam/
Tommy Robinson found at: http://fusion.net/story/285163/europe-right-wing-donald-trump-islam/
Mischaël Modrikamen found at: http://www.tpnn.com/2016/03/25/what-this-belgian-leader-said-about-trump-11-days-before-the-terror-attacks-says-it-all/
Jimmie Åkesson found at: http://www.breitbart.com/london/2016/03/07/sweden-democrats-leader-backs-brexit-stating-nothing-negative-about-leaving-the-eu/

27

THE RULES FOR THE **NEW ECONOMY**

THE NEW ECONOMY REQUIRES SMART PEOPLE who are always thinking out of the box and have a consistent can-do attitude. These are people who tirelessly work hard, day and night, with smart minds. Intelligence is the primary factor in overcoming competition.

By itself, working hard, without this required intelligence, will very rarely bring success.

Lee Kuan Yew is a wonderful example of one who exemplified both the intelligence and the can-do attitude, and he was able to elevate the status of his entire country.[294] In 1959, he was sworn into power as the prime minister of Singapore. By using thorough strategic planning and implementation, he completely changed Singapore's economic situation. That advancement of the economy brought forth advancement in all other sectors. It is amazing how this man remained active throughout his career as both prime minister and eventually a member of the cabinet.

He finally resigned from his cabinet position in 2011 at the age of eighty-seven. He amazingly changed the whole status of an entire nation. In looking at a span of just twenty years, we can see that in Singapore the GDP per person rose from approximately $4000 to $16,000 from 1965 to 1985; that is a 400% increase.[295] Such results are only brought about through the successful implementation of combined intelligence and hard work.

Due to changing conditions, the Old Economy of the previous ages will not come back again. Those conditions include technological breakthroughs, improved communications, the world's growing population, and an overall increase in the pace of life. That is why I believe the Fortune 500 companies will surely change during the 21st century, because the rules of the game have changed and a great shift is happening. I believe more and more companies will rival sovereign nations in their wealth and power, with some of them becoming even more powerful than countries.

Let us examine the simple example of Samsung, whose 2014 revenue was 20.4% of the GDP of South Korea. Samsung, a collection of more than sixty divisions, has led some to refer to South Korea as "the

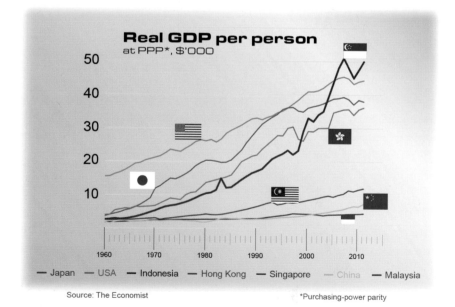

Real GDP per person at PPP*, $'000

— Japan   — USA   — Indonesia   — Hong Kong   — Singapore   — China   — Malaysia

Source: The Economist   *Purchasing-power parity

SINGAPORE IS THE SUCCESS STORY OF A LEADER WHO HAD A STRATEGIC ROAD MAP. AS FOR TRUMP, HE HASN'T BROUGHT ANY REAL PLANS TO ACHIEVE ANY SOLUTIONS; HE ONLY HAS EMPTY SPEECH.

> **IN SINGAPORE THE GDP PER PERSON ROSE FROM APPROXIMATELY $4000 TO $16,000 FROM 1965 TO 1985; THAT IS A 300% INCREASE.**

Republic of Samsung." It began in 1938 with forty employees, exporting rice, dried fish, noodles, and produce before diversifying into insurance, sugar, paper, textiles, property development, and electronics and appliances.[296]

In contrast, those with the disease of Trump do not and will not have adequate programs to create jobs for the nation. Their attitude is one of force and intimidation, and this is not a realistic or feasible method. Trump himself has not suggested any actual strategy that would create jobs for the American people; he simply brags he will make it happen and force companies to hire people. This is similar to how he continually boasts about his intelligence: *"I'm really smart,"*[297] he boasts, and it is as if he truly believes that he possesses the smartest mind in the world while the rest of the world's leaders are nothing but dummies. His shortsightedness and lack of sense deceive him into bringing about more harm than good for the US and global economies.

In his vanity he proclaimed, *"I will be the greatest jobs president that God ever created."*[298]

On September 11, 2015 he even poked fun at his own lack of strategy on the Jimmy Fallon television show. During a mock interview where he was pretending to be interviewed by a mirror image of himself, he was asked about exactly how he would go about creating the much needed jobs for the country. He replied bluntly with a smirk: *"I just will."*[299]

This is the joke that has been propagated throughout his whole campaign. He has been doing nothing but going around and around, pointing his finger in so many directions. He plays

> **TRUMP HIMSELF HAS NOT SUGGESTED ANY ACTUAL STRATEGY THAT WOULD CREATE JOBS FOR THE AMERICAN PEOPLE; HE SIMPLY BRAGS HE WILL MAKE IT HAPPEN AND FORCE COMPANIES TO HIRE PEOPLE.**

the blame game, targeting China, Japan, South Korea, India, Mexico, OPEC, immigrants, migrants, and the Muslims.

Trump refuses to acknowledge that the main root of America's prob-

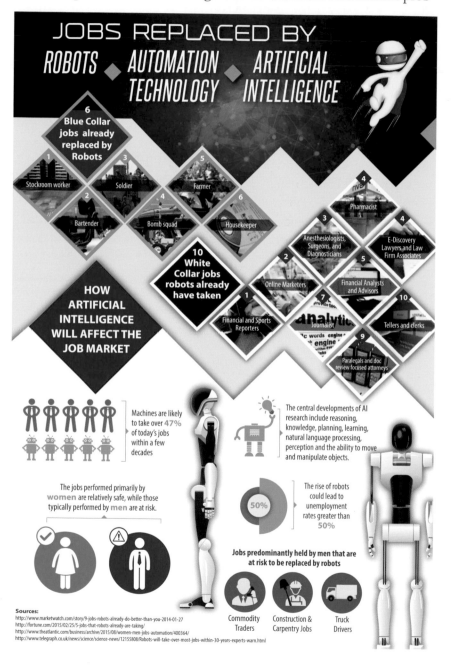

lems also afflicts many other regions of the world. Due to the abundant opportunities for the intelligent people to utilize technology so they may reduce overheads and costs, the world is changing rapidly. Someday, for example, McDonald's may have only a few employees working at each branch (if not zero), in order to cut costs through automation. Many companies throughout the world are dispensing their products through vending machines, rather than live employees. This is because the biggest cost factor in most businesses is labor.

In my opinion, a government body needs to be established, similar to the National Aeronautics and Space Administration (NASA), the agency of the US federal government responsible for the civilian space program as well as aeronautics and aerospace research. I propose a similar government body to manage the changes that have come about as a result of the New Economy. America is the third most populous nation in the world, so it is critical to bring about real solutions. This new body would be even more important than NASA. This is the future we are facing and the challenges it holds, and this council is needed to help create the jobs which are actually needed in the 21st century.

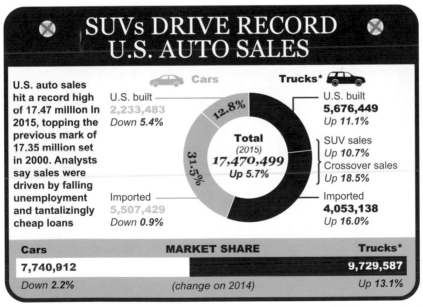

SUVs DRIVE RECORD U.S. AUTO SALES

U.S. auto sales hit a record high of 17.47 million in 2015, topping the previous mark of 17.35 million set in 2000. Analysts say sales were driven by falling unemployment and tantalizingly cheap loans

Cars

U.S. built
2,233,483
Down 5.4%

Imported
5,507,429
Down 0.9%

Total (2015)
17,470,499
Up 5.7%

12.8%

31.5%

Trucks*

U.S. built
5,676,449
Up 11.1%

SUV sales
Up 10.7%
Crossover sales
Up 18.5%

Imported
4,053,138
Up 16.0%

Cars	MARKET SHARE	Trucks*
7,740,912		9,729,587
Down 2.2%	(change on 2014)	Up 13.1%

Sources: Motor Intelligence, Autodata Corp., GN   *Including crossover/SUV

WHEN THE UNEMPLOYMENT RATE OF A COUNTRY GOES DOWN, IT MEANS AN UPTURN FOR THE REST OF THE ECONOMY. IT IS THIS AREA WHICH REQUIRES DETAILED AND FOCUSED PLANS, NOT A BIG MOUTH.

28

COOPERATION TOWARDS
STOPPING THE SPREAD
OF TRUMP'S DISEASE

T HERE IS A NECESSITY FOR ALL THE WORLD'S
population, not just Americans, to immunize themselves from
Trump. This is because the US is the strongest nation on earth,
and it would be too dangerous if this man was given the opportunity to
wield this level of power by becoming its president. The influential leaders of the US should guide its people away from Trump by focusing on
different angles – why he is so dangerous for the youth, for the future,
and for the world's stability. The people need this guidance because they
are of various levels in their mental capacities, in their problems, and in
their opportunities.

A recent forecast by the Intelligence Unit of *The Economist* identified
a Trump Presidency as one of the Top Ten Global Risks.[300] The edito-

A RECENT FORECAST BY THE ECONOMIST INTELLIGENCE UNIT IDENTIFIED A TRUMP PRESIDENCY AS ONE OF THE TOP TEN GLOBAL RISKS.

rial committee of the magazine has done a commendable job highlighting the danger of Trump for the world.

However, I do not agree with statements such as the following, as reported in the *Financial Times*:

"I will take his remarks seriously when he is elected president," said Kuni Miyake, head of the Foreign Policy Institute in Tokyo. "Media overreaction creates people like Trump, who represent the dark side of the US," he added. "I believe in the western democracies — in the end they'll come up with a healthy outcome."[301]

Rather, I believe we must not be complacent. There is a well-known Arab saying, "Do not wait until the axe falls on your head," - similarly, we need to be proactive and highlight the danger that Trump's presidency would pose.

If Trump reaches the White House, that would mean there is a large base who believe in his ideas, and that would also be reflected in both the Congress and Senate. To prove this view, look at the presidential candidates. One was a notable neurosurgeon, successful author, and an African American; but we find that he pulled out of the presidential race and endorsed Trump. What does this mean? It goes to show that there is even a class of highly educated doctors who have been affected with this Trump–Hitler–KKK–ISIS–Al-Qaeda disease!

My observation over the last few years has been that many people in Kuwait have been affected by Trump's disease. I've seen doctors, engineers, and teachers from universities who vote for these kinds of sick people.

People around the world must unite to stop the spread of this warped ideology. They should do this by using available modern communications, which are the very same means that can spread this disease if misused. None should let their bias or prejudice about certain issues become an excuse for them to support Trump. For example, don't support Trump just because he is not a Democrat, or because you assume the economy is not doing well. The damage he would cause is not worth the risk.

I read an article in *Time* magazine: "Why Would Democrats Vote for Trump? It's all about Trade." This article highlighted what people were saying about the lack of employment opportunities. A retired union autoworker said, "My son is in his 20s... He can fill out application after application, and it just isn't going to happen. Meaning, he believes there is zero chance of being hired."[302]

> # NONE SHOULD LET THEIR BIAS OR PREJUDICE ABOUT CERTAIN ISSUES BECOME AN EXCUSE FOR THEM TO SUPPORT TRUMP.

They propagate this in the media in a certain way and with a certain meaning. Let's examine one of the root causes of this problem.

In my opinion, many of these young people have become lazy and they don't want to work, even if you give them the opportunity. They don't want to have pressure, and at the end of the day, they hide their

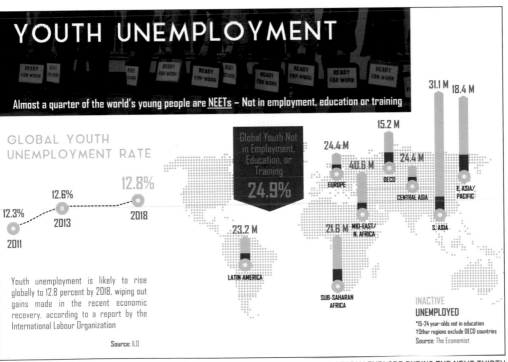

THIS IS THE REAL DANGER WHICH THE WORLD IS FACING. IT'S A BOMB THAT WILL INEVITABLY EXPLODE DURING THE NEXT THIRTY YEARS. IT MAY COME SOONER OR LATER, BUT THIS IS WHAT I EXPECT, UNLESS EFFECTIVE SOLUTIONS ARE IMPLEMENTED.

Forbes also reported:

Sixty percent of all foreign born graduate students in the United States are presently immersed in obtaining degrees in the science and engineering fields. Some portion of the over 300,000 mainland Chinese studying here must be among them.

Meanwhile, the growth rate of American students specializing in the STEM fields is "the lowest of any academic category." It is believed there will be 2.8 million job openings in STEM industries by 2018, of which 800,000 will require a master's degree in some STEM field. Here is an Opportunity Target. Certainly, careers in these areas of experience should involve compensation in the top 10% to 20% of wage-earners in the U.S.[307]

> **THE GROWTH RATE OF AMERICAN STUDENTS SPECIALIZING IN THE STEM FIELDS IS "THE LOWEST OF ANY ACADEMIC CATEGORY.**

These statistics prove that the opportunities are there, and not just any opportunities. There are an estimated 2.8 million jobs that will need filling, and the holders of those jobs can expect to be earning in the top ten to twenty percent of all US wage earners. So the opportunities are there, but who are the ones preparing themselves to benefit from these opportunities? The numbers show that it's the immigrants who are putting in the necessary efforts, while Americans are passing them by – by their own choice.

The Prophet Mohammad (may God's Peace & Blessings be upon him) would say often:

"O God, I seek refuge in you from inability and laziness."

The smartphone, TV, other digital technologies, and the media all help this disease to grow within many families. While in Germany, I was in a business meeting with a German man who has his own private jet. He said to me, "Mohammad, the young German people have become lazy." And I agree with him. That is what I have seen from the employees in the multinational companies when I compare their current condition with their productivity over the last thirty years. It was so much more before.

In early 2000, one of the managers who used to work for me moved to the United States. He and his family found work and are quite successful. Why? Because they are from the old school of Americans who were hardworking and determined.

In the beginning of this year, 2016, I was in a meeting in the US with a company that sells products to Mercedes and Lexus. During the meeting, I proposed a joint business project to the head of the company. His answer was, "I am a lazy man," and he smiled; he was not even ashamed to say that he was lazy. I say this is a huge disease!

This has become a new way of life for many Americans nowadays. They believe that Trump will change things around for them. Too many Americans want to have fun, sleep, and achieve success without investing in their productivity. The situation has become like many people in the developing world with whom we have been interacting for many years.

The Intelligence Unit of *The Economist* said, "Although we do not expect Mr. Trump to defeat his most likely Democratic contender, Hillary Clinton, there are risks to this forecast, especially in the event of a terrorist attack on US soil or a sudden economic downturn."[308]

I believe the risk for a sudden economic downturn is not so likely. The last speech from Janet Yellen of the Federal Reserve will demonstrate that the current economic state of the US is not as grim as those with the Trump disease would try to present. As was reported in *Bloomberg Business* in March 2016:

'A RANGE OF RECENT INDICATORS, INCLUDING STRONG JOB GAINS, POINTS TO ADDITIONAL STRENGTHENING OF THE LABOR MARKET,'

"Officials maintained their forecast for a 4.7 percent U.S. unemployment rate in the fourth quarter of this year. "The median projection for 2017 fell to 4.6 percent from 4.7 percent, and in 2018 to 4.5 percent from 4.7 percent. The rate stood at 4.9 percent in February.

"'A range of recent indicators, including strong job gains, points to additional strengthening of the labor market,' the Fed-

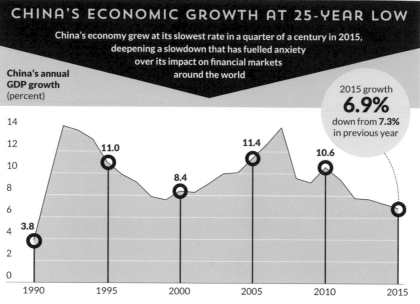

Sources: World Bank, GN

ONE OF AMERICA'S STRONGEST ADVANTAGES IN THE GLOBAL MARKET IS THE NEARLY UNCOUNTABLE AR-
RAY OF MAJOR BRANDS OWNED BY ITS COMPANIES. HOWEVER, CHINA IS VERY WEAK IN THIS REGARD; ITS
COMPANIES HAVE FOCUSED PRIMARILY ON MANUFACTURING EFFICIENCY, RATHER THAN BUILDING KNOWN
AND TRUSTED BRANDS. BRAND OWNERSHIP ALLOWS AMERICAN COMPANIES TO MAINTAIN HIGHER PROFIT
MARGINS THAN CHINESE COMPANIES. JACK MA, FOUNDER OF ALIBABA.COM, SUCCEEDED IN BUILDING A
POWERFUL BRAND IN CHINA, BUT HUNDREDS OR THOUSANDS MORE ARE NEEDED.

eral Open Market Committee (FOMC) said.

"The Fed reiterated that the 'stance of monetary policy remains accommodative, thereby supporting further improvement
in labor market conditions and a return to 2 percent inflation.'

"The domestic U.S. economy has mostly been solid, however. Payroll gains have averaged 235,000 over the last six months
as the jobless rate matched the Fed's goal for maximum employment...

"U.S. stock markets, which had slumped by more than 10
percent by mid-February from the start of the year, have also
regained ground, with the Standard and Poor's 500 Index now
down just 1.4 percent this year."[309]

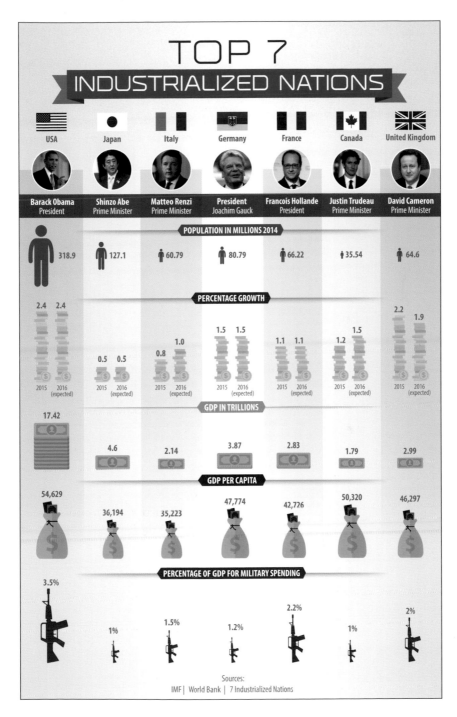

TOP 7
INDUSTRIALIZED NATIONS

USA	Japan	Italy	Germany	France	Canada	United Kingdom
Barack Obama President	**Shinzo Abe** Prime Minister	**Matteo Renzi** Prime Minister	**President** Joachim Gauck	**Francois Hollande** President	**Justin Trudeau** Prime Minister	**David Cameron** Prime Minister

POPULATION IN MILLIONS 2014

| 318.9 | 127.1 | 60.79 | 80.79 | 66.22 | 35.54 | 64.6 |

PERCENTAGE GROWTH

2015	2016 (expected)	2015	2016 (expected)	2015	2016 (expected)	2015	2016 (expected)	2015	2016 (expected)	2015	2016 (expected)	2015	2016 (expected)
2.4	2.4	0.5	0.5	0.8	1.0	1.5	1.5	1.1	1.1	1.2	1.5	2.2	1.9

GDP IN TRILLIONS

| 17.42 | 4.6 | 2.14 | 3.87 | 2.83 | 1.79 | 2.99 |

GDP PER CAPITA

| 54,629 | 36,194 | 35,223 | 47,774 | 42,726 | 50,320 | 46,297 |

PERCENTAGE OF GDP FOR MILITARY SPENDING

| 3.5% | 1% | 1.5% | 1.2% | 2.2% | 1% | 2% |

Sources:
IMF | World Bank | 7 Industrialized Nations

THEY BELIEVE THAT TRUMP WILL CHANGE THINGS AROUND FOR THEM.

And on the other hand, we see that China which is the second strongest economy, has been experiencing twenty-five year lows.

These are truly optimistic economic predictions for the US, which demonstrate that the situation is much better than Trump would have his supporters believe. Terrorists are still a huge problem, of course. They love to find a sick man like Trump — he is in their benefit because he becomes an excuse for them.

29

DOES TRUMP KNOW
MANUFACTURING?

TRUMP SAYS HE IS GOING TO BRING BACK MANU-facturing from China and Mexico to "Make America great again," without any understanding or explanation as to exactly how he would do it and what would be the consequences. He's merely spewing these claims, without suggesting any real strategies to make it happen or to create jobs which are actually needed by these companies. Is it comprehensible that someone without a single success in the field of manufacturing can guide America's manufacturing activities? America has the strongest brand names in the world and its products are revered for their qual-

> **IS IT COMPREHENSIBLE THAT SOMEONE WITH NOT ONE SINGLE SUCCESS IN THE FIELD OF MANUFACTURING CAN GUIDE AMERICA'S MAN-UFACTURING ACTIVITIES?**

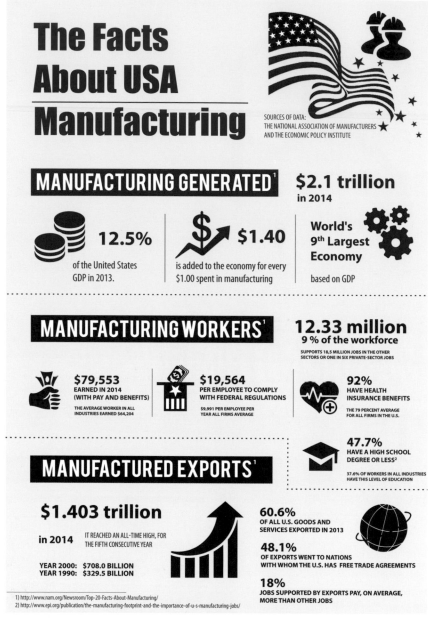

The Facts About USA Manufacturing

SOURCES OF DATA:
THE NATIONAL ASSOCIATION OF MANUFACTURERS
AND THE ECONOMIC POLICY INSTITUTE

MANUFACTURING GENERATED[1]

$2.1 trillion
in 2014

12.5%
of the United States GDP in 2013.

$1.40
is added to the economy for every $1.00 spent in manufacturing

World's 9th Largest Economy
based on GDP

MANUFACTURING WORKERS[1]

12.33 million
9 % of the workforce

SUPPORTS 18,5 MILLION JOBS IN THE OTHER SECTORS OR ONE IN SIX PRIVATE-SECTOR JOBS

$79,553
EARNED IN 2014 (WITH PAY AND BENEFITS)
THE AVERAGE WORKER IN ALL INDUSTRIES EARNED $64,204

$19,564
PER EMPLOYEE TO COMPLY WITH FEDERAL REGULATIONS
$9,991 PER EMPLOYEE PER YEAR ALL FIRMS AVERAGE

92%
HAVE HEALTH INSURANCE BENEFITS
THE 79 PERCENT AVERAGE FOR ALL FIRMS IN THE U.S.

47.7%
HAVE A HIGH SCHOOL DEGREE OR LESS[2]
37.6% OF WORKERS IN ALL INDUSTRIES HAVE THIS LEVEL OF EDUCATION

MANUFACTURED EXPORTS[1]

$1.403 trillion
in 2014   IT REACHED AN ALL-TIME HIGH, FOR THE FIFTH CONSECUTIVE YEAR

YEAR 2000: $708.0 BILLION
YEAR 1990: $329.5 BILLION

60.6%
OF ALL U.S. GOODS AND SERVICES EXPORTED IN 2013

48.1%
OF EXPORTS WENT TO NATIONS WITH WHOM THE U.S. HAS FREE TRADE AGREEMENTS

18%
JOBS SUPPORTED BY EXPORTS PAY, ON AVERAGE, MORE THAN OTHER JOBS

1) http://www.nam.org/Newsroom/Top-20-Facts-About-Manufacturing/
2) http://www.epi.org/publication/the-manufacturing-footprint-and-the-importance-of-u-s-manufacturing-jobs/

MANUFACTURING IS UNDOUBTEDLY ONE OF THE STRENGTHS OF AMERICA.

ity. Just the manufacturing sector of the US is the 9th largest economy in the world. It is ridiculous that Trump speaks about the manufacturing industry while he clearly doesn't understand it. It's no simple matter to shut down whole factories and supply chains which have already been established overseas in order to bring them back to the US. It is as if he believes these factories are toys which can be picked up and moved around without considering the far reaching consequences.

As mentioned by *Forbes*, Ford spokesman Karl Henkel said: "Mark Fields [CEO of Ford] sent Mr. Trump an email with information about Ford, including the $6.2 billion we have invested in our US plants since 2011 and our hiring of nearly 25,000 U.S. employees."[310]

INDEED THE MANUFAC-TURING STRENGTH OF AMERICA IS UNRIVALED IN MANY ASPECTS.

Indeed the manufacturing strength of America is unrivaled in many aspects. Let's examine the simple example of Coca Cola which is a global brand built upon a product consisting of primarily water and sugar. Keep in mind that just about every country in the world has access to these two resources, but no other country has been able to establish anything close to Coke. With water and sugar, America was able to build this single company whose revenue rivals that of nations.

30

TRUMP'S RIDICULOUSLY SHORTSIGHTED VIEW ON IMMIGRANTS

G REAT SUCCESS HAS BEEN BROUGHT TO THE US economy through the results of immigration. In fact, a report from the Partnership for a New American Economy showed more than forty percent of America's Fortune 500 companies were founded by immigrants or the children of immigrants. Eighteen percent (or 90) of the 500 companies had immigrant founders. The children of immigrants started another 114 companies. The revenue generated by Fortune 500 companies founded by immigrants or children of immigrants is greater than the GDP (gross domestic product) of every country in the world outside the U.S., except China and Japan. These Fortune 500 companies had combined revenues of $4.2 trillion in 2010, $1.7 trillion which come from immigrant-founded companies. The report also notes, "Many of America's greatest brands – Apple, Google, AT&T, Colgate, eBay, General Electric, IBM, and McDonald's to name just a few – owe their origin to a founder who was an immigrant or the child of an immigrant."[311]

Let's look at the example of Steve Jobs, the famous co-founder of Apple, who is the child of an immigrant father from Syria. It is truly amazing what this Arab guy, Steve, has done for the US economy. According to Apple's website:

> As of December 2015, Apple is responsible for creating and supporting 1.9 million jobs. Nearly three-quarters of those jobs — 1.4 million — are attributable to the iOS ecosystem. Our spend and investment with thousands of US-based suppliers supports 361,000 jobs, and we now directly employ more than 76,000 people in the US.[312]

Likewise, the tax revenue paid by Apple to the US government was $7.68 billion in 2011. This is a tremendous annual boost to the economy. This Arab guy is the cause for billions of dollars annually in tax revenue contributing to the upkeep of America's roads, military, and government. Now, compare what this Arab guy, Steve, has done for America, even after his death, in comparison to Trump's contributions in his sixty-nine years of age. Indeed every fair and just person would agree that what the Arab guy, son of an immigrant, has accomplished and contributed far outweighs what Trump has done for the US. That was the son of a Syrian immigrant.

On April 25, 2016 while Trump was at his rally in the state of Rhode Island, he said:

"Now here's one I don't like," reading off a piece of paper. *"Syrian refugees are now being resettled in Rhode Island."* The crowd booed loudly. He continued: *"...We can't let this happen. But you have a lot of them resettling in Rhode Island. Just enjoy your — lock your doors, folks."*[313]

Likewise, we have the example of Michael DeBakey the father of modern cardiovascular surgery, another son of Arab immigrants. He saved thousands in his seventy-year career and invented scores of medical procedures and instruments. DeBakey stopped performing surgery at age 90, after more than 60,000 operations. His legacy lives on among the thousands of surgeons he trained, many of whom now lead hospital and medical school departments.

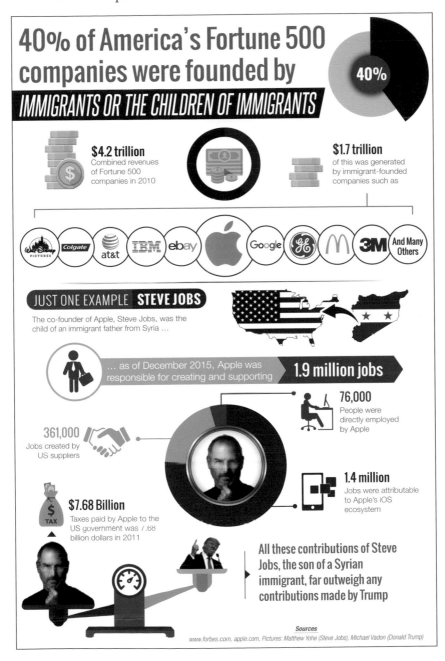

40% of America's Fortune 500 companies were founded by
IMMIGRANTS OR THE CHILDREN OF IMMIGRANTS

40%

$4.2 trillion
Combined revenues of Fortune 500 companies in 2010

$1.7 trillion
of this was generated by immigrant-founded companies such as

Walt Disney PICTURES · Colgate · at&t · IBM · ebay · Apple · Google · GE · McDonald's · 3M · And Many Others

JUST ONE EXAMPLE   STEVE JOBS

The co-founder of Apple, Steve Jobs, was the child of an immigrant father from Syria ...

... as of December 2015, Apple was responsible for creating and supporting **1.9 million jobs**

76,000
People were directly employed by Apple

361,000
Jobs created by US suppliers

1.4 million
Jobs were attributable to Apple's iOS ecosystem

$7.68 Billion
Taxes paid by Apple to the US government was 7.68 billion dollars in 2011

All these contributions of Steve Jobs, the son of a Syrian immigrant, far outweigh any contributions made by Trump

Sources
www.forbes.com, apple.com, Pictures: Matthew Yohe (Steve Jobs), Michael Vadon (Donald Trump)

President Lyndon B. Johnson awarded Dr. DeBakey the Presidential Medal of Freedom. He'd proven himself to be one of the great scientific minds of his generation. In the years since, that status had been reaffirmed by the many honors he has received, including the National Medal of Science, induction into the Health Care Hall of Fame, a lifetime achievement award from the United Nations, and a "living legend" citation from the Library of Congress.[314]

DEBAKEY STOPPED PERFORMING SURGERY AT AGE 90, AFTER MORE THAN 60,000 OPERATIONS

In 1996, only five years after the Cold War ended, Dr. DeBakey traveled to Moscow and arranged Boris Yeltsin's quintuple bypass. President Yeltsin spoke for many of Dr. DeBakey's patients when he called him, "a man with a gift of performing miracles."[315]

Dr. DeBakey advised a number of presidents about health issues and consulted in the personal care of two of them: Lyndon B. Johnson and Richard M. Nixon. He was born on Sept. 7, 1908, the oldest of five children of Lebanese immigrants who moved to the United States. Indeed he was able to reach what he achieved through tireless efforts and high intelligence.[316]

We have the amazing example of Elon Musk, who was born South African. At the early age of twelve, he created a video game and sold it to a computer magazine. In 1988, after obtaining a Canadian passport, Musk left South Africa because he was unwilling to support apartheid through compulsory military service and because he sought the greater economic opportunities available in the United States. Musk attended Queen's University in Kingston, Ontario, and in 1992 he transferred to the University of Pennsylvania, Philadelphia, where he received bachelor's degrees in physics and economics in 1995. He enrolled in graduate school in physics at Stanford University in California, but he left after only two days because he felt that the Internet had much more potential to change society than work in physics.

That same year he founded Zip2, a company that provided maps and business directories to online newspapers. In 1999 Zip2 was bought by the computer manufacturer Compaq for $307 million, and Musk then founded an online financial services company, X.com, which later became PayPal, which specialized in transferring money online. The online auction eBay bought PayPal in 2002 for $1.5 billion.

The Example of the Immigrant

ELON MUSK...

and the Amazing Opportunities He and Those Like Him Can Bring for America

Net Worth $12.7 Billion

Elon Musk is planning SpaceX **mission to Mars by 2018** to learn how to land the sorts of large payloads humans would need should they ever colonize the red planet

Direct Jobs 6,500
Indirect jobs 16,200

Direct Jobs 600

Value to Nevada's Economy $97 billion

Investment in Nevada's K-12 education system $37.5 million

Annual Salaries $50 million

He is the chairman and chief executive officer of, the electric car manufacturer Tesla Motors which incorporates an artificial intelligence autopilot claimed to be almost twice as safe as a human driver.

He went on to found the maker of launch vehicles and spacecraft SpaceX, which succeeded in the first vertical rocket landing on a drone ship at sea in April 2016.

TESLA MOTORS

SPACEX
Space Exploration Technologies

zip2

PayPal

Employees 15,800

Elon Musk founded Zip2, that provided maps and business directories to online newspapers.

Musk also founded an online financial services company, X.com, which later became PayPal, which specialized in transferring money online.

SolarCity

HYPERLOOP

New York Governor Andrew Cuomo has signed off on $750 million in spending on building infrastructure and the facility SolarCity will operate in Buffalo

Musk likewise popularized the idea of hyperloops in 2013. The plan is to eventually hurtle train-like capsules through a tube at over 680 miles per hour.

Local Jobs 3,000

Hundreds of Jobs and great value to the citizens of California

680 miles per hour.

Sources
http://www.britannica.com/topic/Tesla-Motors, http://www.telegraph.ce.uk/technology/2016/04/25/elon-musk-teslas-autopilot-makes-accidents-50pc-less-likely/, http://fortune.com/2016/03/23/elon-musk-hyperloop-las-vegas/, http://idsino.streetwise.co/2016/01/07/where-elon-musk-hiring-spacex-tesla-jobs-cities/, http://www.britannica.com/biography/Elon-Musk, http://britannica.com/topic/Compaq-Computer-Corporation, http://www.britannica.com/topic/SpaceX, http://www.bloomberg.com/news/articles/2016-04-08/musk-s-reusable-rocket-dream-comes-true-with-d, https://www.theguardian.com/technology/2016/apr/27/elon-musk-space-x-mars-mission-tesla

WHAT WOULD TRUMP'S ANTI-IMMIGRATION POLICIES DUE TO AMERICA? THEY WOULD EASILY BE THE CAUSE FOR THESE KINDS OF INNOVATORS MOVING TO OTHER COUNTRIES INSTEAD, AND SKYROCKETING THOSE ECONOMIES INTO THE FUTURE.

He went on to found the maker of launch vehicles and spacecraft SpaceX, which succeeded in the first vertical rocket landing on a drone ship at sea in April 2016. He was also one of the first significant investors in, as well as chairman and chief executive officer of, the electric car manufacturer Tesla Motors which incorporates an artificial intelligence autopilot claimed to be almost twice as safe as a human driver. Musk likewise popularized the idea of hyperloops in 2013. The plan is to eventually hurtle train-like capsules through a tube at over 680 miles per hour. Since then, researchers and a handful of companies have been trying to figure out how to actually build such a system that would create an entirely new form of transportation; tests conducted in May 2016 have proven to be positive.[317]

In this example, we see a man who fled his own country, fed up with the situations that he didn't agree with, so he could seek out better economic opportunities. And what tremendously innovative opportunities he has brought about for America and its people! This clearly proves wrong the closed-door policies Trump seeks to popularize and thus prevent America from benefitting from this type of innovator.

Trump is so terribly shortsighted in comparison to Musk, who said in January 2016 that his aerospace company plans on sending astronauts to Mars in just nine years. You read that correctly; *nine years*. This is the type of thinking America and the rest of the world needs.

Of course, it's impossible to ever know in advance who will be the next Steve Jobs, Elon Musk, or Google cofounder Surgey Brin. Each is from a different background, with a heritage rooted in different continents from around the globe. What would Trump's anti-immigration policies do to America? They would easily be the cause for these kinds of innovators moving to other countries instead, and skyrocketing those economies into the future.

31

TRUMP'S BAN ON MUSLIMS

A TRUMP CAMPAIGN PRESS RELEASE REPORTED Trump's words: *"Donald J. Trump is calling for a total and complete shutdown of Muslims entering the United States until our country's representatives can figure out what is going on."* [318]

I expect that if Trump reaches the White House, he will seek to implement several initiatives to create such a ban. These initiatives would require the issuance of new passports, which would specify each citizen's religion and sect. This of course would be imposed upon American citizens, and pressure would be applied to the international community to do the same. How else could it be determined who is Muslim and who is not? This is the future of what is to be expected, just to give the readers one example of how deeply disturbing Trump's policies are.

In April 2016, a detailed reply to Trump's proposed ban was published in the Kuwaiti newspaper *Arab Times* by Khalaf Ahmad Al Habtoor, a well-known businessman from the United Arab Emirates:

IT WOULD CREATE A 'THEM-AND-US' CLIMATE WITHIN THE US AND IS GUARANTEED TO ALIENATE MANY OF AMERICA'S TRADITIONAL ALLIES

Republican contenders for the White House who are manipulating voters' fears for their own ends by threatening to shut America's door to Muslim visitors while subjecting American-Muslims to intensive monitoring have failed to count the cost of such an immoral, bigoted policy. Current front-runners Donald Trump and Ted Cruz are shamefully vying with each other to attract xenophobes and Islamophobes into their respective camps in a no-holds barred fashion.

The real shock is the result of a Bloomberg Politics/Purple strategies poll indicating 65 percent of Republican primary voters support the idea and even more concerning, 37 percent of all voters are in agreement with a ban on Muslims. Clearly, they have no clue that such an unprecedented action would shoot America in the foot in more ways than one.

Firstly, it would contravene the constitution that outlaws "religious tests." Secondly, it would create a 'them-and-us' climate within the US and is guaranteed to alienate many of America's traditional allies. Thirdly, it would serve as a gift to terrorist recruiters and America-haters. And, fourthly, it is wholly impractical when most passports do not mention its holder's faith. It is likely, too, that some, if not most, predominately Muslim states would institute reciprocal rules whereby American citizens and corporations would be deemed unwelcome.

However, even when those negative consequences are set aside, placing such a 'Keep Out' sign with respect to all Muslims would, undoubtedly, have devastating consequences for America's economy whose ripples would trigger yet another global economic downturn because, as is well known, when Washington sneezes the rest of the world catches a cold.

For a start, America's tourism industry would suffer a major hit. A study conducted jointly by Singapore-based Crescent Ratings and the US firm Dinar Standard reports that Muslim travelers spend an average of $2,000 more than people of other faiths and forecasts taking into account growth that by 2020 the overall spend relating to Muslim tourism worldwide will reach more than $192bn.

WOULD, UNDOUBTEDLY, HAVE DEVASTATING CONSEQUENCES FOR AMERICA'S ECONOMY WHOSE RIPPLES WOULD TRIGGER YET ANOTHER GLOBAL ECONOMIC DOWNTURN

An article in the *Telegraph*, substantiated with statistics from *Travel and Leisure* magazine and the US National Travel and Tourism Office, suggests a ban on Muslims could cost the US more than $18.4 billion a year "not accounting for the necessary overhaul to border infrastructure to implement such a plan."

American airlines, airports, transport systems, cabs, restaurants, entertainment venues and retailers would certainly feel the pinch. Gulf Arabs are also among the biggest purchasers of luxury goods. *Economy Watch* asserts that GCC states make up the majority of the Middle East's travel spend and together represent thirty seven percent of all Muslim travelers worldwide. Data from the US Department of Commerce, which does not base its statistics on religion, shows that Saudis spent $14.6 billion in the United States between 2005 and 2014.

Let us not forget, too, that there are over 100,000 non-American Muslim students (80,000 of them Saudi nationals) attending US colleges and universities whose fees, accommodation and living expenses contribute billions to the US coffers and go to subsidize the fees of American students from poor families. On average annual tuition and fees charged by private universities are in the region of $32,599, which means they gain approximately $130,396 over a four-year period from a single student.

THOUSANDS OF AMERICANS WOULD LOSE THEIR JOBS.

Untold numbers of Muslims also travel to the US to seek private specialist medical treatment; many arrive with their families so as to combine their health care needs with a family vacation.

American exports could also be affected simply because human nature would dictate that Muslim consumers – all 1.7 billion of them – would be far less likely to purchase 'Made in the USA' automobiles, computers and other high-end items. US exports to Saudi Arabia and the UAE alone exceed $57 billion. Over 1000 US firms have a presence in the UAE and 120 operate in Qatar. Many thousands more are based throughout the Middle East and Asia.

What impact a Muslim ban would have on investments is incalculable but defense contracts and multi-billion dollar weapons and aircraft orders could be at risk. Would Qatar proceed with its plans to invest $35 billion dollars in the US over the coming five-year period? Would billionaire investors liquidate their assets and transfer their funds to more Muslim-friendly markets?

It is worth noting that according to the US Treasury, as of 01 January 2015 oil-exporting countries (including Muslim or predominately Muslim) held $290.8 bn in treasury securities.

Moreover, as the Aspen Institute highlights, "In 2015, four

out of the top ten sovereign wealth funds in the world are situated in the GCC" which manage over \$2.28tn "historically directed towards North America and Europe."

Would a President Trump's ban also be applied to Muslim diplomats, I wonder. In that event the embassies, consulates and educational centers of over thirty Muslim-Majority countries, numbering more than one hundred eight diplomatic facilities around the country would be shuttered. Diplomats and other staff who are nationals make up around five percent of those working in foreign missions; the rest are locally employed US nationals. In that case, thousands of Americans would lose their jobs. Plus restaurants, catering companies, car-hire firms, hotels and apartment complexes in areas in which those embassies and consulates are located would suffer losses.

More importantly, Muslim heads of state, foreign ministers and ambassadors would be unable to attend United Nations General Assembly meetings or international conferences taking place on US soil, threatening world peace as well as America's leading role in global affairs.

ONE THING IS INDISPUTABLE. A BAN ON MUSLIMS WOULD PUNCH A HOLE IN THE US ECONOMY TO THE TUNE OF HUNDREDS OF BILLIONS ANNUALLY IN TERMS OF LOSSES

Neither Mr. Trump nor Mr. Cruz has thought through the implications that banning Muslims would have on their own country in terms of potential bankruptcies and job losses not to mention the tremors that would surely rock the financial sector and stock markets, even supposing Muslim countries declined to implement retaliatory measures.

No wonder the *Economist Intelligence Unit* has rated a Trump presidency high among its Top Ten Global Risks, higher than the UK quitting the EU or a major clash in the South China Sea! He presents the same risk level to the global economy as the rising threat of terrorism. How ironic is that!

However, one thing is indisputable. A ban on Muslims would punch a hole in the US economy to the tune of hundreds of billions annually in terms of losses to the aviation, transport and hotel industries, investments, real-estate, retailing, university and medical fees, defense purchases, exports, notwithstanding the potential for sovereign funds to seek greener pastures and wealthy Muslim companies and individuals transferring their capital out of US banks.

From the US perspective it would be madness, especially since its loss would be others' gain. I will bet that European financial institutions, manufacturers and businesses will be laughing all the way to the bank.[319]

REUTERS/ASHRAF MOHAMMAD

KHALAF AHMAD AL HABTOOR

32

SOME PEOPLE CONSIDER TRUMP A QUICK FIX FOR AMERICA, BUT IN REALITY HE'D BE **THE DEMISE OF AMERICA**

T HE DISEASE OF TRUMP IS SPREADING, AND SOME misguided people hold him to be the solution for their problems. However, they should not try to make the answer for their hatred or disease a bigger disease. Just like those who try to solve their problems with alcohol or drugs, Trump's supporters believe that his means are a reasonable approach.

JUST LIKE THOSE WHO TRY TO SOLVE THEIR PROBLEMS WITH ALCOHOL OR DRUGS, TRUMP'S SUPPORTERS BELIEVE THAT HIS MEANS ARE A REASONABLE APPROACH.

But if you listen to Trump's speeches, he clearly offers no *real* solutions.

His speeches reflect a few common themes.

The four foundations of Trump's speeches are: that he can solve every problem, insults, hateful speech, and his wealth.

How is it that he does not mention any realistic strategy at all? Even in the case of a company with only a few employees, a manager would be required to put forward and explain in detail each and every step of his or her strategic plan to achieve a particular result. That manager would prepare a detailed presentation to be repeated many times to iron out any deficiencies with his or her team. How can it be comprehended that a man could be chosen to solve the problems facing the wealthiest and most powerful nation in the world, without any actual action plans? How can this possibly be accepted from him? This is truly a man who cannot fix the nation's problems because he is without any detailed blueprint.

Even at this late stage leading up to the elections and reviewing that which he has presented, we find that Trump is all talk, and has not put forward anything of substance.

DO NOT LET HATRED TOWARDS IMMIGRANTS, REFUGEES, OR FOREIGN COUNTRIES LEAD YOU TO MAKE THE WRONG CHOICE, HOPING FOR A SOLUTION WHICH SIMPLY IS NOT THERE.

It's very important that you don't make the answer for your hatred or disease a bigger disease. Do not let hatred towards immigrants, refugees, or foreign countries lead you to make the wrong choice, hoping for a solution which simply is not there. How would Trump fix the economy, create jobs, improve international relations, and fight terrorism? Simply put, no practical mathods have been offered.

Anyone who expects to be able to influence organizations, as complex as governments or as simple as companies, must learn to speak in

UNITED KINGDOM BUDGET AT A GLANCE

George Osborne faces an £18 billion hole that has opened up in the UK economy since November

Public sector net borrowing (£ billions)

Deficit: £72.2bn.
Below target
of £73.5bn

£157.7bn — 09-10
£136.8bn — 10-11
£115.9bn — 11-12
£121.1bn — 12-13
£103.0bn — 13-14
£91.9bn — 14-15
15-16

KEY POINTS

Government spending: Further £3.5bn a year of public expenditure cuts to achieve £10.4bn surplus by 2019-20

Fuel duty: Frozen for sixth year in row, whereas taxes on tobacco will rise 2% above inflation

Tax avoidance: Raise £12bn by preventing multinationals from shifting profits overseas to avoid tax. Crackdown on VAT evasion from foreign sellers on internet

Health: New levy on soft drinks industry from 2018 to tackle childhood obesity. £520m raised to be used to boost sport in schools

Capital gains: Top rate cut from 28% to 20%, basic rate 18% to 10%, effective from April 2016

630,000

small businesses will pay no rates from next year – £7 billion tax cut for businesses

17%

Corporation tax: Cut from 20% to 17% by 2020

Sources: HM Treasury, *Office of Budget Responsibility*, Picture: Nathan King / Alamy Stock Photo, GN

THE UNITED KINGDOM HAS OUTLINED KEY POINTS AND STRATEGIES TO ADDRESS THE PROBLEMS IT'S FACING. TRUMP, HOWEVER, HAS OFFERED NOTHING TO COUNTER THREE 'BEASTS' DEVASTATING AMERICAN SOCIETY: ALCOHOL, GUNS, AND ILLEGAL DRUGS.

the language of numbers. When experts are communicating ideas and concepts such as success, joblessness, and poverty, it's necessary they do it in numbers. Some ways these examples are conveyed are: net profits, unemployment levels, and the poverty line. Trump therefore must present detailed programs, as other nations and leaders do.

The three presidents who have overseen the largest average economic expansions since World War Two were Kennedy, Johnson, and Clinton, as presented in the graph below. They truly introduced real, actionable methods to resolve those difficult problems faced in their times.

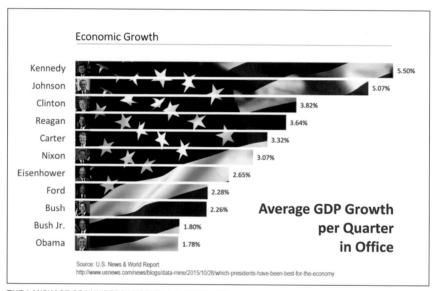

Economic Growth

Kennedy	5.50%
Johnson	5.07%
Clinton	3.82%
Reagan	3.64%
Carter	3.32%
Nixon	3.07%
Eisenhower	2.65%
Ford	2.28%
Bush	2.26%
Bush Jr.	1.80%
Obama	1.78%

Average GDP Growth per Quarter in Office

Source: U.S. News & World Report
http://www.usnews.com/news/blogs/data-mine/2015/10/28/which-presidents-have-been-best-for-the-economy

THE LANGUAGE OF NUMBERS UNCOVERS THE REALITY.

The Economist magazine had divided the Republican candidates into six main categories.[320] Those categories of importance can be summarized into these three:

1. Those who are the true and serious political leaders, and from them is the one who will actually be elected.

2. Those who know that they do not have a serious chance to actually be elected as president. However, they're using their campaign to build recognition and fame in order to get a different position within the government. They want to be on the minds of the other candidates and the public.

3. Those who are like the second group who know they do not have a serious chance to be president, and are not looking for any government job. Rather they are only looking for notoriety and recognition for self-promotion purposes. They have as a goal to use this fame for their business interactions or promoting a book, or other reasons.

According to these experts at *The Economist*, Trump falls into the third category. This clearly shows the great disconnect between these experts and the true condition of those attracted to and indoctrinated by the Trump–Hitler–ISIS–Al-Qaeda–KKK disease.

WHEN EXPERTS ARE COMMUNICATING IDEAS AND CONCEPTS SUCH AS SUCCESS, JOBLESSNESS, AND POVERTY, IT'S NECESSARY THEY DO IT IN NUMBERS.

Trump claims that his whole campaign is completely self-funded and he does not need assistance, because he has his own billions to spend on it. He has his own ways to get things done, as he mentioned many times in his speeches. An example of how he goes about getting things done is when Ben Carson dropped out of his presidential run, Trump promptly offered him a job in his anticipated government. Carson revealed on Newsmax TV that he will work in Trump's administration — at least in an "advisory capacity" — if the Republican presidential front-runner is elected to the White House.[321]

REUTERS/CARLO ALLEGRI

Also there's Chris Christie who was running for the nomination, dropped out, then since resurfaced (as of May 9, 2016) as the head of Trump's transition team, should he win in November.

Trump has not offered anyany systematic approach to rectify what is going wrong with education, the economy, and the many social problems facing ordinary Americans.

He crudely tweeted from his official Twitter account about Mrs. Hillary Clinton, *"If Hillary cannot even satisfy her husband, what makes you think she can satisfy America?"* [322]

COMPARE HOW MANY FAILURES TRUMP HAS HAD IN ESTABLISHING A HOUSEHOLD AND FAMILY. WITH SO MANY DIVORCES, HOW CAN HE SUCCEED IN BUILDING THE COUNTRY?

We would like to compare how many failures Trump has had in establishing a household and family. With so many divorces, how can he succeed in building the country? In "The Top Ten Trump Failures," *Time* Magazine reported:

"For all his success in the boardroom, Donald Trump's life in the bedroom has been messy at best. The real estate magnate married his first wife, Ivana, in 1977, but things got rocky after Trump's affair with actress Marla Maples surfaced in New York City tabloids. 'You b**ch, leave my husband alone!' Ivana told Maples on a ski trip in Aspen, Colo. Ivana's warning fell on deaf ears, and in 1992, Trump left her with a reported $25 million settlement and married his mistress one year later. His marriage to Maples was even shorter-lived, and the couple divorced in 1999. These days, Trump's married to Slovenian supermodel Melania Knauss. Together in marital bliss since 2005, this relationship's proving the third time really is a charm — so far anyway." [323]

His tweet about Mrs. Clinton, which he did not apologize for, and his long history of failed marriages clearly shows another dimension to his disease. Mrs. Hillary Clinton was able to preserve her family and save her marriage despite the great difficulties she faced. It cannot be expected that a man with so many personal problems would be able to cure America's hardships. It is truly surprising that this many people can be rallying for him.

In my opinion, the sudden popularity of Trump is identical to how the Germans were motivated to vote for Hitler. The German people wanted to solve a problem, but they brought about a much bigger problem through their own votes for him. Everyone who is supporting Trump now is responsible for supporting a man who is clearly diseased.

IT CANNOT BE EXPECTED THAT A MAN WITH SO MANY PERSONAL PROBLEMS WOULD BE ABLE TO CURE AMERICA'S HARDSHIPS.

Fear of the risks has spread, as indicated in March 2016 in analysis by the *Economist Intelligence Unit*:

The businessman and political novice, Donald Trump, has built a strong lead in the Republican Party primary, and looks the firm favorite to be the party's candidate in the US presidential election in November.

Analysis

Thus far Mr. Trump has given very few details of his policies – and these tend to be prone to constant revision – but a few themes have become apparent. First, he has been exceptionally hostile towards free trade, including notably NAFTA, and has repeatedly labelled China as a 'currency manipulator.' He has also taken an exceptionally right-wing stance on the Middle East and *jihadi* terrorism, including, among other things, advocating the killing of families of terrorists and launching a land incursion into Syria to wipe out ISIS and acquire its oil. In the event of a Trump victory, his hostile attitude to free trade, and his alienation of Mexico and China in particular, could escalate rapidly into a trade war, and at the least scupper the Trans-Pacific Partnership between the US and eleven other American and Asian states signed in February 2016. His militaristic tendencies towards the Middle East, and his proposed ban on all Muslim travel to the US, would be a potent recruitment tool for *jihadi* groups, increasing their threat both within the region and beyond.

Although we do not expect Mr. Trump to defeat his most likely Democratic contender, Hillary Clinton, there are risks to this forecast, especially in the event of a terrorist attack on US soil or a sudden economic downturn. It is worth noting that the innate hostility within the Republican hierarchy towards Mr. Trump, combined with the inevitable virulent Democratic opposition, will see many of his more radical policies blocked in Congress – albeit such internal bickering will also undermine the coherence of domestic and foreign policymaking. [324]

IT'S CLEAR THAT HE'S A PROTECTIONIST AND NOT AN OPPORTUNIST.

What Trump claims to be solutions are in reality not solutions at all. In speech after speech, interview after interview, his approaches remain empty of any real plan of action. In spite of this, the number of his followers and supporters continues to grow. It is the nature of mankind that people want someone to follow and believe in, but it becomes dangerous for everyone when the one being followed is not worthy. These leaders whom people choose have a unique combination of characteristics; they are strong public speakers, highly charismatic, and are versatile actors.

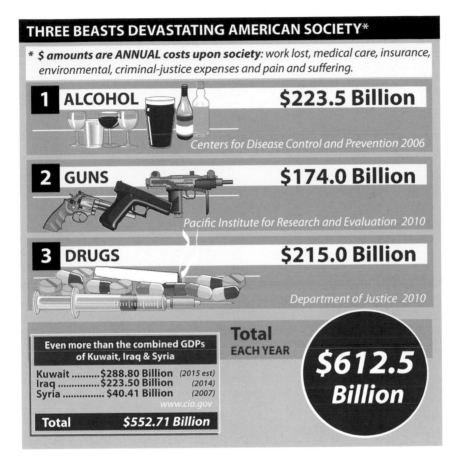

THESE NUMBERS CLEARLY SHOW THE DEPTH OF DAMAGE INFLICTED UPON THE US ECONOMY, FOR WHICH NO ONE IS PUTTING FORWARD ANY REAL SOLUTIONS TO TREAT. THAT IS IN ADDITION TO THE DANGERS THEY POSE TO BOTH HEALTH AND RELATIONSHIPS.

U.S. record pot crop

Marijuana has become the largest cash crop in the United States, exceeding traditional harvests such as wheat, corn and soybeans, says a new report. U.S. growers produce nearly $35 billion worth of the illegal drug annually

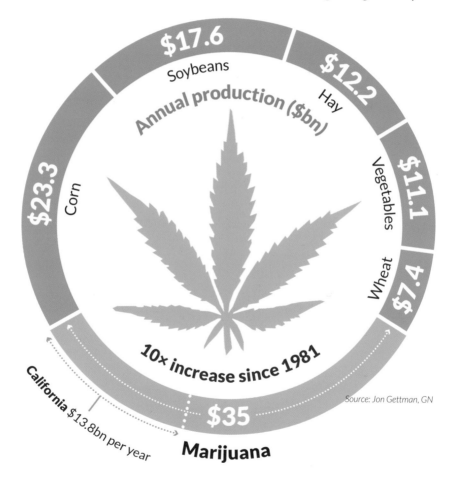

$17.6 Soybeans

$12.2 Hay

$11.1 Vegetables

$7.4 Wheat

$23.3 Corn

Annual production ($bn)

10x increase since 1981

$35 Marijuana

California $13.8bn per year

Source: Jon Gettman, GN

DESTRUCTION OF THE AMERICAN ECONOMY, IN THE LANGUAGE OF NUMBERS.

A DANGEROUS PRESIDENT

33

TRUMP'S **HOSTILITY** TOWARDS OTHER NATIONS AND ITS IMPACT **ON THE** GLOBAL ECONOMY

ONE OF THE LOW POINTS IN THE RECENT HISTO-ry of the global economy was the financial crisis of 2007-08, when the Dow Jones and NASDAQ market indices came crashing down.

The Federal Reserve was in great need of contacting its allies for help. The official news agency of the United Arab Emirates, WAM Dubai, reported on 2nd Nov. 2008:

"Shelling out Dh44 billion ($12 billion) by Abu Dhabi, Qatar, and some other Gulf states to bail out a foreign financial institution takes a lot of courage and honest intention, especially at a difficult time when the Gulf states themselves require additional cash injection to keep the cycle of their economies running, the UAE paper (Gulf News) commented today.

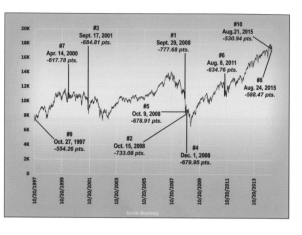

"Once again, the Gulf states have shown their goodwill and renewed commitment to stand by the global community in difficult times,' wrote *Gulf News* in today's editorial."

THE US FEDERAL RESERVE LOOKED TO AMERICA'S ALLIES SUCH AS THE GULF NATIONS FOR CASH FLOW TO INJECT LIQUIDITY INTO THE AILING US ECONOMY.

"This big bailout, the Dubai-based daily said, came nearly ten months after Abu Dhabi had injected $7.5 billion to save Citibank after it was forced to write down a hefty amount due to subprime losses. The latest rescue package comes a few days after Deputy US Treasury Secretary Robert Kimmitt appealed to the Gulf States to inject cash into the US markets to save troubled institutions."[325]

The US Federal Reserve looked to America's allies such as the Gulf nations for cash flow to inject liquidity into the ailing US economy. This eased market turbulence and allowed US financial institutions some respite. Had it not been for the Fed stepping in with these measures to subdue the crash, recovery might have taken even longer.

This is similar to a stroke patient being injected with aspirin, an immediate treatment given in the emergency room to reduce the likelihood of having another stroke.

Adel Al-Jubeir, the Saudi foreign minister, reminded lawmakers in Washington of the up to $750 billion owned by the kingdom in treasury securities and other assets in the US, as reported by the *New York Times*.[326]

Another example is the Black Monday crash of 1987, when Wall Street markets crashed. According to CNBC at the time, "Stocks opened sharply lower and continued to fall for most of the session, as the Dow shed 507 points, or

> **SAUDI FOREIGN MINISTER, RE-MINDED LAWMAKERS IN WASHINGTON OF THE UP TO $750 BILLION OWNED BY THE KINGDOM IN TREASURY SECURITIES AND OTHER ASSETS IN THE US**

22%, the largest-ever one-day percentage decline in the Dow. Overseas markets play catch up to Wall Street as exchanges from Australia to Japan plunge a day after the crash."[327]

The Economist reported, "Central banks around the world responded quickly to the crash, some cutting interest rates, others pumping money into the system."[328]

CNBC concluded, "The chain reaction makes it clear that a global market has emerged."[329]

In 2015, when Chinese shares tumbled 7%, Reuters News Agency reported, "Confronted with a plunge in its stock markets, China's central bank swiftly reached out to the U.S. Federal Reserve, asking it to share its play book for dealing with Wall Street's 'Black Monday' crash of 1987. The request came in a July 27 email from a People's Bank of China official with a subject line: 'Your urgent assistance is greatly appreciated!'

In a message to a senior Fed staffer, the PBOC's New York-based chief representative for the Americas, Song Xiangyan, pointed to the day's 8.5 percent drop in Chinese stocks and said, 'my Governor would like to draw from your good experience.'"[330]

> **IN TODAY'S WORLD, COUNTRIES ARE INTERCONNECTED BY THEIR RELIANCE ON EACH OTHER, AND ESPECIALLY IN TIMES OF CRISES. NATIONS MUST COEXIST AND CONSIDER THE REALITIES OF GLOBALIZATION.**

All this goes to show that, in today's world, countries are interconnected by their reliance

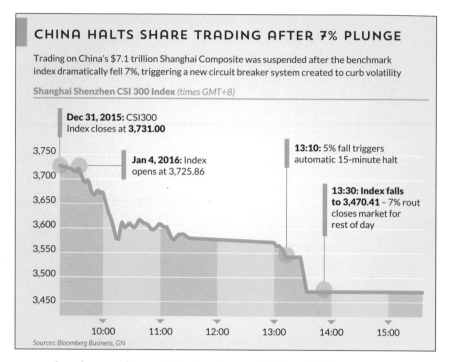

CHINA HALTS SHARE TRADING AFTER 7% PLUNGE

Trading on China's $7.1 trillion Shanghai Composite was suspended after the benchmark index dramatically fell 7%, triggering a new circuit breaker system created to curb volatility

Shanghai Shenzhen CSI 300 Index *(times GMT+8)*

Dec 31, 2015: CSI300
Index closes at **3,731.00**

Jan 4, 2016: Index opens at 3,725.86

13:10: 5% fall triggers automatic 15-minute halt

13:30: Index falls to 3,470.41 – 7% rout closes market for rest of day

Sources: Bloomberg Business, GN

on each other, and especially in times of crises. Nations must coexist and consider the realities of globalization. Does Trump, with his myopic economic ignorance and bullying attitude, recognize the need for co-operation between countries? To listen to his plans on foreign policy, it does not appear to be so. No matter the strength of the investor, whether they invested $10,000, $1000, $100, or one dollar, he or she would have benefited from those injections from the friendly countries.

Trump speaks as if America lives alone in this world. The population of the earth is over seven billion, and with America contributing less than 4.5%, it would be missing out on over 95% of the opportunities.

Investors and stable markets go hand in hand. The former expect secure and reliable market conditions in which to do business, unencumbered by strange and shortsighted individuals like Trump, who have the potential to influence market policies. Global financial collaboration must be considered, especially given that foreign investment in US debt is exorbitant. There are more investments in America made by foreign countries than by American debt holders. On October 28, 2014, Mike Patton of *Forbes* magazine explained:

"According to the U.S. Treasury Department, at the end of August 2014, more than a third of the debt was owned by foreign countries (34.4%). The largest foreign holders of U.S. debt were Mainland China (7.2%) and Japan (7.0%). What is the consequence of having such a large percentage of debt held by foreign nations? It depends. It depends on the relationship between the U.S. and the specific foreign country. It also depends on the global interest rate environment. Finally, it depends on the geo-political climate and the degree of fear around the globe. This is the case because when fear rises, money flows into the U.S. Treasury, which is viewed as a safe place to invest. The percentage of debt owned by countries that are less friendly to America is about 10%. This includes China, several oil exporters (Ecuador, Venezuela, Iran, Iraq, Libya, etc.), and a few others.

GLOBAL FINANCIAL COLLABORATION MUST BE CONSIDERED, ESPECIALLY GIVEN THAT FOREIGN INVESTMENT IN US DEBT IS EXORBITANT.

The worst case would materialize if the largest holders decided to sell their Treasury securities at the same time. This could potentially decrease demand, which would push yields higher. If yields rose, the federal government would find it more difficult to service the debt, pushing the deficit higher. If the deficit rose, the total debt burden would accelerate and, unless demand for U.S. debt were to increase, it could get ugly."[331]

The strength of the US dollar is the backbone of the US economy. In fact, the dollar is the world's international currency, which is used for the majority of global transactions. Commodities such as rice, chemicals, metals, airplanes, computers, cars, and even securities are bought in dollars more often than in any other currency. This shows how the leaders of the US have succeeded over the years in making all of life's necessities available through the American economy. So why increase tensions between the countries to make them want to abandon the US dollar? The role of the president should be to constantly *improve* relations and to *increase* international trade, thus raising the status of the US dollar.

This tremendous economy was established with the contributions of many ethnicities and nationalities, for which the leaders were applauded. However, Trump seeks to dismantle its strength by provoking conflicts

TRUMP SEEKS TO DISMANTLE ITS STRENGTH BY PROVOKING CONFLICTS AMONGST THE NATIONS.

amongst the nations. This is truly from the ill effects of his disease.

Regarding the Japanese, Trump has been speaking against them for decades.

"They come over here, they sell their cars, their VCRs. They knock the hell out of our companies," he told Oprah Winfrey in 1988. [332]

In a *Playboy* interview in 1990, he said, *"First they take all our money with their consumer goods, then they put it back in buying all of Manhattan."* [333]

"If Japan gets attacked, we have to go to their defense and start World War III," he said in a speech in February, 2016. *"If we get attacked, Japan doesn't have to do anything."* [334]

In April 2015 Trump tweeted, *"The Trans-Pacific Partnership is an attack on America's business. It does not stop Japan's currency manipulation. This is a bad deal."* [335]

He also said at a rally, *"They are taking our jobs. China is taking our jobs. Japan is taking our jobs. India is taking our jobs. It is not going to happen anymore, folks!"* [336]

"I'll bring back our jobs from China, from Mexico, from Japan, from so many places," Trump said when he kicked off his campaign in June 2015. [337]

In Trump's March 2016 interview with *The New York Times*, while discussing Japan, he said about the current state of America, *"We're a country that doesn't have money. You know, when we did these deals, we were a rich country. We're not a rich country. We were a rich country with a very strong military and tremendous capability in so many ways. We're not anymore."* [338]

As Trump affirms that this is the true state of the US economy, it is completely nonsensical that he uses the following tone and distasteful meaning like this, with one of its primary trading partners: *"Listen, you motherf**ers, we're going to tax you twenty-five percent,"* he declared to a roaring crowd, describing what he is planning to say to China. [339]

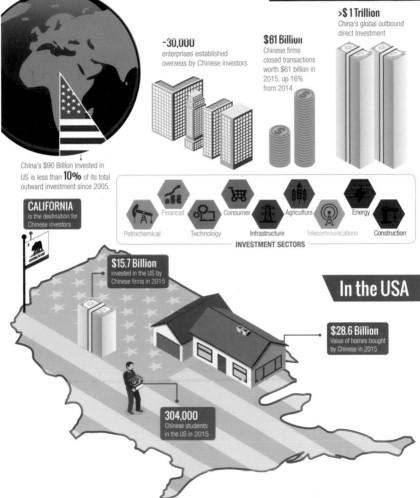

CHINESE
Foreign Direct Investment

In The Global Market

>$1 Trillion
China's global outbound direct Investment

~30,000
enterprises established overseas by Chinese investors

$61 Billion
Chinese firms closed transactions worth $61 billion in 2015, up 16% from 2014

China's $90 Billion invested in US is less than **10%** of its total outward investment since 2005.

CALIFORNIA is the destination for Chinese investors

Financial   Consumer   Agriculture   Energy

Petrochemical   Technology   Infrastructure   Telecommunications   Construction

INVESTMENT SECTORS

$15.7 Billion invested in the US by Chinese firms in 2015

In the USA

$28.6 Billion Value of homes bought by Chinese in 2015

304,000 Chinese students in the US in 2015

AMERICA SHOULD STRIVE TO INCREASE TRADE WITH CHINA DUE TO THE TREMENDOUS BUSINESS OPPORTUNITIES IT HAS TO OFFER. TRUMP HOWEVER, DOES NOT WANT TO TAKE ADVANTAGE OF THIS, THUS LEAVING THE OPPORTUNITIES OPEN AND AVAILABLE FOR OTHER COUNTRIES INSTEAD.

Toshihiro Nakayama, professor of American politics and foreign policy at Keio University in Tokyo had this to say: "We have been watching the rise of Mr. Trump as political entertainment, but it's no longer a joke.... His views are a geo-political threat to Japan and the way he talks is very difficult for us to understand."[340]

Trump also speaks with very disgraceful words about trading partners such as China and Saudi Arabia.

He has tweeted about China:

"China is not our friend. They are not our ally."[341]

> "WE HAVE BEEN WATCHING THE RISE OF MR. TRUMP AS POLITICAL ENTERTAINMENT, BUT IT'S NO LONGER A JOKE.... HIS VIEWS ARE A GEO-POLITICAL THREAT TO JAPAN

It seems Trump wants to wage economic trade war against China, the world's most populous country (1.364 billion) and, with a GDP of $10.35 trillion, the number two economy in the world.[342]

And to Saudi Arabia he plans to say in regards to their oil sales, *"You're not gonna raise that fuc*in' price!"*[343]

The demise of America would come about because the main contributors to the nation are those whom Trump speaks against, as reported by *Bloomberg Business*:

> As a matter of policy, the Treasury has never disclosed the holdings of Saudi Arabia, long a key ally in the volatile Middle East, and instead groups it with fourteen other mostly OPEC nations including Kuwait, the United Arab Emirates and Nigeria. For more than a hundred other countries, from China to the Vatican, the Treasury provides a detailed breakdown of how much U.S. debt each holds."

> They range from the $3 million stake held by the island nation of the Seychelles, to the $69.7 billion investment from the oil-producing economy of Norway, and those of China and Japan, which are both in excess of $1 trillion.[341]

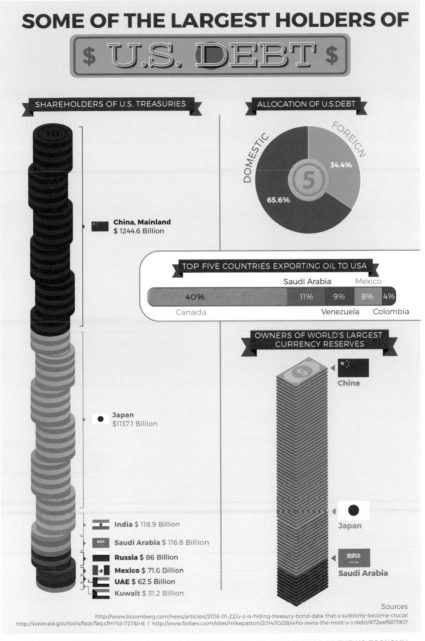

SOME OF THE LARGEST HOLDERS OF
$ U.S. DEBT $

SHAREHOLDERS OF U.S. TREASURIES

China, Mainland
$ 1244.6 Billion

Japan
$1137.1 Billion

India $ 118.9 Billion

Saudi Arabia $ 116.8 Billion

Russia $ 86 Billion

Mexico $ 71.6 Billion

UAE $ 62.5 Billion

Kuwait $ 31.2 Billion

ALLOCATION OF U.S.DEBT

FOREIGN 34.4%

DOMESTIC 65.6%

TOP FIVE COUNTRIES EXPORTING OIL TO USA

Saudi Arabia | Mexico

Canada 40% | 11% | 9% | 8% | 4%

Venezuela | Colombia

OWNERS OF WORLD'S LARGEST CURRENCY RESERVES

China

Japan

Saudi Arabia

Sources
http://www.bloomberg.com/news/articles/2016-01-22/u-s-is-hiding-treasury-bond-data-that-s-suddenly-become-crucial
http://www.eia.gov/tools/faqs/faq.cfm?id=727&t=6 | http://www.forbes.com/sites/mikepatton/2014/10/28/who-owns-the-most-u-s-debt/#72eef8871907

THESE FIGURES MAKE IT CLEAR THAT THESE COUNTRIES ARE AN ACTIVE PART OF THE US ECONOMY.

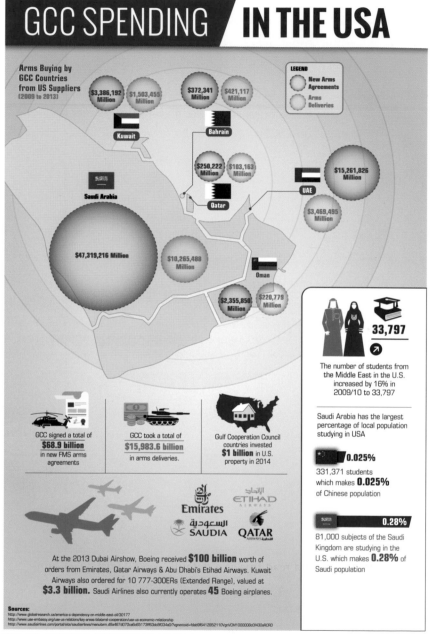

GCC SPENDING / IN THE USA

Arms Buying by GCC Countries from US Suppliers
(2009 to 2013)

$3,386,192 Million — $1,503,455 Million — Kuwait

$372,341 Million — $421,117 Million — Bahrain

LEGEND
New Arms Agreements
Arms Deliveries

$250,222 Million — $103,163 Million — Qatar

Saudi Arabia

$15,261,826 Million — UAE

$3,469,495 Million

$47,319,216 Million

$10,265,488 Million

Oman

$2,355,850 Million — $220,779 Million

33,797

The number of students from the Middle East in the U.S. increased by 16% in 2009/10 to 33,797

Saudi Arabia has the largest percentage of local population studying in USA

0.025%
331,371 students which makes **0.025%** of Chinese population

0.28%
81,000 subjects of the Saudi Kingdom are studying in the U.S. which makes **0.28%** of Saudi population

GCC signed a total of **$68.9 billion** in new FMS arms agreements

GCC took a total of **$15,983.6 billion** in arms deliveries.

Gulf Cooperation Council countries invested **$1 billion** in U.S. property in 2014

Emirates   **ETIHAD** AIRWAYS

SAUDIA   **QATAR** AIRWAYS

At the 2013 Dubai Airshow, Boeing received **$100 billion** worth of orders from Emirates, Qatar Airways & Abu Dhabi's Etihad Airways. Kuwait Airways also ordered for 10 777-300ERs (Extended Range), valued at **$3.3 billion.** Saudi Airlines also currently operates **45** Boeing airplanes.

Sources:
http://www.globalresearch.ca/america-s-dependency-on-middle-east-oil/30177
http://www.uae-embassy.org/uae-us-relations/key-areas-bilateral-cooperation/uae-us-economic-relationship
http://www.saudiairlines.com/portal/site/saudiairlines/menuitem.d9a467d070ca6c65173f63dc8f034a0/?ignextoid=fdab96412852110Vgn/OM1000008c0f430aRCRD

THE GCC COUNTRIES RECOGNIZE THE STRENGTH OF THE AMERICAN ECONOMY AND THE OPPORTUNI-
TIES IN THIS MARKET. GCC INVESTMENTS CREATE MANY JOBS FOR THE US WORK FORCE AND HELP
THE US ECONOMY GROW, AS DO OTHER INTERNATIONAL INVESTORS. THEY ARE LOOKING FOR WIN-WIN
SITUATIONS FOR ALL COUNTRIES INVOLVED, AS OPPOSED TO THE SHORTSIGHTEDNESS OF TRUMP, WHO
BELIEVES HE NEEDS TO WIN ONLY AT THE COST OF OTHERS.

(The US Treasury has recently released, in May 2016, for the first time in forty years, a *detailed* breakdown of major foreign holders of treasury securities, including Saudi Arabia, the UAE and Kuwait, amongst the others.)

In May, 2016, Trump came out with many statements which proved his ignorance of the global financial markets, especially pertaining to foreign debt.

> *"I'm the king of debt. I love debt."*
>
> *"I would borrow, knowing that if the economy crashed, you could make a deal."*
>
> *"First of all, you never have to default because you print the money."* [345]

CNN Money, presented a detailed breakdown as to why his suggestions are so reckless.

"MR. TRUMP DOESN'T HAVE A COHERENT IDEA OF WHAT HE'S TALKING ABOUT,"

The reaction on Wall Street and in Washington was that Trump can't be serious. U.S. bonds are seen as one of the safest (if not THE safest) places to put your money in the world. Tinkering with that would almost certainly hurt America for years to come.

"Mr. Trump doesn't have a coherent idea of what he's talking about," says Michael Strain, an economic policy expert at the American Enterprise Institute, a conservative think tank. "This is the bond market equivalent of *'we're going to build a wall and have Mexico pay for it.'*"

Paying creditors back anything less than the full amount calls into question the "full faith and credit" of the United States.

"People would read this as a default," says Maya MacGuineas, president of the Committee for a Responsible Federal Budget. "It's saying we're not repaying you what you're owed."

Strain, MacGuineas and many others say it would be a disastrous tactic for the United States government.

CHINA IS SPENDING BILLIONS ON AMERICAN BUSINESSES

IT WOULD ALSO HARM MILLIONS OF AMERICANS WHO HOLD U.S. BONDS IN THEIR RETIREMENT AND SAVINGS ACCOUNTS.

First of all, businesses typically buy back debt when they are in trouble. It's seen as a red flag. Investors agree to accept less money because they would rather get 80 cents on the dollar than nothing. The U.S. would have to be in terrible economic shape for this scenario to be an appealing idea.

Second, it would alarm investors in the U.S. and around the world to see the trusted U.S. Treasury playing games in the bond market. It could cause huge uncertainty, and possibly raise U.S. borrowing costs for years as investors demand higher interest payments. Other nations like China might even retaliate with trade sanctions or other economic tactics.

Third, if Trump buys back bonds at a lower price, it doesn't just hurt the Chinese and Japanese who hold the debt. It would also harm millions of Americans who hold U.S. bonds in their retirement and savings accounts.

Fourth, the federal government doesn't have any money to buy debt back with. The U.S. already has $19 trillion in debt. Trump's plan would require the U.S. Treasury to issue new debt to buy old debt. Or it would require the Federal Reserve (America's central bank) to buy the debt. That can cause inflation (or even hyperinflation), and send prices of everything from food to rent skyrocketing.

"TRUMP'S RECKLESSNESS HAS NO LIMITS, EVEN TO THE POINT OF SUGGESTING TREASURY DEBT RESTRUCTURING. HE'S PLAYING WITH MATCHES IN A VERY ARID FOREST,"

And that's to say nothing of the fact that the president doesn't control the Fed, so it's unclear how Trump could even get more money into the economy that way.

"Trump's recklessness has no limits, even to the point of suggesting Treasury debt restructuring. He's playing with matches in a very arid forest," wrote Greg Valliere, chief investment strategist at Horizon Investments.[346]

Time Magazine reported that Trump, when discussing oil prices on air with ABC's George Stephanopoulos, blustered on about the scheming malfeasance of OPEC and the kingdom of Saudi Arabia.

Trump insisted the US could leverage its military supremacy to persuade OPEC to lower prices. In his words: *"I'm going to look 'em in the eye and say, 'Fellas, you'd have your fun. Your fun is over."*[347]

But this rather naive suggestion of bullying this most essential and longstanding American ally in the Middle East — not to mention the recent customer in a megabillion dollar US weapons sale that would create tens of thousands of American jobs — was comparatively harmless when set against his next suggestion. Trump bemoaned US costs sustained during its wars in the Middle East and floated the idea of "taking" Iraqi oil.

Stephanopoulos countered incredulously, "So, we steal an oil field?"

Trump responded, *"Excuse me. You're not stealing anything. You're taking — we're reimbursing ourselves."*[348]

Given how many U.S. leaders have had to stress to their Middle East interlocutors that they're not in it simply for the oil, Trump would be starting off regional relations on pretty slippery ground.

On September 28, 2015, Pratheek Rebala, writing in *Time* Magazine, also provided very detailed information about China's state-owned companies, which are pouring billions of dollars into projects in the United States:

Michigan has welcomed more than $600 million in Chinese investment over the past four years. Overall, Chinese firms sent $6.4 billion to the U.S. in the first half of this year, according to Rhodium Group. China is the fastest-growing national investor in America, targeting real estate, hospitality and technology services, in particular, also according to Rhodium.

Earlier this month, China's Commerce Ministry predicted that the country's global outbound direct investment would exceed $1 trillion this year for the first time ever. Last year, Chinese investors established almost 30,000 enterprises overseas, according to the Commerce Ministry. For all the cash pouring in, the U.S. is still playing catch-up to Europe and the developing world.[349]

Whether Trump likes it or not, the US State Department has emphasized the close economic ties between the US and Mexico, as presented in this *Fact Sheet* from May 2015:

> U.S. relations with Mexico are strong and vital. The two countries share a 2,000-mile border, and bilateral relations

"TRUMP COULD SPOOK THE STOCK MARKET. TRUMP'S UNPREDICTABILITY INTRODUCES A NEW LEVEL OF UNCERTAINTY. IT'S A HUGE NEGATIVE FOR INVESTORS

> between the two have a direct impact on the lives and livelihoods of millions of Americans, whether the issue is trade and economic reform, education exchange, citizen security, drug control, migration, entrepreneurship and innovation, or the environment. The scope of U.S.-Mexican relations is broad and goes beyond diplomatic and official relations. It entails extensive commercial, cultural, and educational ties, with some 1.4 billion dollars of two-way trade and hundreds of thousands of legal border crossings each day. In addition, a million American citizens live in Mexico. U.S. tourists to Mexico numbered over 20 million in 2013 making Mexico the top destination of U.S. travelers. Mexican tourists to the U.S. were over 14 million in 2013, and they spent an estimated $10.5 billion.

THE REACTION OF THE COUNTRIES LIKE JAPAN, CHINA, INDIA, BRAZIL, MEXICO AND OTHERS WOULD BE TO TAKE ANY NUMBER OF ACTIONS AGAINST THE US IN RETALIATION.

Mexico is the United States' second-largest export market (after Canada) and third-largest trading partner (after Canada and China). In 2013, two-way trade in goods and services was more than $550 billion. Mexico's exports rely heavily on supplying the US market, but the country has also sought to diversify its export destinations. Nearly eighty percent of Mexico's exports in 2013 went to the United States. In 2013, Mexico was the third-largest supplier of foreign crude oil to the United States, as well as the largest export market for U.S. refined petroleum products and a growing market for US natural gas. Top US exports to Mexico include electrical machinery, nuclear equipment, motor vehicle parts, mineral fuels and oils, and plastics. Stock foreign direct investment by U.S. companies in Mexico stands at $101 billion, while Mexican investment is $17.6 billion, and has grown by over 35 percent the past five years. It is the seventh fastest growing investor country in the United States.

Education Exchange

In May 2013, President Obama and President Peña Nieto announced the US-Mexico Bilateral Forum on Higher Education, Innovation and Research (herein referred to as the Bilateral Forum) to expand opportunities for educational exchanges, scientific research partnerships, and cross-border innovation to help both countries develop a 21st century workforce for both our mutual economic prosperity and sustainable social development. The Bilateral Forum complements President Obama's 100,000 Strong in the Americas initiative, which seeks to increase student mobility between the United States and the countries of the Western Hemisphere, including Mexico. It also complements Mexico's program Proyecta 100,000 that aims to send 100,000 Mexican students to the United States and to bring 50, 000 US students to Mexico by 2018.

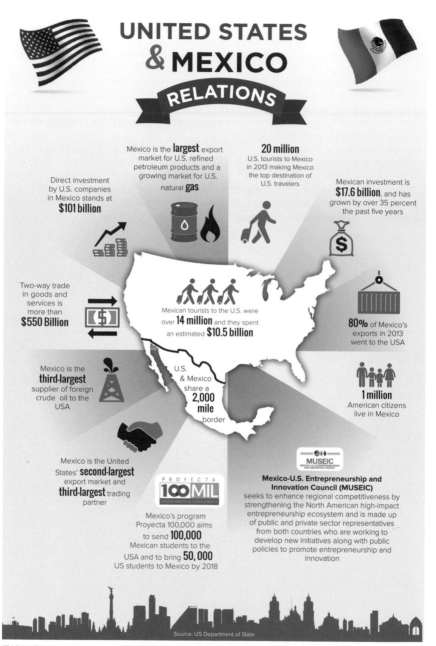

UNITED STATES
& MEXICO
RELATIONS

Mexico is the **largest** export market for U.S. refined petroleum products and a growing market for U.S. natural **gas**

Direct investment by U.S. companies in Mexico stands at **$101 billion**

20 million U.S. tourists to Mexico in 2013 making Mexico the top destination of U.S. travelers

Mexican investment is **$17.6 billion**, and has grown by over 35 percent the past five years

Two-way trade in goods and services is more than **$550 Billion**

Mexican tourists to the U.S. were over **14 million** and they spent an estimated **$10.5 billion**

80% of Mexico's exports in 2013 went to the USA

Mexico is the **third-largest** supplier of foreign crude oil to the USA

U.S. & Mexico share a **2,000 mile** border

1 million American citizens live in Mexico

Mexico is the United States' **second-largest** export market and **third-largest** trading partner

PROYECTA **100 MIL** REGIÓN ABIERTA AL CONOCIMIENTO

Mexico's program Proyecta 100,000 aims to send **100,000** Mexican students to the USA and to bring **50, 000** US students to Mexico by 2018

MUSEIC

Mexico-U.S. Entrepreneurship and Innovation Council (MUSEIC) seeks to enhance regional competitiveness by strengthening the North American high-impact entrepreneurship ecosystem and is made up of public and private sector representatives from both countries who are working to develop new initiatives along with public policies to promote entrepreneurship and innovation

Source: US Department of State

IT IS UNBELIEVABLE THAT A PRESIDENTIAL CANDIDATE IN THE US WOULD SPEAK AS TRUMP DID AGAINST MEXICO WITH ALL THIS COOPERATION AND COORDINATION ON THE TABLE.

Entrepreneurship And Innovation

Another effort is the Mexico - U. S. Entrepreneurship and Innovation Council (MUSEIC), which seeks to enhance regional competitiveness by strengthening the North American high-impact entrepreneurship ecosystem. MUSEIC is made up of public and private sector representatives from both countries who are working to develop new initiatives along with public policies to promote entrepreneurship and innovation. This work through the Bilateral Forum and MUSEIC builds upon and augments the many existing productive educational and research linkages between U.S. and Mexican academic institutions, civil society, and the private sector.[350]

TRADE DEFICITS IN MANUFACTURES HAVE PLAYED ONLY A PARTIAL ROLE IN REDUCING EMPLOYMENT—AND ALMOST NO ROLE OVER THE PAST DECADE.

Likewise, Donald Trump terrifies Wall Street, as reported by Matt Egan for *CNN Money*:

Trump could spook the stock market. Trump's unpredictability introduces a new level of uncertainty. It's a huge negative for investors, who want to map out likely outcomes before committing money to investing in the future.

"Wall Street likes knowns, not variables. And Donald Trump is a variable. I would dare to say he is a wildcard," said Peter Kenny, a thirty-year veteran of Wall Street who is chief market strategist at The Clear Pool Group, a financial technology company.

A Trump White House "would be more of a shoot-from-the-hip kind of administration," said Sam Stovall, chief investment strategist at S&P Capital IQ. "If you're concerned about uncertainty, I would be very concerned about a Trump presidency."[351]

Donald Trump's presidential campaign is built on his business acumen. But some of the Wall Street funds that he has invested in have proven less successful, underperforming industry benchmarks in the last fifteen months. Eighteen out of twenty-one hedge funds and mutual funds in Trump's portfolio lost money in 2015, and seventeen of them are down so far this year, according to public disclosures and private performance data seen by Reuters.

IN FACT, TRADE HAS TYPICALLY BOOSTED EMPLOYMENT DURING DOWNTURNS BECAUSE U.S. RECESSIONS HAVE USUALLY STARTED AT HOME—NOT IN ITS EXPORT MARKETS.

People like Trump would create game plans which in the end, would reflect back to harm the country. As the English say, "penny-wise and pound-foolish"; while he is worried about saving small amounts of money, he's extremely wasteful and foolish regarding more important matters. To clarify this point, the reaction of the countries like Japan, China, India, Brazil, Mexico and others would be to take any number of actions against the US in retaliation. As a reaction to Trump's policies, it would be highly likely for them to put high taxes on American imported products. However, Trump would not accept this reaction, as you see when he replied about the building of a wall on the border with Mexico. When the Mexicans replied in anger that they would not pay for it, as Trump insists they will, Trump turned around and said, *"The wall just got ten feet taller, believe me. It just got ten feet taller."* [352]

To further clarify the necessity of continually promoting international trade and demonstrating that it is not the core reason for American job loss, *Harvard Business Review* published:

Trade deficits in manufactures have played only a partial role in reducing employment—and almost no role over the past decade. Using input-output tables that list the job content of production, we found that in 1998 and 2010, replacing imports with domestically produced goods would have increased manufacturing employment by 2.6 million and 2.9 million in each of those years, respectively. However, over that period, manufacturing employment would have declined by 5.7 million jobs with balanced trade—just 5% less than the 6 million jobs that were lost with the trade deficits that the U.S. actually experienced.

The main cause, again, is the increasing growth in labor productivity. In current dollars, the manufacturing trade deficit was twice as large in 2010 as it was in 1998, but the output per worker was higher, so the job content of each dollar of deficit has been falling rapidly. Even if the U.S. had enjoyed balanced trade in the past two decades, the share of manufacturing in employment would still have tumbled.

Free-trade critics claim that imports have been an important contributor to unemployment, especially during the recent recession. However, we found that the association between employment growth and import growth has been positive. When Americans spend more, they create more jobs at home and they buy more final products and inputs from abroad. In fact, trade has typically boosted employment during downturns because U.S. recessions have usually started at home—not in its export markets. Even in the years after free-trade agreements were signed, employment growth in the United States has been strong. This suggests that, whatever their net effect on employment, these pacts have affected aggregate unemployment in only a modest way. [353]

At the end of March 2016, Trump scaremongered and warned against visiting Europe when he said to ABC,

"I don't think Bruss - England or I don't think that Europe is a safe place. No, I don't. I think there are a lot of problems in Europe that are very, very severe. When you look at Brussels, when you look at the way they've handled things from law enforcement standpoints, when you look at Paris, when you look at so many other places, no, it's not (safe)." [354]

This is the language of someone who exposes his scaremongering for everyone to see. He does not spare anyone in his verbal attacks, and surprisingly, this is while he is merely a candidate running for office. What about if he actually became president and dealt with the other nations of the world in a bullying, aggressive, and demeaning way? He has spoken against Japan, Mexico, China, South Korea, India, Saudi Arabia, and the continent of Europe. Surely he poses a tremendous threat for the stability and advancement of the global economy.

34

TRUMP AND **PUTIN**

TRUMP HAS SPREAD ENMITY AND SPOKE AGGRESsively and disrespectfully regarding various nations, such as Mexico, Japan, China, South Korea, India, Saudi Arabia, Europe, Kuwait, and all the Muslims in general. It is truly amazing that the foreign leader to which he has the highest level of esteem and synergy with is Vladimir Putin of Russia. *Forbes* published the following, detailing why Putin isn't necessarily the best ally to be getting close to.

SEVEN WARNINGS TO DONALD TRUMP ABOUT VLADIMIR PUTIN

by Paul Roderick Gregory of *Forbes* Magazine:

Vladimir Putin's praise of Donald Trump as "a very outstanding man, unquestionably talented" has been reciprocated by Trump's calling Putin "a man so highly respected within his own country and beyond" that they "would get along very well." Trump has shrugged off warnings of Putin's perfidy by citing lack of proof that Putin "kills journalists, political opponents and …invades countries." Only the naïve would know there will be no such proof when the Kremlin controls prosecution, justice and the secret police. Putin's hybrid warfare and its plausible deniability complicates proof of crimes against the international order, despite obvious Russian military engagement in Georgia and Ukraine. Killing journalists and political opponents is only one reason for Trump to be leery of Putin. Trump should heed seven red flags when considering how to respond to Putin's flattery:

First, Trump must know that Putin ordered the hybrid war against Ukraine that has, according to conservative United Nations estimates, killed more than 9,000 and wounded nearly 21,000. Combatants and civilians are being killed daily despite a so-called truce brokered by Russia. More than one and a half million people have been displaced and almost four million are living under desperate circumstances.

SECOND, TRUMP MUST KNOW THAT PUTIN HAS CONSISTENTLY DECLARED THE UNITED STATES AS ENEMY NUMBER ONE SINCE HIS FEBRUARY 2007 SPEECH IN MUNICH.

Second, Trump must know that Putin has consistently declared the United States as enemy number one since his February 2007 speech in Munich. In Putin's world, the United States and its NATO allies are intent on surrounding and dismembering Russia. Any aggressive actions of Russia – Georgia, Crimea, Ukraine – are therefore purely defensive in nature designed to protect Mother Russia from the world's main source of evil. How will Trump "get along very well" with a negotiating partner, whose regime's very existence requires that the U.S. play the role of Russia's major enemy?

Third, Trump must heed the classic scholarly work of noted historian John Dunlop: "The Moscow Apartment Bombings of September 1999." Dunlop uses the various commission and investigative reports that were prepared in that lost time of relative press and political freedom to present convincing evidence that Putin, the FSB (which Putin headed) and the Yeltsin regime deliberately blew up apartment buildings in three Russian cities, including Moscow. More than 300 were killed and 1,700 wounded. The bombings paved the way for the Second Chechen war, on the basis of which Putin was elected president in 2000. Prior to the bombings and the war, Putin had a minuscule favorability rating and stood little chance of being elected.

Fourth, Trump must note that Putin does not hesitate to lie publicly about important political matters, such as his April press conference statement that "there are no Russian troops in Ukraine." (He backtracked this statement at his December press conference.) Putin lied that the March 2014 annexation of Crimea was a spontaneous act of the Crimean people; no Russian troops were involved. Only later did Putin publicly admit that he had ordered work on "returning Crimea" to begin at an all-night meeting on February 22. Russia's armed annexation of Crimea was the first violation of the basic principle of secure sovereign boundaries on which the postwar international order is based.

Fifth, Trump must note that Russia is rated by the Committee to Protect Journalists in 7th place, just after Pakistan, as the most dangerous country for journalists. Iraq and Syria are at the top, and Russia is the only European country on the top list at 56 killed with motive confirmed since 1992. Only lower-level paid killers, if any, have been convicted. Russia with its armies of secret police, FSB agents and informants knows who is responsible. That Putin's KGB state has not brought any of the guilty [to trial] tells us that the Kremlin does not want these cases solved and is hence itself complicit.

Sixth, Trump must note that under Putin there have been at least eight political assassinations of national importance, not counting the murders of numerous regional and local politicians. The two most prominent murders were of opposition politician Boris Nemtsov (February 2015) and of ex-KGB agent and British citizen Alexander Litvinenko (November 2006).

The investigation of Nemtsov's murder is at the usual standstill. High-level suspects hiding in Chechnya have not been interrogated. Only low-level assassins will take the fall citing improbable Islamic-fundamentalist outrage. A London high court is currently hearing the Litvinenko case, which includes the polonium trail of the presumed assassins from and back to Russia. The London court has heard evidence of "a "*prima facie* case" of the culpability of the Russian state." The two presumed assassins are safe in Russia; one has been granted parliamentary immunity. Of particular interest is the Russian March 2006 law which allows state assassination of those who threaten national security. The Russian secret service would not assassinate a UK citizen on British soil without permission from the highest levels.

Seventh, Trump should know that, as documented in Karen Dawisha's book *Putin's Kleptocracy: Who Owns Russia?*, Putin and his inner circle have stolen a large portion of Russia's wealth. Dawisha shows that Putin runs Russia as a criminal enterprise in which "the right to property is entirely conditional upon the property owner's loyalty…" Putin's own wealth will never be known, but it would likely place him among thewealthiest in Europe if not in the world. Russia's top ten billionaires have a cumulated wealth of $125 billion. It is unlikely that their "boss" would be satisfied with less. Would Trump welcome the praise of national thieves like Marcos, Mobutu and Duvalier? I doubt it. Trump is proud he made his fortune. He did not steal it as did Putin.

A savvy negotiator must be able to size up his opponents and decide with whom to associate. [355]

35

TRUMP IS ALREADY BRINGING CHANGE – FOR THE WORSE

FOR THOSE OF US WHO KEEP OUR EYES AND EARS open, we can already see terrible shifts across different groups of people. People are changing for the worse by expressing their prejudices and acting on their repressed racist or xenophobic emotions. Trump brings this to the surface, and the fact that he is a wealthy and powerful graduate of the Wharton School of Business provides him with an air of legitimacy – the kind of example some want to follow.

In cities and towns across America, minorities are reporting a rise in hate-related oppression and threats.

One example is the small town of Pocatello, Idaho. There are 87,380 students from Saudi Arabia studying in the United States, and many of them live here.

A comfortable town that's loved by its residents, until recently the visiting students from Saudi Arabia and Kuwait were welcomed harmoniously into the community. There was even a documentary produced in 2014 featuring students of Idaho State University, ISU. The documentary highlighted how comfortable, friendly, and relaxed the community was.

IN CITIES AND TOWNS ACROSS AMERICA, MINORITIES ARE REPORTING A RISE IN HATE-RELATED OPPRESSION AND THREATS.

But in April 2016, anti-Muslim hate crimes flared up that were unlike what had ever been seen there before. This included distribution of anti-Muslim CDs and messages, home invasions, and burglaries of Muslim homes. It has been reported by ABC News that at the time of this writing, these actions are being investigated by the Idaho US Attorney's office as hate crimes.[356]

Due to these reports of discrimination, Kuwait's minister of higher education will no longer give scholarships to ISU; likewise, the Saudi Arabian Cultural Mission has suspended scholarships too.

ISU and city officials all agree that international students are a benefit to the community, and that it's not the entire community who feel this hatred. The current mayor, Brian Blad, says the community should value its international students because of the culture they bring; he doesn't want to see that go away. "If you want to wipe away all the diversity out of a community, then you have a very narrow minded and narrow focused people."

Kent Tingey, ISU's vice president of advancement, said, "It's a tremendous richness; it enhances not just the university, but the whole community so that people can understand someone who may come from a different situation. And it just makes life more rich and better for everybody."

In a letter, ISU's president said, "Our international students will carry messages home about what America and Americans are like." He hopes that ISU and Pocatello can be a good example.

Mayor Blad said that if the international students were to leave ISU, it could cost the city between three hundred to four hundred million dollars every year.[357]

These hate crimes are something completely new and previously alien to this tight-knit community. We believe there are good reasons to blame the rise of Trump for encouraging these toxic sentiments.

This is just one case study of what's happening in one town. How devastating to the US economy would the effects be if

MAYOR BLAD SAID THAT IF THE INTERNATIONAL STUDENTS WERE TO LEAVE ISU, IT COULD COST THE CITY BETWEEN THREE HUNDRED TO FOUR HUNDRED MILLION DOLLARS EVERY YEAR.

the same were to happen in one hundred towns or cities? That could mean a loss of thirty to forty billion dollars annually, severely hurting the economies of those affected states. The demise and total collapse of the Soviet Union was due to its economic difficulties, and likewise the US threatens itself with the very same type of collapse if it does not reject those propagating Trump's disease. Those Trumpians would jeopardize hundreds of American jobs and cause great hardships for both the government and its citizens. I'm warning my readers to beware of allowing the same disaster which happened to the Soviet Union happen to America, by the actions of those carrying Trump's same way of thinking.

36

TRUMP LEADS TO **WORLD WAR**

TRUMP'S IGNORANCE COULD LEAD TO A WORLD war. We understand from the disease in Trump's speech and ideas that he wants to spend more to build up the military, as he has mentioned. However, the question here is: Is this really the way to help strengthen and build the US economy as he claims? From Trump's naivety and arrogance, he believes that being the biggest bully is a viable approach to cure the nation's problems. Maybe this attitude was successful in the boardroom where he may have employed strong-arm tactics while negotiating a business deal. But it is not only money on the table to be won or lost; it is the lives of human

> FROM TRUMP'S NAIVETY AND ARROGANCE, HE BELIEVES THAT BEING THE BIGGEST BULLY IS A VIABLE APPROACH TO CURE THE NATION'S PROBLEMS.

GLOBAL MILITARY SPENDING GROWS

Global military spending rose in 2015 to nearly $1.7 trillion, the first increase since 2011, driven by Middle East conflicts including the battle against Islamic State, the Saudi-led war in Yemen and fears about Iran

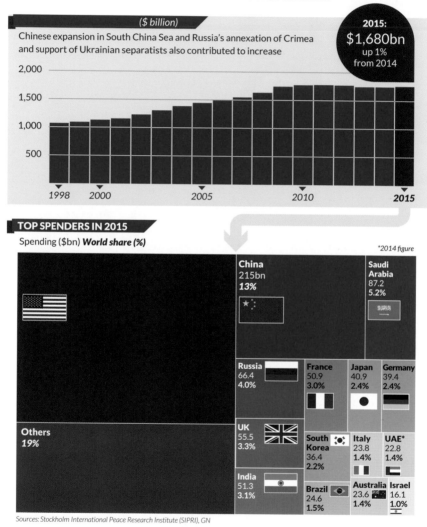

Sources: Stockholm International Peace Research Institute (SIPRI), GN

THESE NUMBERS SHOW CLEARLY THAT AMERICA IS TRULY A WORLD POWER BOTH MILITARILY AND ECONOMICALLY. THE MANUFACTURING SECTOR OF THE US ALONE IS THE 9TH LARGEST ECONOMY IN THE WORLD.

beings that he is excited to be gambling with.

Trump says: *"I'm gonna build a military that's gonna be much stronger than it is right now,"* and, *"It's gonna be so strong, nobody's gonna mess with us."* [358]

This is what he claims to be the path to success. But indeed this is clearly not the path to strengthening international relations; rather it is a language that leads to confrontations and wars. For example, let's examine his aggressive and hostile intention of building a wall between the United States and Mexico:

Trump has made these statements, and more:

"When do we beat Mexico at the border? They're laughing at us, at our stupidity. And now they are beating us economically. They are not our friend; believe me." [359]

"Mexico does not like us. Mexico is not our friend. Mexico is the new China." [360]

"They're killing us at the border and they're killing us on jobs and trade. FIGHT!" [361]

"We get the killers, drugs, and crime, they get the money!" [362]

"We're going to build a great wall & Mexico will pay for it." [363]

Can you believe that this is the language he uses with his neighbor? Trumps speaks like this even though Mexico is the largest export market for US petroleum products, and in 2013 the two-way trade of goods and services with Mexico was more than $550 billion.

Then he immediately followed up with:
"Nobody would be tougher on ISIS than Donald Trump." [364]

Yes, everyone should be tough on ISIS, but look how he speaks about Mexico and ISIS at the same time, in the same tone, and in the same way. Why? They are not the same and not even similar! Using this type of language will lead America to a war that is of no benefit at all for America.

Trump was asked on *CBS This Morning* about how he would handle the ruler of North Korea, he replied that he would *"Get China to make that guy disappear in one form or another very quickly"* and also said:

USING THIS TYPE OF LANGUAGE WILL LEAD AMERICA TO A WAR THAT IS OF NO BENEFIT AT ALL FOR AMERICA.

"China has control, absolute control, of North Korea. They don't say it but they do. And they should make that problem disappear. China is sucking us dry. They're taking our money, they're taking our jobs, they're doing so much. We have built China with what they have taken out. We have power over China." [365]

A Trump campaign press release said, *"Donald J. Trump is calling for a total and complete shutdown of Muslims entering the United States until our country's representatives can figure out what is going on."* [366]

This plan was promptly denounced by many of America's closest allies. "I think his remarks are divisive, stupid and wrong," remarked UK Prime Minister David Cameron, "and I think if he came to visit our country, he'd unite us all against him." [367]

Does America really want to enter more wars? Whether it likes it or not, America has a leadership role in maintaining peace in the world. This is because it is the most powerful country and has the necessary influence to keep most of the world's problems under control. If the United States were to take a step back, surely the world would face a disaster. This would not stop in the Middle East; it would spread to Europe, Asia, Africa, and into the United States itself. If the US did not lead in being both

IF THE UNITED STATES WERE TO TAKE A STEP BACK, SURELY THE WORLD WOULD FACE A DISASTER.

just and stable, the world would not be just and stable either. If the US did not take responsibility, disaster would result. It would be too difficult for all the world's militaries to control the chaos.

To help point out the reality of this risk, let us look to the mentalities of some countries who arm themselves with nuclear weapons, in preparation for war, despite the poverty and direness of their situations and populations.

One example of such a country is Iran. Many people in Iran travel to work in the Gulf countries to earn money to help pay for chemotherapy for their loved ones. Why would they do this? Let us look to how the World Bank has described the situation in Iran:

> The unemployment rate has remained stubbornly high and rose slightly in 2014. The unemployment rate reached 11.4% in 2014, up from 10.4% in 2013. The unemployment rate was much more elevated among women (20.3% for women against 8.7% for men), among the population between the ages of 15 and 29 (17.9% for men and 39% for women in this age cohort) and in urban areas (11.7% in urban areas and 7.4% in rural areas). This weak labor market performance took place within a context of a subdued and declining labor force participation rate with only 37.2% of the country's population being economically active in 2014, down from 37.6% in 2013 (62.9% for men and 11.8% for women). The incidence of underemployment has also become more prevalent, with an estimated 9.5% of workers being considered underemployed (10.3% for men and 4.8% for women). Underemployment is largely concentrated among the youth population.

> Stimulating private sector growth and job creation is a mounting challenge for the new government considering the number of workers who should enter the labor market in the coming years, including women and youth. Weak labor market conditions are exacerbated by the large number of youth entering the labor market and low female labor force participation rate. This trend is expected to be maintained in line with the evolving socio-economic profile with the demographics of the country characterized by a disproportionately high youth population with over 60% of Iran's population of 77 million individuals estimated to be under the age of 30 in 2013. The government estimates that 8.5 million jobs should be created in the following two years to reduce the unemployment rate to 7% by 2016. Tackling youth unemployment in particular is a pressing policy issue.

> In 2005, poverty was 1.45% in Iran using a poverty line of US$1.25 per day (PPP). World Bank projections estimate that only 0.7% of the population (half a million people) lived under

Iran's High Military Funding & Its Sources

BASIC FACTS:

Tehran

Name: Islamic Republic of Iran
Capital: Tehran
Population: 81,824,270

Armed Forces of Iran include:

Islamic Republic of Iran Army
Size: 420,000 personnel

Iranian Revolutionary Guard Corps (IRGC)
Size: 125,000 personnel

Law Enforcement Force of Islamic Republic (Police)
Size: 500,000 personnel

DEFENSE BUDGET[1]

THE IRGC GETS 60%

2015 $10 billion   2016 $11-12 billion

up 32% from 2014

$54.5 billion[2]   **OIL STABILIZATION FUND**

February 2014

and its supplement National Development Fund

THE MILITARY CAN GET MONEY FOR SPECIAL OR URGENT PROJECTS. THE OIL FUND IS NOT TRANSPARENT

FINANCIAL ACTIVITIES   **$15-18 billion[3]**

20% of the Tehran Stock Exchange

OWNERSHIP OF THOUSANDS OF COMPANIES IN THE MOST LUCRATIVE SECTORS OF IRAN'S ECONOMY

$60 billion[4]   **UNDERGROUND ECONOMY**

Assuming a conservative 15%

including smuggling, drug trafficking

HAS BEEN ESTIMATED FROM 6% TO 36% OF IRAN'S GDP THE IRGC IS IN THE BEST POSITION TO HAVE THE LARGEST SHARE

Sources of data: 1) Proposal of the budget for the 2015 fiscal year made by Iranian President Hassan Rouhani. http://www.reuters.com/article/us-iran-economy-idUSKBN0JL0H120141207; 2)Columbia Center on Sustainable Investment's research: http://ccsi.columbia.edu/files/2014/04/nrf_Iran_February_2014_RWI_VCC.pdf; 3) Center for the National Interest's Report: http://nationalinterest.org/feature/who-really-controls-irans-economy-12925?; 4) The Business Insider's Report: http://www.businessinsider.com/how-irans-mafia-like-revolutionary-guard-rules-the-countrys-black-market-2015-12

this poverty line in 2010, although a large proportion of people are living close to it. Indeed, raising the poverty line by US$0.5 (from US$2 to US$2.50 and from US$3 to US$3.50) could put 4%-6% of the population – over 4.5 million people - in poverty.

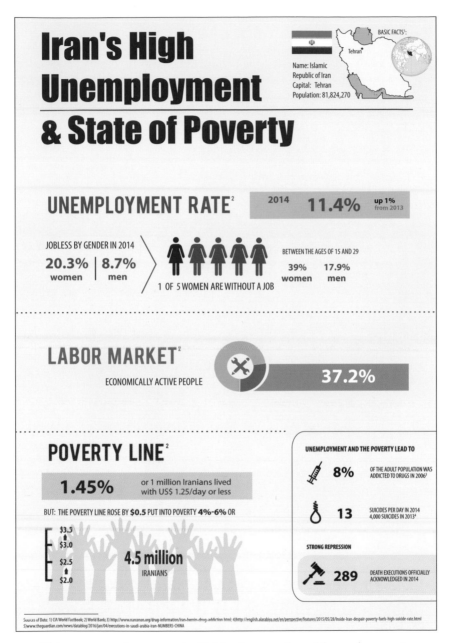

Iran's High Unemployment & State of Poverty

Name: Islamic Republic of Iran
Capital: Tehran
Population: 81,824,270

BASIC FACTS[1]:
Tehran

UNEMPLOYMENT RATE[2]

2014 **11.4%** up 1% from 2013

JOBLESS BY GENDER IN 2014
20.3% | **8.7%**
women | men

1 OF 5 WOMEN ARE WITHOUT A JOB

BETWEEN THE AGES OF 15 AND 29
39% **17.9%**
women men

LABOR MARKET[2]

ECONOMICALLY ACTIVE PEOPLE

37.2%

POVERTY LINE[2]

1.45% or 1 million Iranians lived with US$ 1.25/day or less

BUT: THE POVERTY LINE ROSE BY **$0.5** PUT INTO POVERTY **4%-6%** OR

$3.5
$3.0
$2.5
$2.0

4.5 million IRANIANS

UNEMPLOYMENT AND THE POVERTY LEAD TO

8% OF THE ADULT POPULATION WAS ADDICTED TO DRUGS IN 2006[3]

13 SUICIDES PER DAY IN 2014 4,000 SUICIDES IN 2013[4]

STRONG REPRESSION

289 DEATH EXECUTIONS OFFICIALLY ACKNOWLEDGED IN 2014

Sources of Data: 1) CIA World Factbook; 2) World Bank; 3) http://www.narconon.org/drug-information/iran-heroin-drug-addiction.html; 4)http://english.alarabiya.net/en/perspective/features/2015/05/28/Inside-Iran-despair-poverty-fuels-high-suicide-rate.html 5)www.theguardian.com/news/datablog/2016/jan/04/executions-in-saudi-arabia-iran-NUMBERS-CHINA

This suggests that many individuals are vulnerable to changes in their personal disposable income and to the persistent rise in the cost of living.[368]

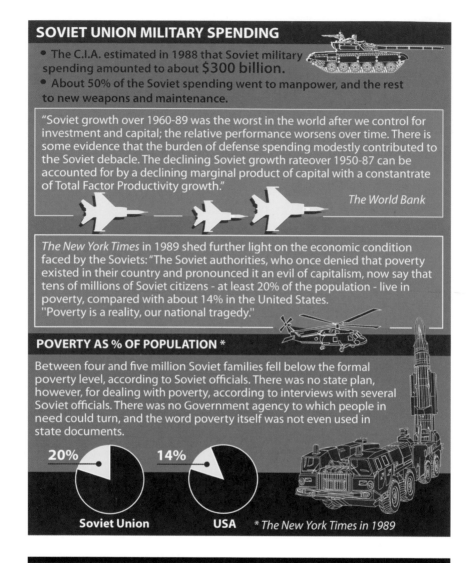

SOVIET UNION MILITARY SPENDING

- The C.I.A. estimated in 1988 that Soviet military spending amounted to about $300 billion.
- About 50% of the Soviet spending went to manpower, and the rest to new weapons and maintenance.

"Soviet growth over 1960-89 was the worst in the world after we control for investment and capital; the relative performance worsens over time. There is some evidence that the burden of defense spending modestly contributed to the Soviet debacle. The declining Soviet growth rateover 1950-87 can be accounted for by a declining marginal product of capital with a constantrate of Total Factor Productivity growth."

The World Bank

The New York Times in 1989 shed further light on the economic condition faced by the Soviets: "The Soviet authorities, who once denied that poverty existed in their country and pronounced it an evil of capitalism, now say that tens of millions of Soviet citizens - at least 20% of the population - live in poverty, compared with about 14% in the United States. "Poverty is a reality, our national tragedy."

POVERTY AS % OF POPULATION *

Between four and five million Soviet families fell below the formal poverty level, according to Soviet officials. There was no state plan, however, for dealing with poverty, according to interviews with several Soviet officials. There was no Government agency to which people in need could turn, and the word poverty itself was not even used in state documents.

20%   14%

Soviet Union   **USA**   * The New York Times in 1989

THE SOVIET UNION, WHICH SPENT BILLIONS ON ITS PLANES, BOMBS, AND MILITARY, YET IT DID NOT POSSESS ENOUGH MONEY TO PAY REGULAR SALARIES TO ITS EMPLOYEES. FINALLY, IT COMPLETELY BROKE DOWN BECAUSE OF ITS ECONOMIC PROBLEMS.

Do you believe a country with all of these disastrous economic factors would actually want to arm itself with nuclear weapons and to fund its military so heavily? No one would expect it, but this is the actual situation we are facing. The madness of some leaders is astonishing.

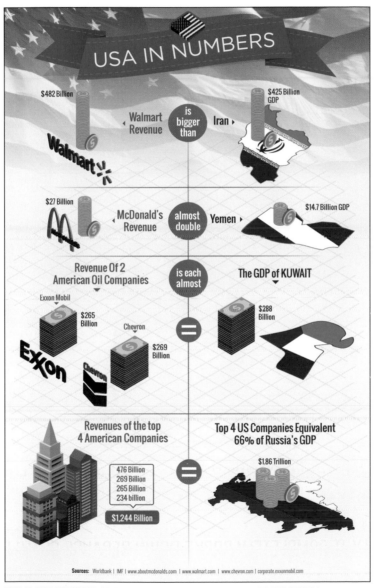

THIS IS THE STRENGTH OF AMERICA IN NUMBERS, COMPARED TO THE OTHERS.

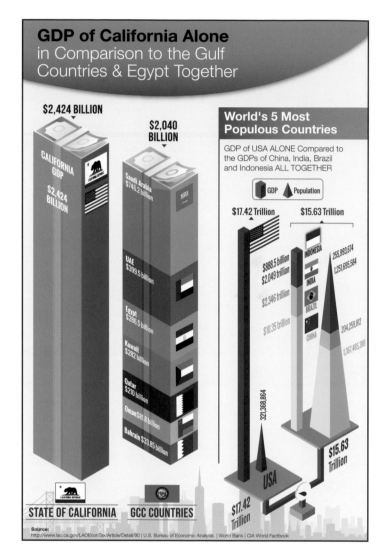

A second example is the former Soviet Union, which spent billions on its planes, bombs, and military, yet it did not possess enough money to pay regular salaries to its employees. Finally, it completely broke down because of its economic problems.[369]

Between four and five million Soviet families fell below the formal poverty level, according to Soviet officials, who nonetheless refused to use the word "poverty" in state documents.[370]

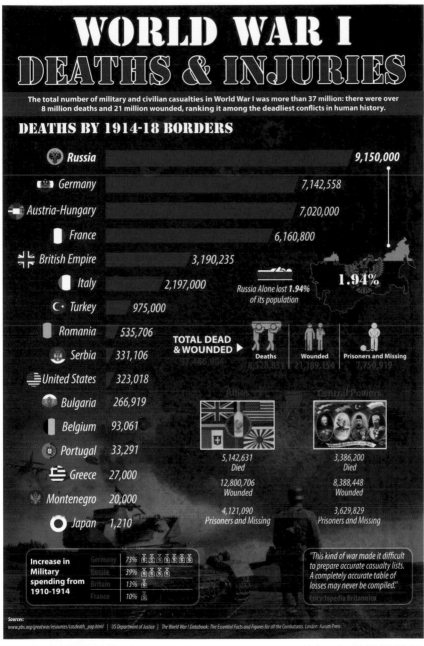

WORLD WAR I
DEATHS & INJURIES

The total number of military and civilian casualties in World War I was more than 37 million: there were over 8 million deaths and 21 million wounded, ranking it among the deadliest conflicts in human history.

DEATHS BY 1914-18 BORDERS

Russia	9,150,000
Germany	7,142,558
Austria-Hungary	7,020,000
France	6,160,800
British Empire	3,190,235
Italy	2,197,000
Turkey	975,000
Romania	535,706
Serbia	331,106
United States	323,018
Bulgaria	266,919
Belgium	93,061
Portugal	33,291
Greece	27,000
Montenegro	20,000
Japan	1,210

Russia Alone lost **1.94%** of its population

1.94%

TOTAL DEAD & WOUNDED ▶

Deaths · Wounded · Prisoners and Missing

Allies

5,142,631 Died
12,800,706 Wounded
4,121,090 Prisoners and Missing

Central Powers

3,386,200 Died
8,388,448 Wounded
3,629,829 Prisoners and Missing

Increase in Military spending from 1910-1914	Germany	73%
	Russia	39%
	Britain	13%
	France	10%

"This kind of war made it difficult to prepare accurate casualty lists. A completely accurate table of losses may never be compiled."
Encyclopedia Britannica

Sources:
www.pbs.org/greatwar/resources/casdeath_pop.html | US Department of Justice | The World War I Databook: The Essential Facts and Figures for all the Combatants. London: Aurum Press

DESPITE THE TERRIBLE LOSS OF LIFE BROUGHT ABOUT BY THE FIRST WORLD WAR, HITLER DIDN'T RE-FLECT UPON IT AND ONLY SOUGHT TO FEED HIS EGOTISTICAL CRAVING FOR POWER BY ANY MEANS NEC-ESSARY.

WHAT IF THE ENEMIES OF AMERICA WERE TO SEND THEIR WEAPONS TO MEXICO OR OTHER NEIGHBORING COUNTRIES, JUST AS THE SOVIET UNION PREVIOUSLY ARRANGED WITH CUBA?

This has been the mindset of those Iranians and Soviets, spending money to gain power, even if the population becomes destitute. To emphasize this point and show the gravity of the Soviet Union's financial weakness, modern day Russia, which has advanced substantially since the Soviet era, has a GDP which is dwarfed by that of the United States. The revenue of just four of America's largest companies totals $1.244 trillion, while the total GDP of Russia is $1.86 trillion. Those four companies alone are equivalent to a whopping 66% of Russia's total GDP.[371]

Do you think that if the United States took a step back, chaos would not ensue? What if the enemies of America were to send their weapons to Mexico or other neighboring countries, just as the Soviet Union previously arranged with Cuba?

The countries of the world have become even closer to each other due to the many advancements in technology and communications. It is too dangerous to push the world away from the United States.

The status of the United States as the leading world power comes at a price the country must pay with its wealth, its citizens, and its efforts. This is the "leadership tax." And if Americans say "no" and reject this responsibility, there is a greater price as an alternative – but that would mean destruction. Without US involvement, the world can neither handle it nor afford it. America is the strongest and richest nation in the world, and also has the largest companies, universities, and military. As Bloomberg reported, it also has the history of being the most innovative. Due to its success, it needs to bear the cost of actualizing justice in the world.

IT WAS HIS CRAVING FOR WEALTH AND POWER BY ANY MEANS NECESSARY THAT DROVE HIM INTO STARTING THE SECOND WORLD WAR.

Consider the reason for World War II, which was similar to what Trump is trying to accomplish. Trump clearly wants to build up America's military strength in order to overpower and take the resources of other nations. This is the same way of thinking which led to WWII, when Hitler was seeking resources and power for Germany. The war was virtually unprecedented in the slaughter, carnage, and destruction it caused.

THE WORLD CAN SEE WITH OPEN EYES THAT TRUMP'S PLAN FOR AMERICA RESEMBLES THOSE VERY SAME STEPS AND DIRECTION WHICH HITLER TOOK

Hitler did not learn from the First World War, so he put himself and the people into a terrible situation. It was his craving for wealth and power by any means necessary that drove him into starting the Second World War. His goal was to utilize his military strength and power to overcome other nations in order to strengthen Germany's economy and make it great again.

Trump said, *"We're not in the position we used to be – I think that we were a very powerful, a very wealthy country; we're a poor country now, a debtor nation."* [372]

On Twitter, he said, *"Trump is not afraid of anything or anyone – the President of the USA needs to unite us & knock the socks off our enemies!"* [373]

To clarify the disease of Trump-Hitler even more, when Trump was asked about taking Iraqi oil, he was asked, "So, we steal an oil field?"

He responded, *"Excuse me. You're not stealing anything. You're taking — we're reimbursing ourselves."* [374]

"I would do things that would be so tough that I don't even know if they'd be around to come to the table. I would take away their wealth. I would take away the oil. What you should be doing now is taking away the oil." [375]

The world can see with open eyes that Trump's plan for America resembles those very same steps and direction which Hitler took, only decades ago – but in another way.

Likewise we must examine how Trump responded when he was asked about his plans to withdraw US troops from Japan and South Korea, and that they should begin taking responsibility for their own security. He said: *"Now, **does that mean nuclear? It could mean nuclear. It's a very scary nuclear world."*** [376] This stance was firmly rejected by the leaders of both those countries, as the proliferation of nuclear weapons only makes the world a more dangerous place for everyone.

It was a touchstone of British propaganda during World War II that "Careless talk costs lives". To this we might add that careless talk may cause wars as well!

37

VISUALIZING TRUMP'S PRESIDENCY

O N SUNDAY, APRIL 9, 2016, THE HIGHLY RESPECT-
ed *Boston Globe* published an imaginary front page that forecast
the first day of a Trump presidency. The headline across the top
of the page announced, "DEPORTATIONS TO BEGIN." The subhead read,
"Curfews extended in multiple cities."

Another story was headlined, "Markets sink as trade war looms." Yet
another headline read, "US soldiers refuse orders to kill ISIS families."

To accompany this shocking preview of a Trump presidency, the editorial board of the *Globe* wrote:

> Donald J. Trump's vision for the future of our nation is as
> deeply disturbing as it is profoundly un-American.
>
> It is easy to find historical antecedents. The rise of demagog-
> ic strongmen is an all too common phenomenon on our small
> planet. And what marks each of those dark episodes is a failure

to fathom where a leader's vision leads, to carry rhetoric to its logical conclusion. The satirical front page of this section attempts to do just that, to envision what America looks like with Trump in the White House.

It is an exercise in taking a man at his word. And his vision of America promises to be as appalling in real life as it is in black and white on the page. It is a vision that demands an active and engaged opposition. It requires an opposition as focused on denying Trump the White House as the candidate is flippant and reckless about securing it.

DONALD J. TRUMP'S VISION FOR THE FUTURE OF OUR NATION IS AS DEEPLY DISTURBING AS IT IS PROFOUNDLY UN-AMERICAN.

After Wisconsin, the odds have shrunk that Trump will arrive in Cleveland with the requisite 1,237 delegates needed to win the nomination outright. Yet if he's denied that nomination for falling short of the required delegates, Trump has warned, "You'd have riots. I think you'd have riots." Indeed, who knows what Trump's fervent backers are capable of if emboldened by the defeat of their strongman at the hands of the hated party elite.

But the rules are the rules — and if no candidate reaches that magic number, the job of choosing a nominee falls to those on the convention floor.

That's not a pretty picture. But then nothing about the billionaire real estate developer's quest for the nation's highest office has been pretty. He winks and nods at political violence at his rallies. He says he wants to "open up" libel laws to punish critics in the news media and calls them "scum." He promised to shut out an entire class of immigrants and visitors to the United States on the sole basis of their religion.

The toxic mix of violent intimidation, hostility to criticism, and explicit scapegoating of minorities shows a political movement is taking hold in America. If Trump were a politician running such a campaign in a foreign country right now, the US State Department would probably be condemning him."

What follows is the satirical front page of Donald Trump's America. What you read on this page is what might happen by 2017 if the GOP frontrunner can put his ideas into practice and his words into action. Many Americans might find this vision appealing, but the Globe's editorial board finds it deeply troubling.[377]

'IF TRUMP WERE A POLITICIAN RUNNING SUCH A CAMPAIGN IN A FOREIGN COUNTRY RIGHT NOW, THE US STATE DEPARTMENT WOULD PROBABLY BE CONDEMNING HIM.'

The Boston Globe

Sunday, April 9, 2017

DEPORTATIONS TO BEGIN

President Trump calls for tripling of ICE force; riots continue

Curfews extended in multiple cities

PRESIDENT TRUMP has set in motion one of his most controversial campaign promises, calling on Congress to fund a "massive deportation force" by tripling the number of federal Immigration and Customs Enforcement agents.

The president made the announcement in a nationally televised address last night from the Old Post Office building in Washington, D.C., now a Trump International Hotel. In a surprise move after the speech, Trump invited Attorney General Chris Christie to stand right next to him at the podium to field questions. "#no_side_eye for Christie this time," tweeted Fox News Channel reporter Megyn Kelly, who was covering the speech from a sports bar near Rockefeller Center because she has been placed on a White House blacklist.

Although Trump reiterated his promise to eject some 11.3 million illegal workers on a two-year timetable — "so fast that your head will spin" — he also promised to "do it humanely." He said he intends to flesh out the policy with special adviser George Papadopoulos, just as soon as the 2009 college grad returns from a preplanned Model UN session in Geneva.

The $400 billion deportation program promises to be one of the most disruptive government actions attempted since desegregation. Economists estimated ICE would need more than 900,000 agents to complete the deportations in the next two years.

Thousands of protesters remain camped outside the Trump International Hotel and around the fence of

the White House. Singing and chanting have been audible inside the executive mansion day and night for weeks. The scent of tear gas pervades Lafayette Square. After Trump vowed to strip federal funding from sanctuary cities during his campaign, round-the-clock protests in Cambridge, Mass., shut down the Red Line temporarily, forcing scores of attendees at an elite Harvard/MIT techfest to evacuate Kendall Square and

take the MBTA's #1 Bus across the Charles River to an alternate site in Boston.

Already in California, armed ICE agents confronted 30 illegal strawberry pickers on a Santa Barbara County farm and bused them to a detention center to await prosecution and a government-chartered flight back to Mexico. State officials held a press conference shortly after the raid to express concern about the economic impact if

"dishes go unwashed in the kitchens of San Francisco restaurants and if our $3 billion strawberry crop is ultimately left to rot."

Trump downplayed fears that the deportations would hurt industries that rely on illegal workers. "Don't forget . . . you have millions of people that are waiting in line to come into this country, and they're waiting to come in legally."

DEPORTATIONS, Page T10

LIVE NOW: PRESIDENT ADDRESSES THE NATION

BREAKING NEWS

TRUMP: DEPORT ILLEGALS 'SO FAST YOUR HEAD WILL SPIN'

Markets sink as trade war looms

WORLDWIDE STOCKS plunged again Friday, completing the worst month on record as trade wars with both China and Mexico seem imminent.

Markets from the Dow to the FTSE to the Nikkei have sunk on speculation that China is dumping some of its US Treasury holdings after the Trump administration announced tariffs as high as 45 percent for all Chinese imports and 35 percent for some Mexican goods.

"I don't mind trade wars when we're losing $58 billion a year," the president said last year. But Chinese officials have made it no secret that they will not let tariffs go unanswered. The Asian giant is the largest holder of US debt, owning some

Dow declines at record pace

$1.4 trillion worth, according to Federal Reserve figures.

The tariffs — and any retaliatory actions — directly threaten American supply chains, especially in the country's auto and agriculture industries.

Investors are spooked, and global recession now seems possible. "Imposing tariffs or putting up trade barriers may sound good, but it will hurt our economy and credibility," Wendy Cutler, the former acting deputy US trade representative told Reuters in 2016.

It's been long feared China could sink the US economy if it were to unload its holdings of US Treasuries, sending borrowing costs skyrocketing. "No one sees how we get out of this spiral if Trump doesn't let up," one Bloomberg economist said.

STOCKS, Page T8

In the news

Bank glitch halts border wall work

LAREDO, Texas — Construction on the new border wall with Mexico stopped suddenly on Friday, dealing a major setback to one of President Trump's key campaign promises, after Mexico refused to pay.

Hastily hired work crews had already been building sections of the wall along stretches of arid borderland in Texas, Arizona, and New Mexico. The shortfall means that Trump may have to turn to Congress to kick in back wages and repay the short-term loans he arranged with government-authorized cement contractors working out of a social club in Queens, N.Y.

Trump on Nobel prize short list

IT'S NOT MIDDLE East peace, at least not yet. But Nobel-watchers were abuzz with speculation that President Trump might be on the short list for the coveted 2017 peace prize when awards are announced in October. His feat? Healing a 1,385-year-old schism between Sunni and Shi'ite Muslims, which has fueled bloody conflicts across the globe for centuries.

Editor's note

This is Donald Trump's America. What you read on this page is what might happen if the GOP front-runner can put his ideas into practice, his words into action. Many Americans might find this vision appealing, but the Globe's editorial board finds it deeply troubling. Read our editorial on Page K2 for more on the dangers of Trump's vision.

US soldiers refuse orders to kill ISIS families

> 'We have a civilian-controlled military for a reason'
>
> — SENIOR ADMINISTRATION OFFICIAL

THE MILITARY FACES "a crisis of good order and discipline," Pentagon officials said yesterday, after days of widespread unrest in the ranks over White House orders to kill relatives of ISIS militants.

More protests were planned in support of two Army Special Forces soldiers who disobeyed direct orders to kill everyone in an ISIS compound. An Air Force drone pilot will face lesser charges in connection with the raid near Raqqa, Syria. Two militants were killed in a firefight, but three women and two children were left alive, contrary to orders issued directly by President Trump.

"When the president promised to take out families of radical Islamic terrorists, he meant it," a senior administration official told reporters traveling on Air Force One. "We have a civilian-controlled military for a reason."

A clash between the military and the White House has been brewing since the campaign, when former CIA chief General Michael Hayden explicitly warned that "American armed forces would refuse to act" if Trump ordered an attack on terrorist families.

New libel law targets 'absolute scum' in press

Legislation could supplant state laws

A REPUBLICAN-CONTROLLED Congress last night passed sweeping changes to libel law in the United States, moving the bill to the desk of the new president who has promised to sign it. The legislation, a fulfillment of a Trump campaign promise, will make US libel law similar to Great Britain's and is expected to expose journalists to frequent high-dollar lawsuits. Hundreds of the country's top legal scholars called the law "an evisceration of the First Amendment," temporarily eliciting a rare note of sympathy for trial lawyers and journalists.

Both the House and Senate support the so-called LAME Act [Limiting American Media Entitlement Act], named for the epithet that conservatives love to hurl at the press. "Seventy to 75 percent of reporters are absolutely dishonest. Absolute scum. Remember that. Scum. Scum. Totally dishonest people," Trump said in a ceremony on Capitol Hill with WWE star Hulk Hogan, who won a $140 million lawsuit against Gawker.com for release of a sex tape. "And I haven't even gotten to privacy yet," Trump said.

lawsuit has a better chance of prevailing. The United States has had no federal libel laws to "open up" as Trump suggested. But the laws voted on this week would change that, supplanting current state laws that are considered more press-friendly.

LIBEL, Page T4

GETTY IMAGES

China's President Xi Jinping and his wife, Peng Liyuan, waved as they boarded an Air China plane in 2015.

PRESIDENT TRUMP, who campaigned on a platform to reform trade relations with China and to "make America great again," touched off a diplomatic crisis last week after insulting Peng Liyuan, the fashionable first lady of China who has been dubbed the "Chinese Kate Middleton." Trump tweeted out a photo of his new pet shar-pei, a wrinkly puppy named Madame Peng. But he was unrepentant, saying his foreign policy needs to be "unpredictable." Trump added: "I don't know why she's so offended, I love cute puppies and I love women! It's not like I tweeted out a photo of a Rottweiler named Merkel."

SHUTTERSTOCK

Inside

NASA engineers halted the launch of an unmanned probe amid fears that its new gold leaf trim would interfere with radio communications. **T3**

Japanese Emperor Akihito formally censured Ambassador Kid Rock for a speech calling on US allies to "Let the [expletive] business guy run the [expletive] country like a [expletive] business." **T6**

Heavy spring snow closed Yellowstone National Park for the first time since it dropped its loser name, Yellowstone, in January. **T7**

Education Secretary Omarosa Manigault summoned PBS officials to Capitol Hill to discuss remaking "Celebrity Apprentice" using hand puppets. **T8**

"A Trumping to Remember," the president's first romance novel, was yanked from the shelves after the publisher acknowledged portions were cribbed from a May 1986 edition of Penthouse. **T9**

CONCLUSIONS

38

CAN AN INDIVIDUAL OF A NATION, ACTING ALONE, BRING ABOUT ITS RECTIFICATION?

"GIVE TRUMP A CHANCE"

THERE ARE THOSE WHO SAY AMERICA SHOULD "give Trump a chance," but the presidential role is not a game in which you can merely give someone a chance. The leader of America, by necessity, becomes the leader of the strongest military with the strongest nuclear weapons, the strongest stock exchange, banks, universities, currency, and the strongest global influence. The president is responsible for the well being of more than 330 million Americans. This

is a very serious matter, and it would be foolish to gamble with someone who is unpredictable and reckless. Everyone who votes to put Trump into the White House is responsible for that choice and the grave outcomes that can be expected. If he's elected, the nation will be stuck with him and his policies for four whole years. It's not worth the risk – it's a serious responsibility.

Don't be faced with the agony of regret that will be felt by those who choose to put Trump into power. Not just any power, but the power to influence nations from the east to the west.

What is contained in this book is sufficient for a person of intellect to recognize the danger Trump poses, especially if he's given the opportunity to control tremendous power. The loss of lives and livelihoods across the world would be too terrible and costly. It's not something to just try.

> *"Whatsoever a man soweth, that shall he also reap."*
> *– Galatians 6: 7-8 (King James Version).*

CAN AN INDIVIDUAL OF A NATION, ACTING ALONE, BRING ABOUT ITS RECTIFICATION?

This chapter heading raises an important issue that's not addressed by political analysts. Societies are always looking for the person who will solve the problems they're facing, discover new opportunities for their populations, and be their hero. As Singapore's Lee Kuan Yew reputedly said, "Fighting corruption is like cleaning stairs: To be successful, one has to start at the top."[378] At first glance, it may appear to be a correct statement, but the reality is much more complicated than how he phrased it. The reason is that merely replacing the head of a government is never enough to bring about positive change.

It is never, and will never, really be that simple for Trump's supporters to accomplish everything they are trying to do in the current situation, and here's why. As discussed previously, Trump has only reached this level of

HE IS THEIR PREJUDICE, BIGOTRY, SHORTSIGHTEDNESS, HASTINESS, GREED, DISTRUST, SUSPICION, AND HYPERNATIONALISM.

success in grabbing the Republican presidential nomination because he is a reflection of who is supporting him. He is the embodiment of who they are. He is their prejudice, bigotry, shortsightedness, hastiness, greed, distrust, suspicion, and hypernationalism. A people's nominee will only ever be the one whose characteristics and attributes are the ones they agree with, are attracted to, and expect to be emulated.

So long as the people are affected with this disease, it should not be expected that their leader will rectify their situation or bring success for them, because the leader himself is a reflection of them. Conversely, you find that leaders who are just, fair, take correct stances, and bring about rectification, are those whose societies are likewise just and forward thinking. Thus it is society's responsibility to correct their own manners and outlook, if they expect to have a leader exemplifying those characteristics.

SOCIETIES ARE ONLY RECTIFIED BY COMPREHENSIVE MEANS.

We see a beautiful example in God's sending of the prophets (may God's peace be upon them all). They were always sent amongst the general population, calling their societies to that which was good and upright. They were not sent only as kings or of a ruling class. Their message was for all the society, and the rectification of a society engenders uprightness in its leadership.

Societies are only rectified by comprehensive means. Look at the example of Japan, which, after two decades of economic stagnation, has found that its return to growth is hampered by the twin challenges of an aging population and the mountain of public debt built up during years of on-and-off deflation. The country's main bet is to focus on higher growth, rather than fiscal consolidation, to tackle the world's largest public debt of 246 percent of GDP. Progress has been slow and the sharp division between regular workers with jobs for life, and part-timers with no security, has muted the effect on wages. In 2014 Japan's trade deficit was the worst on record, as the weaker yen has meant the country has been hit by a painful rise in the cost of imports. This came as the country was forced to import more fossil fuels.[379]

Another little-known statistic about Japan is that approximately twenty five percent of men over thirty years old are virgins.[380] This is a strong indication of their strong moral standards. The Japanese are also intensely hardworking, to the extent that the *Washington Post* reported that death from too much work is so commonplace in Japan that there is a word for it – *karoshi*. There is a national *karoshi* hotline, a *karoshi* self-help book, and a law that funnels money to the widow and children of a salaryman (it's almost always a man) who works himself into an early *karoshi* for the good of his company. This problem became prevalent "in the boom years of the late 1970s, as the number of Japanese men working more than sixty hours a week soared. Thirty years later, overtime rules remain so nebulous and so weakly enforced that the United Nations International Labor Organization has described Japan as a country with no legal limits on the practice."[381]

Japan has almost no immigration, as just *two percent* of the population is of foreign origin.[382] This situation would be ideal in the eyes of those who share Trump's mindset in reducing immigration. There is *literally nobody* to "take away" jobs from the Japanese, and this is evident in the 3.2% unemployment rate,[383] which is incredibly low.

THE ISSUE OF BUILDING A SUCCESSFUL NATION IS INCREDIBLY COMPLICATED AND INTRICATE, AND CANNOT BE REDUCED DOWN TO SIMPLISTIC NOTIONS

Even with all these characteristics often viewed by many as positive, such as high standards of education and moral character, being hard working, having an excellent record in manufacturing, and not having foreign competition in the labor market, Japan is still struggling and falling behind. It has not kept up in being innovative and forward-thinking, as it once was decades ago. It needs to create more out-of-the-box breakthroughs. This is what is required in these times we live in, similar to how Apple stretched the boundaries of innovation and developed the unexpected for the hungry global marketplace. Just as Apple did, only a few years ago, Japan needs to build new success stories for itself.*

The issue of building a successful nation is incredibly complicated and intricate, and cannot be reduced down to simplistic notions like building a wall, banning Muslims, badmouthing other nations, or hik-

---

* I will be releasing a book in the future with a focus on Japan, God willing!

ing import tariffs. It requires a rich combination of intelligence, strong values, hard work, and strategic planning – all of which Trump has still not demonstrated.

REUTERS/JONATHAN ERNST

39

CLOSING THOUGHTS

A S I WRITE THESE CLOSING THOUGHTS IN JUNE of 2016, five months before the general election in November, Trump has achieved astonishing popularity amongst large groups of the electorate and, as described in the preface, his ascendency has been a phenomenon.

Yet it is clear Trump is unqualified to lead this great nation forward, especially due to the highly complex nature of the time we're living in. If he is successful in reaching the Oval Office, it means that America has taken a step backward and regressed.

The stakes are very high. In these turbulent times, the challenges faced by the United States are significant.

The UK's Office for National Statistics estimates the average life expectancy for males and females born in 2015 will be ninety-one and ninety-four, respectively. [384] This will produce huge burdens on the Social Security system, and extensive planning needs to be done in preparation of that.

Through innovations in artificial intelligence and other innovative breakthroughs, there will emerge a large number of new jobs that have not been invented yet, so great planning and development in the education sector must be done also.

America will be facing new challenges from the developing partnership between Russia and China. Their respective leaders, Vladimir Putin and Xi Jinping, have had meetings with each other over a dozen times since 2013. They are the only two countries to be members of all five of these organizations: APEC, BRICS, G20, Shanghai Cooperation Organization, and the United Nations Security Council. Both nations have used at least six corresponding vetoes in the UN Security Council.

Trade has increased between them six hundred percent over the past decade. Under a contract signed in 2014, China agreed to buy Russian gas worth $400 billion over 30 years[385] — a deal that's been called the

largest in its history. Russia has also said it is ready to grant Chinese investors majority stakes in oil and gas exploration projects. A Chinese consortium is expected to grab a massive contract to build a high-speed rail link between Moscow and the southern city of Kazan.[386] The summer of 2014 included two striking events: Russian and Chinese warships puttering about together in the eastern Mediterranean, in a gaming war; and Russian and Chinese presidents standing shoulder to shoulder in Beijing for the 70th anniversary of the end of the Second World War.[387]

In 2015, China's vice foreign minister Cheng Guoping said previously that Beijing plans to boost its cooperation with Russia in a number of areas, including space. Russian deputy prime minister Dmitry Rogozin confirmed this by stating that both parties share "deep mutual understanding and mutual interests" in space-related projects.[388]

As recently as May 2016, a U.S. Navy admiral explained to an audience at the Navy League's Sea, Air and Space symposium that the term "near-peer" is a misnomer, because in some cases the Russian and Chinese have the advantage over American forces. "Our near-peer competitors are no longer near peers," said Rear Adm. Mike Darrah, Naval Air Systems Command's program executive officer for unmanned systems and strike weapons. "In some cases, they have gone beyond us."[389]

> HIS DISEASED MINDSET IS LIKE THE MINDSET OF HITLER WHO SOUGHT SELF-PROMOTION TO THE EXTENT THAT HIS COUNTRY, AND ALL THOSE AROUND IT, WERE DRAGGED INTO A HORRIBLE WAR.

So how robust is the Russia-China axis?

The growing ties between Russia and China are made clear through these examples, and they aren't all merely surface-level dealings. Rather, they illustrate the building of a deep and close relationship.

America is still incredibly powerful, as it contributes to thirty-six percent of global military spending, in comparison to China and Russia's combined contribution of seventeen percent. *Politico* Magazine reported that "despite recently closing hundreds of bases in Iraq and Afghanistan, the United States still maintains nearly eight hundred military bases in more than seventy countries and territories abroad—from giant 'Little

Americas' to small radar facilities. Britain, France and Russia, by contrast, have about thirty foreign bases combined."[390]

Finding the solutions to these and many other challenges requires a keen intellect, steady hand, and unwavering moral compass. Can it really be expected that the most wealthy, innovative, and powerful nation in the world, with a population of over 330 million people, would consider handing itself over to a dangerous charlatan like Trump? What he has suggested to *"make America great again"* is pathetically childish and doomed to fail. Just a few of his incomprehensible policy points include building the wall, the escalation of enmity and conflict between nations, and buying back US debt at lower prices to shortchange investors.

TRUMP HIMSELF WILL MOVE ON LIKE THE BLOWING OF THE WIND

His diseased mindset is like the mindset of Hitler, who sought self-promotion to the extent that he propelled his country, and most of the civilized world, into a horrible war. The German people only wanted their nation's situation to be improved, but look where he led them and the world instead. Hitler was empowered through the voting process, as was Mussolini. The voting process may also carry Trump into power, and if it does, it will show the regression of a sad majority in America today.

All that being said, due to my trust in the American people, I believe Trump will not be successful in reaching the White House. He is diseased, and the more he exposes that to the people, the more they will realize that he is not the answer to their problems, nor the nation's. A person of intellect would be able to know him and evaluate him after hearing him only once; so what about this whole drawn-out campaign of countless statements, actions, and speeches? Trump has shown the world exactly who he is and that he is by no means presidential material. It can never be claimed or expected that he will begin acting presidential once he's ready, because it will be just that, only an act. At seventy years of age, it would be completely unrealistic for this leopard to change his spots. I hope Americans heed the warning on the cover that the question of Trump is a serious one, and the answer is truly scary!

Trump himself will move on like the blowing of the wind, and his incitements to violence, propagation of xenophobia, and misidentification of the real problems facing us may soon be forgotten. However,

KENA BETANCUR/AFP/GETTY IMAGES

the underlying diseases will remain. They will continue to be apparent in two main groups. First, those who accepted his bait and supported Trump and his ways in the past and present. Second, those who are the likes of Junior Trumpians being raised and groomed in this corrupt way of thinking. This is the mentality of bigotry, distrust, and corruption shared by Trump, Hitler, the KKK, ISIS, Al-Qaeda, and those right-wing groups currently on the rise.

ENDNOTES

1. Trump, Donald J. "Get Tough" *Time to Get Tough*. Washington, DC: Regnery Publishing, 2011. pg 2. Print.

2. Trump, Donald J. Interviewed by George Stephanopoulos. *Good Morning America*. ABC. 17 June 2015. Television to Web Transcript. Web: 22 May 2016. <http://www.abcnews.go.com>

3. Churchill, Winston. "The Truth About Hitler" *The Strand Magazine*, Nov 1935: p.10. Web: 22 May 2016. <https://hansberndulrich.wordpress.com>

4. Churchill, 1935, p.17.

5. Churchill, 1935, p.17.

6. Churchill, 1935, p.16.

7. Churchill, 1935, p.16.

8. Churchill, 1935 p.21.

9. Associated Press. "Article Dealt with Purges" (30 Oct 1935) in *Gegen den Strom*, 11 Oct 2012. Web: 22 May 2016. <https://hansberndulrich.wordpress.com>

10. Churchill, 1935 p.17.

11. "1938: 'Peace for Our Time' – Neville Chamberlain" *On This Day*, BBC News. 30 Sep 2008. Web: 22 May 2016. <http://news.bbc.co.uk/onthisday/>

12. Trump, Donald J. "Get Tough" *Time to Get Tough*. Washington, DC: Regnery Publishing, 2011. pg 5. Print.

13. Tani, Maxwell. "Donald Trump: 'If I get Elected, you may get bored with winning.'" *Business Insider.* 9 Sep 2015. <http://www.businessinsider.com>

14. Stelter, Brian. "This is your brain on Donald Trump" *CNN Money.* 26 Mar 2016. Web: 6 Jun 2016. <http://money.cnn.com>

15. Matthews, David M. "Jim Jones' followers enthralled by his skills as a speaker" *CNN.* 13 Nov 2008. Web: 6 Jun 2016. <http://www.cnn.com>

16. Matthews, 13 Nov 2008.

17. Salisbury, Drew. "You can't unsee this photo of Trump and his 15-year-old daughter" *Death and Taxes.* 1 Feb 2016. Web: 27 May 2016. But the comment was made on the 6 Mar 2006 episode of *The View,* when Ivanka was 24 years old. <http://www.deathandtaxesmag.com>

18. Salisbury, Drew. "Donald Trump's favorite thing he has in common with his daughter is gross" *Death and Taxes.* 2 Feb 2016. Web: 27 May 2016. <http://www.deathandtaxesmag.com>

19. Trump, Donald J. [@realDonaldTrump]. "If Hillary Clinton can't satisfy her husband what makes her think she can satisfy America?" 16 Apr 2015. Web: 22 Jun 2016. Tweet.

20. Moyer, Justin William. "Donald Trump's 'schlonged': A linguistic investigation" *The Washington Post.* 22 Dec 2015. Web: 25 May 2016. <http://www.washingtonpost.com>

21. Nelson, Libby. "Here are all Donald Trump's insults to women that Megyn Kelly asked about" *Vox.* 6 Aug 2015. Web: 25 May 2016. <http://www.vox.com>

22. Cohen, Claire. "Donald Trump sexism tracker: Every offensive comment in one place" *The Telegraph* 4 Jun 2016. Web: 23 Jun 2016. <http://www.telegraph.co.uk>

23. Willis, Jackie. "Rosie O'Donnell says Donald Trump's Megyn Kelly Remarks are Part of 'a War on Women'" *ET Online,* Entertainment Tonight. 14 Aug 2015. Web: 23 Jun 2016. <http://www.etonline.com>

24. Kaczynski, Andrew, Nathan McDermott. "Donald Trump Said a Lot of Gross Things about Women on *Howard Stern*" *BuzzFeed.* 24 Feb 2016. Web: 23 Jun 2016. <http://www.buzzfeed.com>

25. Kaczynski, Andrew, Nathan McDermott. 24 Feb 2016.

26. Dagostino, Mark, and Brian Orloff. "Rosie Slams Trump, The Donald Fires Back" *People.* 20 Dec 2006. Web: 23 Jun 2016. <http://www.people.com>

27. Trump, Donald J. [@realDonaldTrump]. "Rosie is crude, rude, obnoxious and dumb - other than that I like her very much!" 11 Jul 2014. Web: 22 Jun 2016. Tweet.

28. Zaru, Deena. "The Donald Trump-Rosie O'Donnell feud: A timeline" CNN. 12 Aug 2015. Web: 23 Jun 2016. <http://www.cnn.com>

29. ETOnline.com. "Donald Trump vs. Rosie O'Donnell" *YouTube.* 20 Dec 2006. Web: 23 Jun 2016. <https://www.youtube.com/watch?v=d32577Hom08>

30. Cohen, Claire. 4 Jun 2016.

31. ETOnline.com. "Donald Trump vs. Rosie O'Donnell" *YouTube*. 20 Dec 2006. Web: 23 Jun 2016. <https://www.youtube.com/watch?v=d32577Hom08>

32. Bellstrom, Kristen. "Donald Trump Says Men Who Take Care of Their Kids are Acting 'Like the Wife'" *Fortune*. 24 Apr 2016. Web: 23 Jun 2016. <http://www.fortune.com>

33. Jordan, Mary. "From playboy to president? Trump's past crude sex talk collides with his White House bid." *The Washington Post*. 10 May 2016. Web: 23 Jun 2016. <http://www.washingtonpost.com>

34. Kaczynski, Andrew, Nathan McDermott. "Donald Trump Said a Lot of Gross Things about Women on *Howard Stern*" *BuzzFeed*. 24 Feb 2016. Web: 23 Jun 2016. <http://www.buzzfeed.com>

35. Nelson, Libby. "Donald Trump's deep insecurity about his 'short fingers' explained" *Vox*. 2 Mar 2016. Web: 25 May 2016. <http://www.vox.com>

36. Friedman, Barry. "Would God be so Good?" *Esquire*. 29 Jul 2013. Web: 25 May 2016. This article includes excerpts from earlier pieces. <http://www.esquire.com>

37. McMorris-Santoro, Evan. "Trump on China: 'Listen You Mother F***ers' (Video)" *TalkingPointsMemo*. 29 Apr 2011. Web: 30 May 2016. <http://talkingpointsmemo.com>

38. Diamond, Jeremy. "Trump: 'We can't continue to allow China to rape our country'" *CNN* Cable News Network. 2 May 2016. Web: 22 May 2016. <http://www.cnn.com>

39. Trump, Donald J. Interviewed by George Stephanopoulos. "*This Week* Transcript: Donald Trump," *This Week*, ABC. 8 May 2016. Web: 23 Jun 2016. <http://www.abcnews.go.com>

40. Trump, Donald J. "Get Tough" *Time to Get Tough*. Washington, DC: Regnery Publishing, 2011. pg 2. Print.

41. Allen, Nick. "El Chapo Guzman 'Vows to make Donald Trump swallow his words'" *The Telegraph*. 13 Jul 2015. Web: 25 May 2016. <http://www.telegraph.co.uk>

42. Trump, Donald J. [@realDonaldTrump]. "I love the Mexican people, but Mexico is not our friend. They're killing us at the border and they're killing us on jobs and trade. *Fight*!" 30 Jun 2015. Web: 25 May 2016. Tweet.

43. Trump, Donald J. "Our Country Needs a Truly Great Leader" *The Wall Street Journal*. Candidacy Announcement: 15 Jun 2015. Web: 10 Jun 2016. <http://www.wsj.com>

44. Trump, Donald J. Interviewed by George Stephanopoulos. *Good Morning America*. ABC. 17 June 2015. Television to Web Transcript. Web: 22 May 2016. <http://www.abcnews.go.com>

45. Trump, Donald J. Candidacy Announcement: 15 Jun 2015.

46. Allen, Michael. "Former Mexican President: Not Paying for Trump's Wall (Video)" *Opposing Views*. 25 Feb 2016. Web: 30 May 2016. Trump made his declaration during a televsed candidates debate on CNN. <http://www.opposingviews.com>

47. Worstall, Tim. "Donald Trump Blows the Trade Argument Again: Blames India for Stealing American Jobs" *Forbes*. 28 Feb 2016. Web: 30 May 2016. <http://www.forbes.com>

48. Holmes, Jack. "Proud F-Word Avoider Donald Trump has said the F-Word a Few Times" *Esquire*. 5 Mar 2016. Web: 30 May 2016. <http://www.esquire.com>

49. Phillips, Amber. "25 people, places and things Donald Trump has denounced" *The Washington Post*. 20 Jul 2015. Web: 29 May 2016. This made #22 on their list! <http://www.washingtonpost.com>

50. Crockett, Emily. "Why Donald Trump keeps calling Elizabeth Warren 'Pocahontas'" *Vox*. 10 Jun 2016. Web: 25 May 2016. <http://www.vox.com>

51. Crockett, 10 Jun 2016.

52. Trump, Donald J. [@realDonaldTrump]. "Goofy Elizabeth Warren is weak and ineffective. Does nothing. All talk, no action -- maybe her Native American name?" 6 May 2016. Web: 22 Jun 2016. Tweet.

53. Nelson, Libby. "Here are all Donald Trump's insults to women that Megyn Kelly asked about" *Vox*. 6 Aug 2015. Web: 25 May 2016. <http://www.vox.com>

54. Trump, Donald J. [@realDonaldTrump]. "Wow, Jeb Bush, whose campaign is a total disaster, had to bring in mommy to take a slap at me. Not nice!" 6 Feb 2016. Web: 22 Jun 2016. Tweet.

55. Trump, Donald J. [@realDonaldTrump]. "@JebBush is a sad case. A total embarrassment to both himself and his family, he just announced he will continue to spend on Trump hit ads!" 2 Jan 2016. Web: 22 Jun 2016. Tweet.

56. Trump, Donald J. [@realDonaldTrump]. "Ben Carson has never created a job in his life (well, maybe a nurse). I have created tens of thousands of jobs, it's what I do." 25 Oct 2015. Web: 22 Jun 2016. Tweet.

57. Trump, Donald J. [@realDonaldTrump]. "Have a good chance to win Texas on Tuesday. Cruz is a nasty guy, not one Senate endorsement and, despite talk, gets nothing done. Loser!" 26 Feb 2016. Web: 22 Jun 2016. Tweet.

58. Trump, Donald J. [@realDonaldTrump]. "Ted Cruz lifts the Bible high into the air and then lies like a dog-over and over again! The Evangelicals in S.C. figured him out & said no" 23 Feb 2016. Web: 22 Jun 2016. Tweet.

59. Trump, Donald J. [@realDonaldTrump]. "Is Cruz honest? He is in bed w/ Wall St. & is funded by Goldman Sachs/Citi, low interest loans. No legal disclosure & never sold off assets." 22 Jan 2016. Web: 22 Jun 2016. Tweet.

60. Trump, Donald J. [@realDonaldTrump]. "Failed presidential candidate Lindsey Graham should respect me. I destroyed his run, brought him from 7% to 0% when he got out. Now nasty!" 7 Mar 2016. Web: 22 Jun 2016. Tweet.

61. Trump, Donald J. [@realDonaldTrump]. "Failed presidential candidate Lindsey Graham should respect me. I destroyed his run, brought him from 7% to 0% when he got out. Now nasty!" 7 Mar 2016. Web: 22 Jun 2016. Tweet.

62. Trump, Donald J. [@realDonaldTrump]. "Watch Kasich squirm --- if he is not truthful in his negative ads I will sue him just for fun!" 19 Nov 2015. Web: 22 Jun 2016. Tweet.

63. Trump, Donald J. [@realDonaldTrump]. "Hillary and Sanders are not doing well, but what is the failed former Mayor of Baltimore doing on that stage? O'Malley is a clown." 14 Nov 2015. Web: 22 Jun 2016. Tweet.

64. Trump, Donald J. [@realDonaldTrump]. "@GovernorPataki couldn't be elected dog catcher if he ran again—so he didn't!" 1 Jul 2015. Web: 22 Jun 2016. Tweet.

65. Trump, Donald J. [@realDonaldTrump]. "Truly weird Senator Rand Paul of Kentucky reminds me of a spoiled brat without a properly functioning brain. He was terrible at DEBATE!" 10 Aug 2015. Web: 22 Jun 2016. Tweet.

66. Trump, Donald J. [@realDonaldTrump]. "@GovernorPerry failed on the border. He should be forced to take an IQ test before being allowed to enter the GOP debate." 16 Jul 2015. Web: 22 Jun 2016. Tweet.

67. Trump, Donald J. [@realDonaldTrump]. "Why would the great people of Florida vote for a guy who, as a Senator, never even shows up to vote - worst record. Marco Rubio is a joke!" 3 Mar 2016. Web: 22 Jun 2016. Tweet.

68. Trump, Donald J. [@realDonaldTrump]. "Sheldon Adelson is looking to give big dollars to Rubio because he feels he can mold him into his perfect little puppet. I agree!" 13 Oct 2015. Web: 22 Jun 2016. Tweet.

69. Trump, Donald J. [@realDonaldTrump]. "Strange, but I see wacko Bernie Sanders allies coming over to me because I'm lowering taxes, while he will double & triple them, a disaster!" 28 Dec 2015. Web: 22 Jun 2016. Tweet.

70. Trump, Donald J. [@realDonaldTrump]. "@CharlesGKoch is looking for a new puppet after Governor Walker and Jeb Bush cratered. He now likes Rubio--next fail." 3 Nov 2015. Web: 22 Jun 2016. Tweet.

71. Kaczynski, Andrew, Nathan McDermott. "Donald Trump Said a Lot of Gross Things about Women on *Howard Stern*" *BuzzFeed*. 24 Feb 2016. Web: 23 Jun 2016. <http://www.buzzfeed.com>

72. Kaczynski, Andrew, Nathan McDermott. 24 Feb 2016.

73. Kaczynski, Andrew, Nathan McDermott. 24 Feb 2016.

74. Kaczynski, Andrew, Nathan McDermott. 24 Feb 2016.

75. Trump, Donald J. [@realDonaldTrump]. "Wacko @glennbeck is a sad answer to the @SarahPalinUSA endorsement that Cruz so desperately wanted. Glenn is a failing, crying, lost soul!" 21 Jan 2016. Web: 22 Jun 2016. Tweet.

76. Trump, Donald J. [@realDonaldTrump]. "Failing host @glennbeck, a mental basketcase, loves SUPERPACS - in other words, he wants your politicians totally controlled by lobbyists!" 29 Oct 2015. Web: 22 Jun 2016. Tweet.

77. Trump, Donald J. [@realDonaldTrump]. "Wacky @glennbeck who always seems to be crying (worse than Bochner) speaks badly of me only because I refuse to do his show--a real nut job!" 8 Oct 2015. Web: 22 Jun 2016. Tweet.

78. Nelson, Libby. "Here are all Donald Trump's insults to women that Megyn Kelly asked about" *Vox*. 6 Aug 2015. Web: 25 May 2016. As the incident is recounted in Ms. Nelson's column, Ms. Beck asked for a *medical break* during deposition, presumably so that she could retreat someplace more private to use the pump – that's not the same as wanting to pump in front of Mr. Trump! Is

he offended or is he flattering himself?<http://www.vox.com>
Trump, Donald J. [@realDonaldTrump]. "@CNN & @CNNPolitics did not say that lawyer Beck lost the case and I got legal fees. Also, she wanted to breast pump in front of me at dep." 29 Jul 2015. Web: 22 Jun 2016. Tweet.

79. Trump, Donald J. [@realDonaldTrump]. "@BrentBozell, one of the National Review lightweights, came to my office begging for money like a dog. Why doesn't he say that?" 22 Jan 2016. Web: 22 Jun 2016. Tweet.

80. Trump, Donald J. [@realDonaldTrump]. "Reading @nytdavidbrooks of the NY Times is a total waste of time, he is a clown with no awareness of the world around him- dummy!" 18 Mar 2016. Web: 22 Jun 2016. Tweet.

81. Trump, Donald J. [@realDonaldTrump]. "While I have never met @nytdavidbrooks of the NY Times, I consider him one of the dumbest of all pundits- he has no sense of the real world!" 18 Mar 2016. Web: 22 Jun 2016. Tweet.

82. Trump, Donald J. [@realDonaldTrump]. "I have watched sloppy Graydon Carter fail and close Spy Magazine and now am watching him fail at @VanityFair Magazine. He is a total loser!" 15 Nov 2015. Web: 22 Jun 2016. Tweet.

83. Trump, Donald J. [@realDonaldTrump]. "Rumor has it that the grubby head of failing @VanityFair Magazine, 'Sloppy' Graydon Carter, is going to be fired or replaced very soon?" 16 Oct 2015. Web: 22 Jun 2016. Tweet.

84. Trump, Donald J. [@realDonaldTrump]. "Why are @JebBush flunkies @ananavarro and @secupp, two of the dumbest people in politics, always on the @CNN panels..and yet Poll:Trump 39" 27 Dec 2015. Web: 22 Jun 2016. Tweet.

85. Trump, Donald J. [@realDonaldTrump]. "Wow, great news! I hear @EWErickson of Red State was fired like a dog. If you read his tweets, you'll understand why. Just doesn't have IT!" 8 Oct 2015. Web: 22 Jun 2016. Tweet.

86. Trump, Donald J. [@realDonaldTrump]. "@EWErickson is a total low life--- read his past tweets. A dummy with no 'it' factor. Will fade fast." 8 Oct 2015. Web: 22 Jun 2016. Tweet.

87. Trump, Donald J. [@realDonaldTrump]. "Small crowds at @RedState today in Atlanta. People were very angry at EWErickson, a major sleaze and buffoon who has saved me time and money" 8 Aug 2015. Web: 22 Jun 2016. Tweet.

88. Trump, Donald J. [@realDonaldTrump]. "@DavidGregory got thrown off of TV by NBC, fired like a dog! Now he is on @CNN being nasty to me. Not nice!" 29 Mar 2016. Web: 22 Jun 2016. Tweet.

89. Trump, Donald J. [@realDonaldTrump]. "@AP has one of the worst reporters in the business -- @JeffHorwitz wouldn't know the truth if it hit him in the face." 23 Nov 2015. Web: 22 Jun 2016. Tweet.

90. Trump, Donald J. [@realDonaldTrump]. "I don't cheat at golf but @SamuelLJackson cheats—with his game he has no choice—and stop doing commercials!" 6 Jan 2016. Web: 22 Jun 2016. Tweet.

91. Trump, Donald J. [@realDonaldTrump]. "Really dumb @CheriJacobus. Begged my people for a job. Turned her down twice and she went hostile. Major loser, zero credibility!" 5 Feb 2016. Web: 22 Jun 2016. Tweet.

92. Trump, Donald J. [@realDonaldTrump]. "Really dumb @CheriJacobus. Begged my people for a job. Turned her down twice and she went hostile. Major loser, zero credibility!" 5 Feb 2016. Web: 22 Jun 2016. Tweet.

93. Trump, Donald J. [@realDonaldTrump]. "The worst show in Las Vegas, in my opinion, is @pennjillette. Hokey garbage. New York show even worse!" 16 Jul 2015. Web: 22 Jun 2016. Tweet.

94. Trump, Donald J. [@realDonaldTrump]. "I loved firing goofball atheist Penn @pennjillette on The Apprentice. He never had a chance. Wrote letter to me begging for forgiveness." 16 Jul 2015. Web: 22 Jun 2016. Tweet.

95. Trump, Donald J. [@realDonaldTrump]. "Highly overrated & crazy @megynkelly is always complaining about Trump and yet she devotes her shows to me. Focus on others Megyn!" 17 Mar 2016. Web: 22 Jun 2016. Tweet.

96. Trump, Donald J. [@realDonaldTrump]. "I refuse to call Megyn Kelly a bimbo, because that would not be politically correct. Instead I will only call her a lightweight reporter!" 27 Jan 2016. Web: 22 Jun 2016. Tweet.

97. Trump, Donald J. [@realDonaldTrump]. "@FrankLuntz is a total clown. Has zero credibility! @FoxNews @megynkelly" 15 Jan 2016. Web: 22 Jun 2016. Tweet.

98. Trump, Donald J. [@realDonaldTrump]. "@FrankLuntz is a low class slob who came to my office looking for consulting work and I had zero interest. Now he picks anti-Trump panels!" 7 Aug 2015. Web: 22 Jun 2016. Tweet.

99. Lee, Jasmine C., and Kevin Quealy. "The 229 People, Places and Things Donald Trump has Insulted on Twitter: A Complete List" The New York Times. 17 Jun 2016. Web: 22 Jun 2016. <http://www.nytimes.com>

100. Trump, Donald J. [@realDonaldTrump]. "Why are @JebBush flunkies @ananavarro and @secupp, two of the dumbest people in politics, always on the @CNN panels..and yet Poll:Trump 39" 27 Dec 2015. Web: 22 Jun 2016. Tweet.

101. Trump, Donald J. [@realDonaldTrump]. "Great job @MariaTCardona on @ThisWeekABC. You made kooky Cokie Roberts and @BillKristol look even dumber than they are. You will be right!" 29 Nov 2015. Web: 22 Jun 2016. Tweet.

102. DelReal, José A. "Trump: Romney a 'choke artist' who would have 'dropped to his knees' for an endorsement" The Washington Post. 3 Mar 2016. Web: 7 Jun 2016. <http://www.washingtonpost.com>

103. Trump, Donald J. [@realDonaldTrump]. "@KarlRove is a biased dope who wrote falsely about me re China and TPP. This moron wasted $430 million on political campaigns and lost 100%" 12 Nov 2015. Web: 22 Jun 2016. Tweet.

104. Trump, Donald J. [@realDonaldTrump]. "Irrelevant clown @KarlRove sweats and shakes nervously on @FoxNews as he talks "bull" about me. Has zero cred. Made fool of himself in '12." 16 Jul 2015. Web: 22 Jun 2016. Tweet.

105. Trump, Donald J. [@realDonaldTrump]. "@BenSasse looks more like a gym rat than a U.S. Senator. How the hell did he ever get elected? @greta" 29 Jan 2016. Web: 22 Jun 2016. Tweet.

106. Trump, Donald J. [@realDonaldTrump]. "Just watched the very incompetent Mitt Romney Campaign Strategist, Stuart Stevens. Now I know why Mitt lost so badly. Stevens is a clown!" 22 Feb 2016. Web: 22 Jun 2016. Tweet.

107. Trump, Donald J. [@realDonaldTrump]. "Stuart Stevens is a dumb guy who fails @ virtually everything he touches. Romney campaign, his book, etc. Why does @andersoncooper put him on?" 13 Jan 2016. Web: 22 Jun 2016. Tweet.

108. Trump, Donald J. [@realDonaldTrump]. "Megyn Kelly has two really dumb puppets, Chris Stirewalt & Marc Threaten (a Bushy) who do exactly what she says. All polls say I won debates" 15 Oct 2015. Web: 22 Jun 2016. Tweet.

109. Trump, Donald J. [@realDonaldTrump]. "@GovernorSununu who couldn't get elected dog catcher in NH forgot to mention my phenomenal biz success rate: 99.2%" 27 Jul 2015. Web: 22 Jun 2016. Tweet.

110. Trump, Donald J. [@realDonaldTrump]. "@GovernorSununu who couldn't get elected dog catcher in NH forgot to mention my phenomenal biz success rate: 99.2%" 27 Jul 2015. Web: 22 Jun 2016. Tweet.

111. Trump, Donald J. [@realDonaldTrump]. "Megyn Kelly has two really dumb puppets, Chris Stirewalt & Marc Threaten (a Bushy) who do exactly what she says. All polls say I won debates" 15 Oct 2015. Web: 22 Jun 2016. Tweet. Notice the pattern of mocking family names – Thiessen becomes "Threaten".

112. Trump, Donald J. [@realDonaldTrump]. "I hear that sleepy eyes @chucktodd will be fired like a dog from ratings starved Meet The Press? I can't imagine what is taking so long!" 12 Jul 2015. Web: 22 Jun 2016. Tweet.

113. Trump, Donald J. [@realDonaldTrump]. "Sleep eyes @ChuckTodd is killing Meet The Press. Isn't he pathetic? Love watching him fail!" 12 Jul 2015. Web: 22 Jun 2016. Tweet.

114. Trump, Donald J. [@realDonaldTrump]. "Sleep eyes @ChuckTodd is killing Meet The Press. Isn't he pathetic? Love watching him fail!" 12 Jul 2015. Web: 22 Jun 2016. Tweet.

115. Trump, Donald J. [@realDonaldTrump]. "@bobvanderplaats is a total phony and con man. When I wouldn't give him free hotel rooms and much more, he endorsed Cruz. @foxandfriends" 31 Jan 2016. Web: 22 Jun 2016. Tweet.

116. Trump, Donald J. [@realDonaldTrump]. "Weak and totally conflicted people like @TheRickWilson shouldn't be allowed on television unless given an I.Q. test. Dumb as a rock! @CNN" 9 Dec 2015. Web: 22 Jun 2016. Tweet.

117. Trump, Donald J. [@realDonaldTrump]. "@FoxNews is the only network that does not even mention my very successful event last night. $6,000,000 raised in one hour for our VETS." 29 Jan 2016. Web: 22 Jun 2016. Tweet.

118. Trump, Donald J. [@realDonaldTrump]. "Union Leader refuses to comment as to why they were kicked out of the ABC News debate like a dog. For starters, try getting a new publisher!" 10 Jan 2016. Web: 22 Jun 2016. Tweet.

119. Trump, Donald J. [@realDonaldTrump]. "I was so happy when I heard that @Politico, one of the most dishonest political outlets, is losing a fortune. Pure scum!" 8 Oct 2015. Web: 22 Jun 2016. Tweet.

120. Trump, Donald J. [@realDonaldTrump]. "I wonder why somebody doesn't do something about the clowns @politico and their totally dishonest reporting." 7 Oct 2015. Web: 22 Jun 2016. Tweet.

121. O'Reilly, Bill. "Some new polling out of New Hampshire" *Talking Points*, Fox News. 6 Feb 2016. Web: 25 May 2016. <http://www.foxnews.com>

122. Trump, Donald J. [@realDonaldTrump]. "Macy's was very disloyal to me bc of my strong stance on illegal immigration. Their stock has crashed! #BoycottMacys" 12 Nov 2015. Web: 22 Jun 2016. Tweet.

123. Trump, Donald J. [@realDonaldTrump]. "I hope the boycott of @Macys continues forever. So many people are cutting up their cards. Macy's stores suck and they are bad for U.S.A." 16 Jul 2015. Web: 22 Jun 2016. Tweet.

124. Salisbury, Drew. "You can't unsee this photo of Trump and his 15-year-old daughter" *Death and Taxes*. 1 Feb 2016. Web: 27 May 2016. But the comment was made on the 6 Mar 2006 episode of *The View*, when Ivanka was 24 years old. <http://www.deathandtaxesmag.com>

125. Salisbury, Drew. "Donald Trump's favorite thing he has in common with his daughter is gross" *Death and Taxes*. 2 Feb 2016. Web: 27 May 2016. <http://www.deathandtaxesmag.com>

126. Moyer, Justin William. "Donald Trump's 'schlonged': A linguistic investigation," *The Washington Post*. 22 Dec 2015. Web: 25 May 2016. <http://www.washingtonpost.com>

127. Nelson, Libby. "Here are all Donald Trump's insults to women that Megyn Kelly asked about" *Vox*. 6 Aug 2015. Web: 25 May 2016. <http://www.vox.com>

128. Friedman, Barry. "Would God be so Good?" *Esquire*. 29 Jul 2013. Web: 25 May 2016. This article includes excerpts from earlier pieces. <http://www.esquire.com>

129. O'Reilly, Bill. "Some new polling out of New Hampshire" *Talking Points*, Fox News. 6 Feb 2016. Web: 25 May 2016. <http://www.foxnews.com>

130. Nelson, Libby. "Donald Trump's deep insecurity about his 'short fingers' explained" *Vox*. 2 Mar 2016. Web: 25 May 2016. <http://www.vox.com>

131. Blair, Gwenda. Interviewed by Michael Krigge. "What Donald Trump learned from his German grandpa Friedrich Drumpf" *DW News*, DeutscheWelle. 9 Sep 2015. Web: 25 May 2016. <http://www.dw.com>

132. Trump, Donald J. [@realDonaldTrump]. "@SenJohnMcCain should be defeated in the primaries. Graduated last in his class at Annapolis--dummy!" 16 Jul 2015. Web: 6 Jun 2016. Tweet.

133. Trump, Donald J. [@realDonaldTrump]. "@SenJohnMcCain should be defeated in the primaries. Graduated last in his class at Annapolis--dummy!" 16 Jul 2015. Web: 6 Jun 2016. Tweet.

134. Trump, Donald J. [@realDonaldTrump]. "Why does @Greta have a fired Bushy like dummy, John Sununu on- spewing false info? I will beat Hillary by a lot, she wants no part of Trump." 21 Jan 2016. Web: 6 Jun 2016. Tweet.

135. Trump, Donald J. [@realDonaldTrump]. "Isn't it funny that I am now #1 in the money losing @HuffingtonPost (poll), and by a big margin. Dummy @ariannahuff must be thrilled!" 25 Jul 2015. Web: 6 Jun 2016. Tweet.

136. Trump, Donald J. [@realDonaldTrump]. "@NYDailyNews, the dying tabloid owned by dopey clown Mort Zuckerman, puts me on the cover daily because I sell. My honor, but it is dead!" 28 Jun 2015. Web: 6 Jun 2016. Tweet.

137. Trump, Donald J. [@realDonaldTrump]. "Sorry losers and haters, but my I.Q. is one of the highest – and you all know it! Please don't feel so stupid or insecure, it's not your fault" 8 May 2013. Web: 6 Jun 2016. Tweet.

138. Trump, Donald J., with Tony Schwartz. *The Art of the Deal*. New York, NY: Random House, 2009. p.58. Print.

139. Trump, Donald J. [@realDonaldTrump]. "Dopey Prince @Alwaleed_Talal wants to control our U.S. politicians with daddy's money. Can't do it when I get elected. #Trump2016" 11 Dec 2015. Web: 6 Jun 2016. Tweet.

140. Trump, Donald J. [@realDonaldTrump]. "Just out Nevada poll shows Jeb Bush at 1%, he should take his dumb mouthpiece, @LindseyGrahamSC, and just go home." 17 Feb 2016. Web: 6 Jun 2016. Tweet.

141. Trump, Donald J. [@realDonaldTrump]. "Mitt Romney, who was one of the dumbest and worst candidates in the history of Republican politics, is now pushing me on tax returns. Dope!" 25 Feb 2016. Web: 6 Jun 2016. Tweet.

142. Trump, Donald J. [@realDonaldTrump]. "When Mitt Romney asked me for my endorsement last time around, he was so awkward and goofy that we all should have known he could not win!" 24 Feb 2016. Web: 6 Jun 2016. Tweet.

143. Trump, Donald J. [@realDonaldTrump]. "Between Iraq war monger @krauthammer, dummy @KarlRove, deadpan @GeorgezWill, highly overrated @megynkelly, among others, @FoxNews not fair!" 15 Dec 2015. Web: 6 Jun 2016. Tweet.

144. Trump, Donald J. [@realDonaldTrump]. "Something must be done with dopey @KarlRove - he is pushing Republicans down the same old path of defeat. Don't fall for it, Karl is a loser" 12 Dec 2015. Web: 6 Jun 2016. Tweet.

145. Trump, Donald J. [@realDonaldTrump]. "Total fool @KarlRove is part of the Republican Establishment problem. An all talk, no action dummy!" 12 Nov 2015. Web: 6 Jun 2016. Tweet.

146. Trump, Donald J. [@realDonaldTrump]. "@KarlRove is a biased dope who wrote falsely about me re China and TPP. This moron wasted $430 million on political campaigns and lost 100%" 12 Nov 2015. Web: 6 Jun 2016. Tweet.

147. Kilachand, Sean. "Forbes History: The Original 1987 List of International Billionaires" *Forbes*. 21 Mar 2012. Web: 25 May 2016. <http://www.forbes.com>

148. Stump, Scott. "Donald Trump: My dad gave me 'a small loan' of $1 million to get started" *Today*. 26 Oct 2015. Web: 25 May 2016. <http://www.today.com>

149. Trump, Donald J. Interviewed by David Letterman. *Late Night*, NBC. 10 Nov 1987. Television.

150. King Jr, Neil. "Trump on 2012: 'Part of Beauty of Me is I'm Very Rich'" *The Wall Street Journal*. 17 Mar 2011. Web: 3 Jun 2016. <http://blogs.wsj.com>

151. Trump, Donald J. Interviewed by Anderson Cooper. *360 Degrees, CNN*, New York: 28 Dec 2006. Television to Web Transcript: 3 Jun 2016. <http://edition.cnn.com>

152. Haskell, Josh. "Trump Doesn't Expect Violence If He Fails to Win Republican Presidential Nomination" *ABC News*. 17 Apr 2016. Web: 3 Jun 2016. <http://www.abcnews.go.com>

153. Carroll, Lauren. "Is Donald Trump Self-Funding his Campaign? Sort of" *Politifact*. 10 Feb 2016. Web: 17 Jun 2016. <http://www.politifact.com>

154. Carroll, 10 Feb 2016.

155. Trump, Donald J. Interviewed by Don Lemon. Transcription by Chris Cillizza. "The Fix: Here's Your Daily Donald Trump Interview, Annotated" *The Washington Post*. Transcript: 2 Sep 2015. Web: 3 Jun 2015. <http://www.washingtonpost.com>

156. Melter, Ari. "Trump Campaign Could Use New Donations to Pay Donald Trump $36M for Loan" *NBC News*. 13 May 2016. Web: 3 Jun 2016. <http://www.cnbc.com>

157. Cabaniss, Will. "Donald Trump's campaign contributions to Democrats and Republicans" *PunditFact*. 9 Jul 2015. Web: 3 Jun 2015. <http://www.politifact.com>

158. Langley, Monica, and Rebecca Ballhaus. "Donald Trump Won't Self-Fund General-Election Campaign" *The Wall Street Journal*. 4 May 2016. Web: 23 Jun 2016. <http://www.wsj.com>

159. Benen, Steve. "With Adelson ready to invest in Trump, who's the 'puppet' now?" *The Rachel Maddow Show*, MSNBC. 16 May 2016. Web: 23 Jun 2016. <http://www.msnbc.com>

160. Trump, Donald J. [@realDonaldTrump]. "@stranahan: Sheldon Adelson Pledges $100 Million to Elect Trump President - Breitbart" 16 May 2016. Web: 23 Jun 2016. Tweet.

161. Isquith, Elias. "'Just surgically disconnect your shame sensor': What Ted Cruz gets right about how American plutocracy works" *Salon*. 20 Apr 2015. Web: 23 Jun 2016. <http://www.salon.com>

162. Scott, Eugene. "Trump campaign: We're facing an emergency goal of $100,000" CNN. 18 Jun 2018. Web: 23 Jun 2018. <http://edition.cnn.com>

163. DelReal, José A. "Trump: Romney a 'choke artist' who would have 'dropped to his knees' for an endorsement" *The Washington Post*. 3 Mar 2016. Web: 7 Jun 2016. <http://www.washingtonpost.com>

164. Anderson, Stuart. "Trump the Hypocrite: Investing Overseas Fine for Him" *Forbes*. 17 Aug 2015. Web: 3 Jun 2016. <http://www.forbes.com>

165. Anderson, 17 Aug 2015.

166. Miller, Zeke J. "When Donald Trump Praised Hillary Clinton" *Time*. 17 Jul 2015. Web: 3 Jun 2016. <http://www.time.com>

167. Sherfinski, David. "Donald Trump: Hillary Clinton 'an embarrassment to our country'" *The Washington Times*. 16 Mar 2016. Web: 3 Jun 2016. <http://www.washingtontimes.com>

168. Altman, Alex. "How Bush went from 'Winner' to 'Loser' in Trump's Eyes" *Time*. 3 Sep 2015. Web: 3 Jun 2016. <http://www.time.com>

169. Trump, Donald J. [@realDonaldTrump]. "The last thing our country needs is another BUSH! Dumb as a rock!" 18 Dec 2015. Web: 3 Jun 2016. Tweet.

170. Trump, Donald J. Interviewed by Chuck Todd. *Meet the Press*, NBC News. 20 Dec 2015. Television to Web Transcript: 3 Jun 2016. <http://www.nbcnews.com>

171. Staff Writers. "Donald Trump praises Kim Jong-un for his firm hand with executed uncle" *The Telegraph*. 11 Jan 2016. Web: 27 May 2016. <http://www.telegraph.co.uk>

172. Trump, Donald J. Interviewed by Sean Hannity. *Hannity*, FoxNews. 12 Aug 2015. Television to Web Transcript: 25 May 2016. <http://www.foxnews.com>

173. Trump, Donald J. [@realDonaldTrump]. "Druggies, drug dealers, rapists and killers are coming across the southern border. When will the U.S. get smart and stop this travesty?" 19 Jun 2015. Web: 23 Jun 2016. Tweet.

174. Jones, Susan. "Rubio Blasts Trump for Hiring Illegal Aliens; Trump Responds: 'You Haven't Hired Anybody'" *CNSNews.com*. 26 Feb 2016. Web: 27 May 2016. <http://www.cnsnews.com>

175. Jones, 26 Feb 2016.

176. Swanson, Ana. "The myth and the reality of Donald Trump's business empire" *The Washington Post*. 29 Feb 2016. Web: 27 May 2016. <http://www.washingtonpost.com>

177. S.M. "Presidential Candidates compete over their embrace of torture" *The Economist*. 13 Feb 2016. Web: 27 May 2016. <http://www.economist.com>

178. Gass, Nick. "Donald Trump was for the Clintons before he was against them" *Politico*. 29 Dec 2015. Web: 27 May 2016. <http://www.politico.com>

179. Diamond, Jeremy, and Eugene Scott. "Trump asks backers to swear their support, vows to broaden torture laws" *CNN* Cable Network News. 5 Mar 2016. Web: 27 May 2016. <http://www.cnn.com>

180. Becker, Kyle. "Trump's Comment about Chinese Government at Tiananmen Square: The 'Strongman' America Needs?" *Independent Journal*. 12 Jan 2016. Web: 7 Jun 2016. <http://www.ijreview.com>

181. Becker, 12 Jan 2016.

182. Trump, Donald J. [@realDonaldTrump]. "Big protest march in Colorado on Friday afternoon! Don't let the bosses take your vote!" 14 Apr 2016. Web: 7 Jun 2016. Tweet.

183. Lecklider, Aaron. "Donald Trump says He Loves the Poorly Educated, We Should Too" *The Huffington Post*. 26 Feb 2016. Web: 7 Jun 2016. <http://www.huffingtonpost.com>

184. Cardesman, Anthony H. *New Estimates of Iran's Petroleum Exports and Income after the Nuclear Implementation Day and Reductions in Sanctions,* CSIS: Centre for Strategic & International Studies. Third Revision: 26 Jan 2016. Web: 27 May 2016. Cardesman cites the World Bank overview of Iran, which is not itself available online. <http://www.csis.org>

185. Kim, Eun Kyung. "Hillary Clinton attended Donald Trump's Wedding? GOP debate burning questions answered" *Today News.* 7 Aug 2015. Web: 7 Jun 2016. <http://www.today.com>

186. DelReal, José A. "Trump: Romney a 'choke artist' who would have 'dropped to his knees' for an endorsement" *The Washington Post.* 3 Mar 2016. Web: 7 Jun 2016. <http://www.washingtonpost.com>

187. Diamond, Jeremy. "Trump: 'I could shoot somebody and I wouldn't lose voters'" *CNN.* 24 Jan 2016. Web: 7 Jun 2016. <http://www.cnn.com>

188. Gass, Nick. "Reid: With Trump, 'Republicans are reaping what they've sown'" *Politico.* 2 Mar 2016. Web: 15 Jun 2016. <http://www.politico.com>

189. Stark, Holger. "Aiding and Abetting: How an Uncritical Media Helped Trump's Rise" *Der Spiegel International.* 15 Mar 2016. Web: 15 Jun 2016. <http://www.spiegel.de>

190. "Donald J. Trump Endorsed by New Jersey Governor Chris Christie" Press Release. New York, NY: Donald J. Trump for President, Inc. 26 Feb 2016. Web: 20 May 2016. <http://www.donaldjtrump.com>

191. "Donald J. Trump Receives Endorsement of Former VP Candidate & Influential Conservative Sarah Palin" Press Release. New York, NY: Donald J. Trump for President, Inc. 19 Jan 2016. Web: 20 May 2016. <http://www.donaldjtrump.com>

192. "Donald J. Trump Endorsed by Maine Governor Paul LePage" Press Release. New York, NY: Donald J. Trump for President, Inc. 26 Feb 2016. Web: 20 May 2016. <http://www.donaldjtrump.com>

193. Haberman, Maggie. "Gov. Rick Scott of Florida Endorses Donald Trump" *New York Times.* 16 Mar 2016. Web: 20 May 2016. <http://www.nytimes.com>

194. Costa, Robert. "Lou Barletta, an immigration hard-liner in Congress, endorses Trump" *The Washington Post.* 22 Mar 2016. Web: 20 May 2016. <http://www.washingtonpost.com>

195. Diamond, Jeremy. "First Congressman to back Trump: 'We need a chief executive'" *CNN.* 24 Feb 2016. Web: 20 May 2016. <http://www.cnn.com>

196. Morton, Victor. "Rep. Scott DesJarlais of Tennessee endorses Donald Trump" *The Washington Times.* 24 Feb 2016. Web: 20 May 2016. <http://www.washingtontimes.com>

197. Weigel, David. "Rep. Renee Ellmers votes for Trump" *The Washington Post.* 15 Mar 2016. Web: 20 May 2016. <http://www.washingtonpost.com>

198. Gass, Nick. "Trump lands his first congressional endorsements" *Politico.* 24 Feb 2016. Web: 20 May 2016. <http://www.politico.com>

199. Lippman, Daniel. "Trump nabs endorsement from Pennsylvania Rep. Tom Marino" *Politico.* 29 Feb 2016. Web: 20 May 2016. <http://www.politico.com>

200. Gampel, Kelly. "Congressman Tom Reed backs Donald Trump" *StarGazette*. 16 Mar 2016. Web: 20 May 2016. <http://www.stargazette.com>

201. "Donald J. Trump Endorsed by Senator Jeff Sessions" Press Release. New York, NY: Donald J. Trump for President, Inc. 28 Feb 2016. Web: 20 May 2016. <http://www.donaldjtrump.com>

202. Costa, Robert. "Scott Brown to endorse Trump" *The Washington Post*. 2 Feb 2016. Web: 20 May 2016. <http://www.washingtonpost.com>

203. "Donald J. Trump Receives Endorsement from Dr. Ben Carson and Announces Delegate Selection Team" Press Release. NYC, NY: Donald J. Trump for President, Inc. 11 Mar 2016. Web: 20 May 2016. <http://www.donaldjtrump.com>

204. Cillizza, Chris. "Pat Buchanan says Donald Trump is the future of the Republican Party" *The Washington Post*. 12 Jan 2016. Web: 20 May 2016. <http://www.washingtonpost.com>

205. Marans, Daniel. "Trump Advising General Defends Muslim Ban" *Huffington Post*. 19 May 2016. Web: 20 May 2016. <http://www.huffingtonpost.com>

206. Wemple, Erik. "Jeffrey Lord, CNN's very own Trump apologist, strikes again" *The Washington Post*. 18 Sep 2016. Web: 20 May 2016. After his political career, CNN took on Lord as a commentator. <http://www.washingtonpost.com> Revesz, Rachel. "Donald Trump supporter Jeffrey Lord says KKK were Democrats who wanted to advance their own progressive agenda" *The Independent*. 2 Mar 2016. Web: 22 May 2016. <http://www.independent.co.uk>

207. Trump, Donald J. [@realDonaldTrump]. "Humbled to be in Utah with retired General Robert C. Oaks. We are so thankful for his support and endorsement here in SLC." 19 Mar 2016, 5h15. Web: 22 May 2016. Tweet.

208. Rappeport, Alan. "Top Experts Confounded by Advisers to Donald Trump" *New York Times*. 22 Mar 2016. Web: 22 May 2016. <http://www.nytimes.com>

209. Lewis, Paul. "Sheriff Joe Arpaio on Donald Trump: 'My mission is to get him elected'" *The Guardian*. 22 Mar 2016. Web: 19 Jun 2016. <http://theguardian.com>

210. Bumiller, Elisabeth. "McCain Draws Line on Attacks as Crowds Cry 'Fight Back'" *New York Times*. 10 Oct 2008. Web: 27 May 2016. <http://www.nytimes.com>

211. Jacobs, Ben. "Trump's Rochester Rally: Furor over Anti-Muslim Bigotry and a shot at the Pope" *The Guardian*. 18 Sep 2015. Web: 27 May 2016. <http://theguardian.com>

212. Bumiller, 10 Oct 2008.

213. Angelou, Maya. Precise source unknown but first pinned to Maya Angelou by Oprah Winfrey, then by everyone else almost by acclamation. Even if she did not say it first, either she should have or later wished she had!

214. Merritt, Jonathan. "Why Do Evangelicals Support Donald Trump?" *The Atlantic*. 3 Sep 2015. Web: 6 Jun 2016. <http://www.theatlantic.com>

215. Lakoff, George. "Why Trump?" Blog: 2 Mar 2016. Web: 6 Jun 2016. <http://georgelakoff.com>

216. Nelson, Libby. "The strangest line from Donald Trump's victory speech: 'I love the poorly educated!'" *Vox*. 24 Feb 2016. Web: 6 Jun 2016. <http://www.vox.com>

217. Merritt, 3 Sep 2015.

218. Cohn, Nate. "Donald Trump's Strongest Supporters: A Certain Kind of Democrat" *The New York Times*. 16 Mar 2016. Web: 20 May 2016. <http://www.nytimes.com>

219. Edelman, Adam. "Donald Trump supported by former KKK leader David Duke: 'I hope he does everything we hope he will do'" *New York Daily News*. 26 Feb 2016. Web: 20 May 2016. <http://www.nydailynews.com>

220. Western Journalism. "David Duke did not Endorse Trump, but will Vote for him" *YouTube*. Video clip online. 1 Mar 2016. Web: 19 Jun 2016. <https://www.youtube.com/watch?v=E3-EP-sPXxE>

221. Thomas, Chris. "KKK leader disavows violent past, declares Trump 'best' for president" *NBC News*. 29 Apr 2016, updated 9 May 2016. Web: 22 May 2016. <http://www.nbc12.com>

222. Vavreck, Lynn. "Measuring Donald Trump's Supporters for Intolerance" *New York Times*. 23 Feb 2016. Web: 20 May 2016. <http://www.nytimes.com>

223. Altman, Alex. "The Billionaire and the Bigots" *Time*. 14 Apr 2016. Web: 22 May 2016. <http://www.time.com>

224. Smith, Candace. "The White Nationalists who Support Donald Trump" *ABC News*. 10 Mar 2016. Web: 19 Jun 2016. <http://abcnews.go.com>

225. Miller, Michael E. "Donald Trump on a protester: 'I'd like to punch him in the face'" *The Washington Post*. 23 Feb 2016. Web: 22 May 2016. <http://www.washingtonpost.com>

226. Jerde, Sara. "Trump to Crowd: 'Knock the Crap out of' Tomato Throwers, I'll Cover Legal Fees" *TalkingPointsMemo*. 1 Feb 2016. Web: 22 May 2016. <http://talkingpointsmemo.com>

227. Scherer, Michael. "Person of the Year: The Short List" *Time*. 21 Dec 2015. Web: 22 May 2016. <http://www.time.com>

228. Smith, Candace. "Clashes Erupt Outside Donald Trump's Missouri Rally" *ABC News*. 11 Mar 2016. Web: 22 May 2016. <http://abcnews.go.com>

229. Trump, Donald J. Interviewed by Chris Cuomo. *New Day*, CNN. 16 Mar 2016. Television to Web Transcript: 22 May 2016. <http://www.cnn.com>

230. Young, Ashley. "Carson predicts 'a lot of turmoil' if Trump is denied nomination" *CNN*. 16 Mar 2016. Web: 22 May 2016. <http://www.cnn.com>

231. White, Daniel. "Trump Supporter: 'Riots aren't Necessarily a Bad Thing'" *Time*. 16 Mar 2016. Web: 22 May 2016. <http://www.time.com>

232. "Riot" Merriam-Webster Dictionary. Web. <http://www.merriam-webster.com>

233. Nelson, Libby. "Watch: Trump supporter yells 'Go to fucking Auschwitz' at protesters" *Vox*. 14 Mar 2016. Web: 29 May 2016. <http://www.vox.com>

234. Nelson, 14 Mar 2016.

235. Moyer, Justin William, and Jenny Starrs, Sarah Larimer. "Trump supporter charged after sucker-punching protester at North Carolina rally" *The Washington Post*. 11 Mar 2016. Web: 29 May 2016. <http://www.washingtonpost.com>

236. "Protester storms stage at Ohio Trump rally" *Fox 5*. 12 Mar 2016. Web: 29 May 2016. <http://www.fox5ny.com>

237. Bobic, Igor. "Donald Trump Rally Turns Ugly: 'Light the Motherf**ker on Fire!'" *The Huffington Post*. 15 Dec 2015. Web: 29 May 2016. <http://www.huffingtonpost.com>

238. Webber, Rod. "Trump Supporter Joe Sylvester Brags of Threat to Kill Daily KOS Writer / Racist Rant" Blog: 12 Aug 2015. Web: 29 May 2016. <http://rodwebber.wordpress.com>

239. Trump, Donald J. Interviewed by Steve Doocy. *Fox and Friends*, Fox News. 11 Aug 2015. Television: 20 Jun 2016. <http://insider.foxnews.com>

240. Atkin, Emily. "To Defeat ISIS, Trump Openly Suggests Committing War Crimes" *ThinkProgress*. 3 Dec 2015. Web: 3 Jun 2016. <http://thinkprogress.org>

241. Krieg, Gregory. "Israeli expert: Trump's Call to Kill Terrorists' Families Immoral, Ineffective" *CNN*. 3 Dec 2015. Web: 3 Jun 2016. <http://www.cnn.com>

242. Trump, Donald J. [@realDonaldTrump]. "Sadly, the overwhelming amount of violent crime in our major cities is committed by blacks and hispanics – a tough subject – must be discussed." 5 Jun 2013. Web: 7 Jun 2016. Tweet.

243. Jacobson, Louis. "Donald Trump: 'The Mexican government ... they send the bad ones over'" *Politifact*. 6 Aug 2015. Web: 7 Jun 2016. <http://www.politifact.com>

244. "1918 flu pandemic" *Wikipedia*. 12 May 2016. Web: 22 May 2016. <http://en.wikipedia.org>

245. Livingstone, Ken. "Text of Statement by Mayor Ken Livingstone" *Financial Times*. 7 Jul 2005. Web: 25 May 2016. <http://www.ft.com>

246. Diamond, Jeremy. "Trump cites story of general who dipped bullets in pigs' blood to deter Muslims" *CNN*. 20 Feb 2016. Web: 25 May 2016. <http://www.cnn.com>

247. McCoy, Barney. "Donald Trump bungles facts, history on General John Pershing, Pigs and Muslims" *JournalCetera*, WordPress. 25 Feb 2016. Web: 25 May 2016. <https://barneymccoy.wordpress.com>

248. Sneed, Tierney. "Trump All for Torturing Terror Suspects: 'He'll Talk Faster with the Torture'" *TalkingPointsMemo*. 22 Mar 2016. Web: 22 May 2016. <http://talkingpointsmemo.com>

249. Kazin, Matthew. "Florida Gov. Rick Scott on Why He's Endorsing Trump" *Fox Business News*. 17 Mar 2016. Web: 22 May 2016. <http://foxbusinessnews.com>

250. "Constitution of the United States" Amendment 2.

251. Trump, Donald J. [@realDonaldTrump]. "We already have tremendous regulations. Now, if you look at my opponents, they're very weak on the Second Amendment. I'm very, very strong." 26 Oct 2015. Web: 22 May 2016. Tweet.

252. Brogan, Jacob. "Shooting Victim: 'We're on this Earth for Such a Short Time'" *The Slatest*, Slate. 12 Jun 2016. Web: 20 Jun 2016. <http://slate.com/blogs/>

253. Kazin, 17 Mar 2016.

254. Steinhauser, Gabrielle, with Matthias Verbergt. "Is Belgium's Interior Minister Copying Trump?" *The Wall Street Journal*. 18 Apr 2016. Web: 22 May 2016. <http://blogs.wsj.com>

255. Silverstein, Jason. "Trump-loving Maine Governor Paul LePage mocks Bulgarian and Indian workers in speech, says they need 'an interpreter'" *New York Daily News*. 25 Apr 2016. Web: 22 May 2016. <http://www.nydailynews.com>

256. Burke, Liz. "Donald Trump's popularity is spreading to Australia, and his supporters are all around us" *news.com.au*. 2 Mar 2016. Web: 22 May 2016. <http://www.news.com.au>

257. "Algeria" and "Islamic Salvation Front" *Wikipedia*. 6 Apr 2016. Web: 12 Jun 2016. <http://en.wikipedia.org>

258. Kriseman, Rick. [@kriseman]. "I am hereby barring Donald Trump from entering St. Petersburg until we fully understand the dangerous threat posed by all Trumps." 7 Dec 2015. Web: 12 Jun 2016. Tweet.

259. Knowles, David. "Donald Trump Adds Saudi Arabia to List of Countries Ripping Off the U.S." *Bloomberg*. 16 Aug 2015. Web: 6 Jun 2016. <http://www.bloomberg.com>

260. U.S. Department of State. "U.S. Relations with Saudi Arabia" Fact Sheet, Bureau of Near Eastern Affairs: 23 Aug 2013. Web: 20 Jun 2016. <http://www.state.gov/r/pa/ei/bgn/3584.htm>

261. Knowles, 16 Aug 2015.

262. Obama, Barack H. Interviewed by Nadia Bilbassy-Charters. "U.S. President Barack Obama on an exclusive interview with Al Arabiya" *AlArabiya*. 15 May 2015. Television to Web Transcript: 6 Jun 2016. <http://english.alarabiya.net>

263. Goldberg, Jeffrey. "The Obama Doctrine" *The Atlantic*: Apr, 2016. Web: 6 Jun 2016. <http://www.theatlantic.com>

264. "US praises sanctions on Hezbollah" *Arab News*. 10 Dec 2015. Web: 6 Jun 2016. <http://www.arabnews.com>

265. "Saudi Arabia tip-off saved UK lives, David Cameron says" *BBC News*. 2 Feb 2015. Web: 6 Jun 2016. <http://www.bbc.com>

266. Al-Faisal, Prince Turki. "Mr. Obama, we are not 'free-riders'" *Arab News*. 14 Mar 2016. Web: 6 Jun 2016. <http://www.arabnews.com>

267. Reuters. "Kuwait Security Chief to Obama: We're not 'free-riders'" *AlArabiya*. 17 Mar 2016. Web: 6 Jun 2016. <http://english.alarabiya.net>

268. Pond, Allison. "A Portrait of Mormons in the U.S." Pew Research Center. 24 Jul 2009. Web: 6 Jun 2016. <http://www.pewforum.org>

269. Ahmed, Kamal. "Ford: 'We assume Apple is working on a car'" *BBC News*. 25 Apr 2016. Web: 29 May 2016. <http://www.bbc.com>

270. Trump, Donald J. [@realDonaldTrump]. "Sorry losers and haters, but my I.Q. is one of the highest – and you all know it! Please don't feel so stupid or insecure, it's not your fault" 8 May 2013. Web: 6 Jun 2016. Tweet.

271. "Donald Trump: British Muslims aren't reporting terror suspects" *The Telegraph*. 23 Mar 2016. Web: 29 May 2016. <http://www.telegraph.co.uk>

272. Alfano, Sean. "Leona Helmsley Leaves $12M to her Dog" *CBS News*, CBS. 29 Aug 2007. Web: 29 May 2016. <http://www.cbsnews.com>

273. Trump, Donald J. Interviewed by Oprah Winfrey. *The Oprah Winfrey Show*. Television. 1988. Embedded video clip: 28 Jul 2015.
Capretto, Lisa. "In 1988, Oprah Asked Donald Trump If He'd Ever Run For President. Here's How He Replied." Huffpost OWN, *The Huffington Post*. 28 Jul 2015. Web: 20 Jun 2016. <http://www.huffingtonpost.com>

274. Nash, James. "California Beats U.S. in Millionaires, Food-Stamp Users" *Bloomberg*. 9 Mar 2014. Web: 29 May 2016. <http://www.bloomberg.com>

275. Sawchuk, Katia. "California has More Billionaires than Every Country Except the U.S. and China" *Forbes*. 4 Mar 2015. Web: 29 May 2016. <http://www.forbes.com>

276. Bohn, Sarah, with Caroline Danielson and Monica Bandy. "Poverty in California" Public Policy Institute of California. Dec 2015. Web: 20 Jun 2016. <http://www.ppic.org>

277. "Happy Birthday! Sweden's Ikea founder turns ninety" *The Local*. 30 Mar 2016. Web: 29 May 2016. <http://www.thelocal.se>

278. Schmitt, Bertel. "It's All About Ghosn: Why the Renault-Nissan Alliance Nearly Collapsed, and Who Comes After Carlos" *Forbes*. 15 Dec 2015. Web: 29 May 2016. <http://www.forbes.com>

279. Capital IQ. "Zein Abdalla" Executive profile summary. *Bloomberg*. n.d. Web: 23 Jun 2016. <http://www.bloomberg.com>

280. Trump, Donald J. Interviewed by Chuck Todd. *Meet the Press*, NBC News. 17 Aug 2015. Television to Web Transcript: 29 May 2016. *The Washington Post*. <http://www.washingtonpost.com>

281. Phillips, Amber. "25 people, places and things Donald Trump has denounced" *The Washington Post*. 20 Jul 2015. Web: 29 May 2016. This made #22 on their list! <http://www.washingtonpost.com>

282. Phillips, 20 Jul 2015.

283. Wright, David. "Trump: Tubman on the $20 bill is 'pure political correctness'" CNN. 21 Apr 2016. Web: 29 May 2016. <http://www.cnn.com>

284. Trump, Donald J. Interviewed by Chris Matthews. *Town Hall*, MSNBC, Green Bay, Wisconsin: 30 Mar 2016. Television to Web Transcript: 12 Jun 2016. <http://info.msnbc.com>

285. *NationMaster*. Web: 12 Jun 2016. <http://www.nationmaster.com>

286. Turck, Mary. "Private prisons, public shame" *Al Jazeera America*. 9 Jun 2015. Web: 12 Jun 2016. <http://america.aljazeera.com>
Godard, Thierry. "The Economics of the American Prison System" *SmartAsset*.

23 Mar 2016. Web: 12 Jun 2016. <http://www.smartasset.com>

287. Rajghatta, Chidanand. "Prospects of a Trump presidency rattles the world" *The Times of India*. 18 Mar 2016. Web: 29 May 2016. <http://timesofindia.indiatimes.com>
Wilders, Geert. [@geertwilderspvv]. "I hope @realDonaldTrump will be the next US President. Good for America, good for Europe. We need brave leaders." 7 Dec 2015. Web: 29 May 2016. Tweet.

288. Kottasova, Ivana. "Smarter robots put 50% of jobs at risk" *CNN Money*. 13 Nov 2015. Web: 29 May 2016. <http:///money.cnn.com>

289. Egan, Matt. "30% of bank jobs are under threat" *CNN Money*. 13 Nov 2015. Web: 29 May 2016. <http:///money.cnn.com>

290. "Generation jobless" *The Economist*. 27 Apr 2013. Web: 29 May 2016. <http://www.economist.com>

291. Devine, Daniel James. "Automatic Employment" *World*, World News Group. 6 Apr 2013. Web: 29 May 2016. <http:///www.worldmag.com>

292. Bender, Ruth. "Germany's AfD Adopts Anti-Islam Stance at Party Conference" *The Wall Street Journal*. 1 May 2016. Web: 29 May 2016. <http://www.wsj.com>

293. "Germany AfD Conference: party adopts anti-Islam policy" *BBC World Service News*, BBC. 1 May 2016. Web: 29 May 2016. <http://www.bbc.com>

294. "Lee Kuan Yew" *Wikipedia*. Web: 6 Jun 2016. <http://en.wikipedia.org>

295. "Singapore" *Wikipedia*. Web: 6 Jun 2016. <http://en.wikipedia.org>

296. Lee, Jungah. "Samsung: Giant in Transition" *Bloomberg*. 4 Feb 2016. Web: 10 Jun 2016. <http://www.bloomberg.com>

297. Parker, Asha. "'I'm speaking with myself because I have a very good brain': Donald Trump is really smart, according to Donald Trump" *Salon*. 28 Apr 2016. Web: 10 Jun 2016. <http://www.salon.com>

298. Trump, Donald J. "Our Country Needs a Truly Great Leader" *The Wall Street Journal*. Candidacy Announcement: 15 Jun 2015. Web: 10 Jun 2016. <http://www.wsj.com>

299. Trump, Donald J. Interviewed by Jimmy Fallon. "Donald Trump Interviews Himself in the Mirror" *The Tonight Show*, NBC. 11 Sep 2015. Television to Web Video Clip: 10 Jun 2016. <http://www.nbc.com>

300. "Donald Trump Wins the U.S. Presidential Election" *The Economist Intelligence Unit*. 18 May 2016. Web: 3 Jun 2016. <http://gfs.eiu.com>

301. Harding, Robin. "Donald Trump's rise sparks alarm in Japan" *Financial Times*. 14 Mar 2016. Web: 3 Jun 2016. <http://next.ft.com>

302. Elliott, Philip. "Why Would Democrats Vote for Trump? It's All About Trade" *Time*. 10 Mar 2016. Web: 3 Jun 2016. <http://www.time.com>

303. "North American Robotics Market Sets New Records in 2012" *Robotics Industry Association*. 5 Feb 2013. Web: 3 Jun 2016. <http://www.robotics.org>

304. Lenzner, Robert. "40% of the Largest U.S. Companies Founded by Immigrants or Their Children" *Forbes*. 25 Apr 2013. Web: 3 Jun 2016. <http://forbes.com>

305. Van, Jon. "Immigrant Children Get Better Grades, Study Finds" *Chicago Tribune*. 23 Feb 1994. Web: 3 Jun 2016. <http://articles.chicagotribune.com>

306. Lunday, Amy. "Children of U.S. immigrants outperforming their peers, study shows" *Hub*, Johns Hopkins University. 13 Sep 2012. Web: 3 Jun 2016. <http://hub.jhu.edu>

307. Lenzner, 25 Apr 2013.

308. "Donald Trump Wins the U.S. Presidential Election" *The Economist Intelligence Unit*. 18 May 2016. Web: 3 Jun 2016. <http://gfs.eiu.com>

309. Randow, Jana. "Fed Scales Back Rate-Rise Forecasts as Global Risks Remain" *Bloomberg Business*. 16 Mar 2016. Web: 3 Jun 2016. <http://www.bloomberg.com>

310. Anderson, Stuart. "Trump the Hypocrite: Investing Overseas Fine for Him" *Forbes*. 17 Aug 2015. Web: 3 Jun 2016. <http://www.forbes.com>

311. "The 'New American' Fortune 500," Partnership for a New American Economy, June 2011: p.2. Print. Web: 20 Jun 2016. <http://www.renewoureconomy.org> Anderson, Stuart. "40 Percent of Fortune 500 Companies Founded by Immigrants or their Children" *Forbes*. 19 Jun 2011. Web: 27 May 2016. <http://www.forbes.com>

312. Elmer-DeWitt, Philip. "What Donald Trump Doesn't Know about Apple could Fill a Stadium" *Fortune*. 19 Jan 2016. Web: 27 May 2016. <http://www.fortune.com>

313. Engel, Pamela. "Trump on Syrian Refugees: 'Lock Your Doors, Folks!'" *Business Insider*. 25 Apr 2016. Web: 27 May 2016. <http://www.businessinsider.com>

314. "Michael E. DeBakey" *Wikipedia*. Web: 6 Jun 2016. <http://en.wikipedia.org>

315. Altman, Lawrence K. "In Moscow in 1996, a Doctor's Visit Changed History" *The New York Times*. 1 May 2007. Web: 27 May 2016. <http://www.nytimes.com>

316. "Michael E. DeBakey" *Wikipedia*. Web: 6 Jun 2016. <http://en.wikipedia.org>

317. "Elon Musk" *Wikipedia*. Web: 20 Jun 2016. <http://en.wikipedia.org>

318. Trump, Donald J. "Statement on Preventing Muslim Immigration" Press Release, New York, NY: Donald J. Trump for President, Inc. 7 Dec 2015. Web: 27 May 2016. <http://www.donaldjtrump.com>

319. Al Habtoor, Khalaf Ahmad. "Barring Muslims would spell a US economic disaster" *Al Arabiya*. 3 Apr 2016. Web: 3 Jun 2016. <http://english.alarabiya.net>

320. "Republican presidential hopefuls: A field guide to 2016" *The Economist*. 25 Apr 2015. Web: 21 Jun 2016. <http://www.economist.com>

321. Hoffman, Bill. "Ben Carson: Trump promised me a job" *Newsmax*. 14 Mar 2016. Web: 25 May 2016. <http://www.newsmax.com>

322. Thompson, Catherine. "Trump Lets His Followers Know 'Hillary Clinton Can't Satisfy Her Husband'" *TalkingPointsMemo*. 17 Apr 2015. Web: 25 May 2016. <http://talkingpointsmemo.com>

323. Sun, Feifei. "Top Ten Donald Trump Failures: The Marriages" *Time*. 29 Apr

2011. Web: 25 May 2016. <http://content.time.com>

324. "Donald Trump Wins the U.S. Presidential Election" *The Economist Intelligence Unit*. 18 May 2016. Web: 3 Jun 2016. <http://gfs.eiu.com>

325. "Gulf states step in again to help world" *Gulf News*. 1 Nov 2008. Web: 30 May 2016. <http://gulfnews.com>

326. Mazzetti, Mark. "Saudi Arabia Warns of Economic Fallout in Congress Passes 9/11 Bill" *The New York Times*. 15 Apr 2016. Web: 30 May 2016. <http://www.nytimes.com>

327. "Remembering the Stock Market Crash of 1987" *CNBC*. 1 Oct 2007. Web: 30 May 2016. <http://www.cnbc.com>

328. "Black marks from Black Monday" *The Economist*. 20 Oct 2012. Web: 30 May 2016. <http://www.economist.com>

329. "Remembering the Stock Market Crash of 1987" *CNBC*. 1 Oct 2007. Web: 30 May 2016. <http://www.cnbc.com>

330. Lange, Jason. "Exclusive: China central bank to the Fed: A little help, please?" *Reuters*. 21 Mar 2016. Web: 30 May 2016. <http://www.reuters.com>

331. Patton, Mike. "Who Owns the Most U.S. Debt?" *Forbes*. 28 Oct 2014. Web: 30 May 2016. <http://www.forbes.com>

332. Capretto, Lisa. "In 1988, Oprah Asked Donald Trump If He'd Ever Run For President. Here's How He Replied." *The Huffington Post*. 28 Jul 2015. Web: 20 Jun 2016. <http://www.huffingtonpost.com>

333. Plaskin, Glenn. "Playboy Interview: Donald Trump (1990)" *Playboy*. 14 Mar 2016. Web: 30 May 2016. <http://www.playboy.com>

334. Spitzer, Kirk. "Trump's Japan-bashing has close U.S. ally in Asia on edge" *USA Today*. 17 Mar 2016. Web: 30 May 2016. <http://www.usatoday.com>

335. Trump, Donald J. [@realDonaldTrump]. "The Trans-Pacific Partnership is an attack on America's business. It does not stop Japan's currency manipulation. This is a bad deal." 22 Apr 2015. Web: 30 May 2016. Tweet.

336. Worstall, Tim. "Donald Trump Blows the Trade Argument Again: Blames India for Stealing American Jobs" *Forbes*. 28 Feb 2016. Web: 30 May 2016. <http://www.forbes.com>

337. Spitzer, 17 Mar 2016.

338. Trump, Donald J. Interviewed by Telephone by Maggie Haberman and David E. Sanger. "Transcript: Donald Trump Expounds on His Foreign Policy Views" *The New York Times*. 26 Mar 2016. Web: 30 May 2016. <http://www.nytimes.com>

339. McMorris-Santoro, Evan. "Trump on China: 'Listen You Mother F***ers' (VIDEO)" *TalkingPointsMemo*. 29 Apr 2011. Web: 30 May 2016. <http://talkingpointsmemo.com>

340. Spitzer, 17 Mar 2016.

341. Trump, Donald J. [@realDonaldTrump]. "China is not our friend. They are not our ally. They want to overtake us, and if we don't get smart and tough soon, they will." 21 Feb 2013. Web: 30 May 2016. Tweet.

342. "China" *World Bank*. Web: 27 May 2016. <http://data.worldbank.org>

343. Holmes, Jack. "Proud F-Word Avoider Donald Trump has said the F-Word a Few Times" *Esquire*. 5 Mar 2016. Web: 30 May 2016. <http://www.esquire.com>

344. Wong, Andrea, and Liz McCormick. "Saudi Arabia's Secret Holdings of U.S. Debt are Suddenly a Big Deal" *Bloomberg*. 23 Jan 2016. Web: 30 May 2016. <http://www.bloomberg.com>

345. Wright, David "Trump: U.S. will never default 'because you print the money'" CNN. 10 May 2016. Web: 21 Jun 2016. <http://www.cnn.com>

346. Long, Heather. "Why Donald Trump's debt proposal is reckless" CNN Money. 9 May 2016. Web: 21 Jun 2016. <http://money.cnn.com>

347. Stephanopoulos, George. "Donald Trump's Solution on Gas Prices: Get Tough with Saudi Arabia, Seize Oil Fields in Libya and Iraq?" ABC News. 18 Apr 2011. Web: 30 May 2016. <http://blogs.abcnews.com/george/>

348. Stephanopoulos, 18 Apr 2011.

349. Rebala, Pratheek, and Hannah Beech. "See Where China is Spending Billions on American Businesses" *Time*. 28 Sep 2015. Web: 30 May 2016. <http://www.time.com>

350. "U.S. Relations with Mexico: Fact Sheet" *U.S. Department of State*. May 2015. Web: 30 May 2016. <http://www.state.gov>

351. Egan, Matt. "Donald Trump Terrifies Wall Street" *CNN Money*, CNN. 16 Sep 2015. Web: 30 May 2016. <http://www.money.cnn.com>

352. Allen, Michael. "Former Mexican President: Not Paying for Trump's Wall (VIDEO)" *Opposing Views*. 25 Feb 2016. Web: 30 May 2016. Trump made his declaration during a televsed candidates debate on CNN. <http://www.opposingviews.com>

353. Lawrence, Robert Z., and Lawrence Edwards. "Shattering the Myths about U.S. Trade Policy" *Harvard Business Review*, March 2012. Web: 30 May 2016. <https://hbr.org>

354. Candea, Ben, and Nicki Rossoll. "Donald Trump: 'I don't think America is a Safe Place for Americans'" ABC News. 27 Mar 2016. <http://abcnews.go.com>

355. Gregory, Paul Roderick. "Seven Warnings to Donald Trump about Vladimir Putin" *Forbes*. 8 Jan 2016 Web: 21 Jun 2016. <http://www.forbes.com>

356. "Idaho U.S. Attorney addresses hate crimes in Pocatello" *ABC News*, KIFI-TV, Pocatello, Idaho: 14 Apr 2016. Video clip: 14 Jun 2016. <http://www.localnews8.com>

357. Inglet, Misty. "Idaho's U.S. Attorney visits Pocatello" KIFI-TV, Pocatello, Idaho: 14 Apr 2016. Video clip: 14 Jun 2016. <http://www.localnews8.com>

358. Trump, Donald J. [@realDonaldTrump]. "I will make our military so big, powerful & strong that no one will mess with us." 24 Jan 2016. Web: 25 May 2016. Tweet.

359. Noriega, Margarita. "Ted Cruz defends Donald Trump: 'He speaks the truth' about immigration" *Vox Xpress*. 30 Jun 2015. Web: 25 May 2016. <http://www.vox.com>

360. Trump, Donald J. Interviewed by George Stephanopoulos. *Good Morning America*. ABC. 17 June 2015. Television to Web Transcript. Web: 22 May 2016. <http://www.abcnews.go.com>

361. Trump, Donald J. [@realDonaldTrump]. "I love the Mexican people, but Mexico is not our friend. They're killing us at the border and they're killing us on jobs and trade. *Fight*! " 30 Jun 2015. Web: 25 May 2016. Tweet.

362. Allen, Nick. "El Chapo Guzman 'Vows to make Donald Trump swallow his words'" *The Telegraph*. 13 Jul 2015. Web: 25 May 2016. <http://www.telegraph.co.uk>

363. Trump, Donald J. "Our Country Needs a Truly Great Leader" *The Wall Street Journal*. Candidacy Announcement: 15 Jun 2015. Web: 10 Jun 2016. <http://www.wsj.com>

364. Trump, Donald J. Candidacy: 15 Jun 2015.

365. Johnson, Jenna. "Donald Trump wants China to make North Korea's Kim Jong-un 'disappear'" *The Washington Post*. 10 Feb 2016. Web: 27 May 2016. <http://www.washingtonpost.com>

366. Trump, Donald J. "Statement on Preventing Muslim Immigration" Press Release, New York, NY: Donald J. Trump for President, Inc. 7 Dec 2015. Web: 27 May 2016. <http://www.donaldjtrump.com>

367. Chorley, Matt. "Donald Trump is 'divisive, stupid and wrong' but we shouldn't ban him from Britain, says David Cameron" *Mail Online*, The Daily Mail. 16 Dec 2015. Web: 27 May 2016. <http://www.dailymail.co.uk>

368. Cardesman, Anthony H. *New Estimates of Iran's Petroleum Exports and Income after the Nuclear Implementation Day and Reductions in Sanctions*, CSIS: Centre for Strategic & International Studies. Third Revision: 26 Jan 2016. Web: 27 May 2016. Cardesman cites the World Bank overview of Iran, which is not itself available online. <http://www.csis.org>

369. Easterly, William, and Stanley Fisher. *The Soviet Economic Decline Dataset*, World Bank, Apr 2001. Web: 27 May 2016. Abstract. <http://go.worldbank.org/2VZYL0N6N0>

370. Fein, Esther B. "Soviet Openness Brings Poverty Out of the Shadows" *The New York Times*. 29 Jan 1989. Web: 27 May 2016. <http://www.nytimes.com>

371. Please see the infographic on the previous page, which was constructed out of data from the WorldBank and IMF.

372. Balz, Dan. "Trump's foreign policy views: A sharp departure from GOP orthodoxy" *The Washington Post*. 21 Mar 2016. Web: 27 May 2016. <http://www.washingtonpost.com>

373. Trump, Donald J. [@realDonaldTrump]. "Trump is not afraid of anything or anyone — that's the President USA needs to unite us & knock the socks off our enemies!" 19 Mar 2016. Web: 27 May 2016. Tweet.

374. Stephanopoulos, 18 Apr 2011.

375. Sherfinski, David. "Donald Trump: 'I'd bomb the hell out of the oil fields'" *The Washington Times*. 9 Jul 2015. Web: 27 May 2016. <http://www.washingtontimes.com>

376. Fifield, Anna. "In Japan and South Korea, bewilderment at Trump's suggestion they build nukes" *The Washington Post*. 28 Mar 2016. Web: 27 May 2016. <http://www.washingtonpost.com>

377. "The GOP must stop Trump" *Boston Globe*. 9 Apr 2016. Web: 9 June 2016. <http://www.bostonglobe.com>

378. McCarthy, Leonard. "Turning the Page: A New Rule Book," ICAC (Independent Commission Against Corruption) Symposium, Hong Kong. Video Address: 11 May 2015. Web: 23 Jun 2016.

379. Cadman, Emily, with Robin Harding and Steve Bernard. "The Japanese economy at a glance" *Financial Times*. n.d. Web: 23 Jun 2016. <https://ig.ft.com>

380. Wakatsuki, Yoko. "Middle-aged virgins: Why so many Japanese stay chaste" CNN. 24 Jun 2015. Web: 23 Jun 2016. <http://edition.cnn.com>

381. Harden, Blaine. "Japan's Killer Work Ethic" *The Washington Post*. 13 Jul 2008. Web: 23 Jun 2016. <http://www.washingtonpost.com>

382. "Bad timing: Japan and immigration" *The Economist*. 20 Feb 2015. Web: 24 Jun 2016. <http://www.economist.com>

383. "Japanese unemployment rate slides in January" *The Financial Times*. 29 Feb 2016. Web: 23 Jun 2016. <http://ft.com>

384. "Life Expectancy at Birth and at Age 65 by Local Areas in England and Wales: 2012 to 2014" Office for National Statistics. 4 Nov 2015. Web: 23 Jun 2016. <https://www.ons.gov.uk>

385. Sands, David R. "New Russia-China alliance latest diplomatic, strategic blow to Obama" *The Washington Times*. 30 Apr 2015. Web: 23 Jun 2016. <http://www.washingtontimes.com>

386. Bennetts, Marc. "Shunned by West, Putin seeks friend, financier on China visit" *The Washington Times*. 23 Jun 2016. Web: 23 Jun 2016. <http://www.washingtontimes.com>

387. Parfitt, Tom. "Russia-China clinch tightens with joint navy exercises in Mediterranean" The Telegraph. 11 May 2015. Web: 23 Jun 2016. <http://www.telegraph.co.uk>

388. Sands, David R. "New Russia-China alliance latest diplomatic, strategic blow to Obama" *The Washington Times*. 30 Apr 2015. Web: 23 Jun 2016. <http://www.washingtontimes.com>

389. Majumdar, Dave."The U.S. Military's Greatest Fear: Russia and China are Catching Up Fast"The National Interest. 17 May 2016. Web: 23 Jun 2016. <http://nationalinterest.org>

390. Vine, David. "Where in the World Is the U.S. Military?" *Politico*: Jul/Aug 2015. Web: 23 Jun 2016. <http://www.politico.com>

INDEX